GW00992834

Conversations with Julian Bar

Literary Conversations Series

Peggy Whitman Prenshaw
General Editor

Conversations with
Julian Barnes

Edited by
Vanessa Guignery and Ryan Roberts

University Press of Mississippi
Jackson

www.upress.state.ms.us

The University Press of Mississippi is a member of the Association of American University Presses.

First printing 2009
∞
Library of Congress Cataloging-in-Publication Data

Barnes, Julian.
    Conversations with Julian Barnes / edited by Vanessa Guignery and Ryan Roberts.
        p.   cm. — (Literary conversations series)
    Includes index.
    ISBN 978-1-60473-203-0 (alk. paper) — ISBN 978-1-60473-204-7 (pbk. : alk. paper)
1. Barnes, Julian—Interviews. 2. Authors, English—20th century—Interviews. I. Guignery, Vanessa. II. Roberts, Ryan. III. Title.
   PR6052.A6657Z55 2009
   823'.914 B—dc22

                                     2008031704

British Library Cataloging-in-Publication Data available

Books by Julian Barnes

Novels

Metroland. London: Jonathan Cape, 1980.
Before She Met Me. London: Jonathan Cape, 1982.
Flaubert's Parrot. London: Jonathan Cape, 1984.
Staring at the Sun. London: Jonathan Cape, 1986.
A History of the World in 10½ Chapters. London: Jonathan Cape, 1989.
Talking It Over. London: Jonathan Cape, 1991.
The Porcupine. London: Jonathan Cape, 1992.
England, England. London: Jonathan Cape, 1998.
Love, etc. London: Jonathan Cape, 2000.
Arthur & George. London: Jonathan Cape, 2005.

Short Story Collections

Cross Channel. London: Jonathan Cape, 1996.
The Lemon Table. London: Jonathan Cape, 2004.

Nonfiction

Letters from London 1990–1995. London: Picador, 1995.
Something to Declare. London: Picador, 2002.
The Pedant in the Kitchen. London: Atlantic, 2003.
Nothing to Be Frightened Of. London: Jonathan Cape, 2008.

Detective fiction under the pseudonym of Dan Kavanagh

Duffy. London: Jonathan Cape, 1980.
Fiddle City. London: Jonathan Cape, 1981.
Putting the Boot In. London: Jonathan Cape, 1985.
Going to the Dogs. London: Viking, 1987.

Translation

The Truth about Dogs. By Volker Kriegel. London: Bloomsbury, 1988.
In the Land of Pain. By Alphonse Daudet. London: Jonathan Cape, 2002.

Contents

Introduction ix

Chronology xvii

Julian Barnes in Interview *Ronald Hayman* 3

Escape from Metroland *Caroline Holland* 7

Julian Barnes *Patrick McGrath* 11

The World's History and Then Some in 10½ Chapters *Bruce Cook* 20

Into the Lion's Mouth: A Conversation with Julian Barnes *Michael March* 23

He's Turned Towards Python (But Not the Dead Flaubert's Parrot Sketch . . .):
    Interview with Julian Barnes Observer 27

"Novels Come out of Life, Not out of Theories": An Interview with Julian Barnes
    Rudolf Freiburg 31

"History in Question(s)": An Interview with Julian Barnes *Vanessa Guignery* 53

Julian Barnes: The Art of Fiction CLXV *Shusha Guppy* 64

Julian Barnes, Etc. *Robert Birnbaum* 83

Interviews: Julian Barnes *Peter Wild* 96

Julian Barnes in Conversation *Vanessa Guignery* 101

Cool, Clean Man of Letters *Nadine O'Regan* 115

Big Ideas—Program 5—"Julian Barnes" *Ramona Koval* 118

"It's for Self-Protection" *Stuart Jeffries* 129

Interview with Julian Barnes *Xesús Fraga* 134

Julian Barnes: Are You an Oldie? *Margaret Crick* 148

Julian Barnes: The Final Interview *Vanessa Guignery and Ryan Roberts* 161

Index 189

Introduction

In 1983, Julian Barnes was selected by the Book Marketing Council as one of the "Best Twenty Young British Novelists" in a list which included Martin Amis, Pat Barker, William Boyd, Kazuo Ishiguro, Ian McEwan, Salman Rushdie, and Graham Swift. Some twenty-five years later, these novelists have all confirmed their talent, and many of their works can easily be considered as classics. Julian Barnes in particular is regarded as one of the most prominent contemporary authors, having met great success with his ten novels, two volumes of short stories, three collections of essays, and four pseudonymously written detective novels. His most recent book *Nothing to Be Frightened Of* (2008) is part essay and part memoir. Julian Barnes's work has been widely translated abroad, and he has won several prestigious literary prizes, including the Somerset Maugham Award (1981), Geoffrey Faber Memorial Prize (1985), E. M. Forster Award from the American Academy and Institute of Arts and Letters (1986), Shakespeare Prize (1993), and the 2004 Austrian State Prize for European Literature. Barnes has won both the Prix Médicis and the Prix Fémina, and in 2004 he became a Commandeur de l'Ordre des Arts et des Lettres in France. Three of his novels have been shortlisted for the Man Booker Prize.

When gathering interviews for this volume, one is constantly reminded of Geoffrey Braithwaite, the narrator of *Flaubert's Parrot*, when he protests, "Why does the writing make us chase the writer? Why can't we leave well alone? Why aren't the books enough?"[1] Indeed, in the final interview of this collection, Julian Barnes echoes this sentiment, stating, "I would warn anyone against taking an interview with a writer, however interesting and seemingly truthful, as a surer guide to the author's intentions than the book itself." Despite his reluctance to take part in extensive promotional work and in spite of his distant or "benign indifference" to academia, literary theory, and criticism, Barnes has been an extremely generous interviewee from the beginning of his writing career. He responds openly and eloquently to questions, and even though he no longer reads reviews of his books and resists becoming too self-conscious about his own work, Barnes is extremely serious and thorough when discussing his literary production. He chooses his words with meticulous care, but also displays a playful, wry, and witty sense of humor and irony, as the following interviews reveal.

Julian Barnes does not have an exhibitionist nature and has always been protective of his private life, which makes the conversations included here all the more unique in that they often provide the reader with a glimpse into select aspects of his personal life and offer insight into the person behind his writing. In a discussion of *Metroland*, which Barnes acknowledges is autobiographical in "spirit" and "topography,"[2] Barnes reveals that, in his late teens and early twenties, he had a "difficult and distant relationship"[3] with his parents, both of whom were French schoolteachers. As an adult, he maintained a "distantly accepting" relationship, but, upon their deaths he became much more aware of their genetic and familial hold on him as an individual: "My ability to be free and discover some particular individual essence, was not entirely a foolish hope but it was bound around by all sorts of governing conditions laid down by my ancestors."[4] In the final interview, Barnes also talks at length about his parents, and more particularly about their political and religious beliefs and the effect, both personal and literary, of their deaths.

The interviews included in this collection reveal that Julian Barnes has a refined and demanding view of literature and the role of writing in his life. When Shusha Guppy asks Barnes, "What is the purpose of fiction?" he answers, "It's to tell the truth. It's to tell beautiful, exact, and well-constructed lies which enclose hard and shimmering truths." He confirms this seemingly paradoxical idea in another interview, stating, "[Y]ou write fiction in order to tell the truth."[5] In a conversation with Nadine O'Regan, he emphasizes the importance of writing in his life: "I don't think I'd be happy if I just stopped writing," he says. "Writing has become necessary to me. It is a necessity as well as a pleasure." Describing this necessity, Barnes provides Rudolf Freiburg and, later, Shusha Guppy a brief description of a typical working day, explaining to Guppy, "I work seven days a week; I don't think in terms of normal office hours—or rather, normal office hours for me include the weekends." He tells Freiburg, "I'm never not a writer. It seems to me that I am in the happy position of having a job, a vocation, a passion that occupies me twenty-four hours of the day and everything is grist to the mill."

Julian Barnes proves equally forthcoming when the subject turns to specifics regarding his work as a novelist, and he willingly discusses the intricacies of the writer's craft, offering insight into the composing and genesis of some of his novels. To Ronald Hayman, Barnes explains in detail why he took several years to modify the various drafts of *Metroland* (his first novel, published when he was thirty-four), to try and make it less "over-instructive" and more "plausible." In interviews with Patrick McGrath in 1987 and with Vanessa Guigney in 2002, Barnes reveals interesting aspects of the genesis of *Flaubert's Parrot*, disclosing, for example, that he dropped a chapter about sex and creativity. During Guigney's interview, Barnes read several extracts from his travel notebook for September 1981, which provide details about the incident which eventually sparked the creation of *Flaubert's Parrot*. In his conversation with Bruce Cook, Barnes unveils the origin of some of the chapters of *A History of the World in 10½ Chapters*, describing the book's varied evolution: "[B]ooks are like teeth—that is, some have one root and some are molars with three or four." When talking with Xesús Fraga, Barnes explains that his original idea for *Arthur & George* was to set two stories in parallel, one set in the past about Arthur Conan Doyle and George Edalji, and the other set in the contemporary world dealing with racial prejudice. He gave up the idea of the contemporary story and also relinquished one of the early titles of the book, *The Skin of Things*, which was highly suggestive, drawing attention to "the surface of the world and what was immediately underneath it and the skin of George and the skin of Arthur."

Adding to these details about the origins of his works, Barnes also remarks that his approach to writing varies depending on whether he's writing fiction or nonfiction. When constructing a novel, Barnes points out, "I never start at the beginning. I tend to start at a central moment and often circle round."[6] Barnes approaches each novel uniquely, believing "each book should try to be something new for you, a challenge."[7] Similarly, he tells Shusha Guppy, "In order to write the novel I'm committed to, I have to pretend that it's not only separate from everything I've written before, but also separate from anything anyone in the history of the universe has written. This is a grotesque delusion and a crass vanity, but also a creative necessity." In his interview with Roberts and Guignery, Barnes also addresses how he approaches the composition of essays and explains in great detail how he chooses his subject matter. For Barnes, a clear distinction exists between fiction and other forms of writing. As he explains to Robert Birnbaum, "Fiction is the supreme fiction. And everybody's autobiography is a fiction but not the supreme fiction. I work as a novelist, and I also work as a journalist. And I am very conscious of the essential difference of the two skills."

The conversations selected for inclusion in this volume address a wide range of issues and several common themes run through them, including death, truth, love, infidelity, jealousy, sexuality, obsession, religion, the relationship between fact and fiction, memory, history, Englishness, and the irretrievability of the past. Barnes sometimes feels rather uncomfortable when critics point out common topics or strategies throughout his novels. He addresses his unease with critical approaches to his writings by clarifying, "You do often feel when you read academic criticism, not that I do it much, or when you hear academics talking about their books, that they forget that theirs is a secondary activity. They forget that however important a critic is, a first-rate critic is always less important, and less interesting, than a second-rate writer."[8]

Despite Barnes's skepticism, the academic interviews included here testify to the ongoing critical debate classifying Barnes's fiction as being representative of postmodernist writing, since his work both resorts to and subverts realistic strategies, is essentially self-reflexive, and celebrates the literary past but also considers it with irony. Rudolf Freiburg in particular addresses the question in a collection of interviews with British contemporary authors entitled *Do You Consider Yourself a Postmodern Author?* However, Julian Barnes invariably sidesteps such discussions of his work and the use of labels which he finds "pointless and irritating," because they tend to imprison his novels in a constructed grid whereas, for him, "novels come out of life, not out of theories." In the same way, he feels slightly annoyed when interviewers question the genre of his books, especially challenging the appellation of *Flaubert's Parrot* and *A History of World in 10½ Chapters* as novels. Barnes finds the whole debate about genre taxonomy out of date, telling Bruce Cook, "The definition of a novel is pretty much an academic question by now." On the other hand, in his conversation with Freiburg, Barnes insists that *The Porcupine* and *England, England* be considered as political novels rather than satire. Both these novels, but also most of Julian Barnes's other books, intertwine reality and fiction, historical figures and imaginary ones. When discussing the collection of short stories *The Lemon Table* with Ramona Koval, Barnes notes, "I quite like putting facts and real things and real stories into my fiction."

The blurring of fact and fiction is one of several issues that inevitably recur in several interviews because they appear in one form or another in the majority of Barnes's work. Thus, Gustave Flaubert is a recurrent topic in the interviews as the French writer is a regular figure in Julian Barnes's fiction and essays. Barnes admires Flaubert's books greatly, telling Patrick McGrath in 1987: "[H]e's the writer whose words I most carefully tend to weigh, who I think has spoken the most truth about writing." More generally, Julian Barnes is very fond of France and French literature, which is why French elements figure so much in his books. In more recent interviews, Barnes answers questions regarding his relation to old age and death as well as to God and religion, issues which are particularly dealt with in his new book, *Nothing to Be Frightened Of.* His position on the question of God, for example, is lucid and finely phrased: "I don't believe in God but I miss Him."[9] The interviews collected in this volume provide Barnes numerous occasions for such self-reflection and clarification of the essential themes of his writing and, taken as a whole, provide the greatest opportunity for readers to understand the complexities of his works.

The following interviews were originally published in a wide variety of locations (Great Britain, North America, Australia, France, Germany, and Spain) and the interviewers, coming from diverse backgrounds in journalism or the academy, offer a wide range of approaches to their subject. In the long interviews (Freiburg, Guppy, Fraga, Guignery, Roberts), Barnes speaks in detail about several of his novels, talking extensively about his creative process but also a wide range of topics, justifying for example his decision to place his archive with the Harry Ransom Center in Austin, Texas, talking about his keen interest in photography (Guignery/Roberts), discussing the new fashionable form of historical fiction and his main literary influences (Guppy), or reflecting on the danger of writers taking up political causes (Fraga). In shorter interviews published in newspapers, magazines, or available on the internet, Barnes discusses specific works upon their publication but also addresses subjects of general interest, such as, for example, his views on reality TV (Birnbaum) or the benefits and disadvantages of being an "oldie" (Crick). The interview with Peter Wild about Barnes's 2002 translation of the French essay *In the Land of Pain* by Alphonse Daudet is original in that it covers not only the art of translation itself and the inevitable loss it entails, but also Barnes's relation to new technology and his view on the mechanics of the Man Booker Prize.

This collection contains interviews spanning a quarter of a century, thus representing various phases of Barnes's career. The first conversation focuses on Barnes's earliest publications, including *Metroland* (1980) and the pseudonymously published *Duffy* (1980), while the most recent interview includes questions related to Barnes's newest publication, *Nothing to Be Frightened Of* (2008). Interviewers invariably and frequently refer to the success of Barnes's novels *Flaubert's Parrot* and *A History of the World in 10½ Chapters*, so special consideration was given by including lengthy interviews devoted to these works, including one interview devoted entirely to *Flaubert's Parrot* (Guignery 2002) and another to themes of history in Barnes's works (Guignery 2000). The rest of the interviews in this collection discuss the full range of Julian Barnes's writings, including pseudonymous pieces, his short stories and essays, and even his translation of Daudet's essay and the creative indexing of Barnes's two essay collections.

As editors, we have selected interviews that we feel to be the most in-depth, substantive, insightful, literate, and wide-ranging, and we have tried to avoid, as much as possible, repetitions, even though the material covered sometimes overlaps. The interviews included here appear in their original form, with only minor editing to improve clarity or to establish uniformity of presentation. They are arranged, as best as we could determine, in the order in which they were conducted, from 1980 to 2007. The interviews originally appeared in a variety of publications, including British national newspapers such as the *Observer* and the *Guardian*, more specialized publications (*Books and Bookmen* and *Bomb*), local newspapers such as the *Islington Gazette* (London) and *Daily News* (Los Angeles), as well as academic journals and scholarly publications such as the *Paris Review* or the French *Sources* and *Cercles*. Some interviews are available online (*New Presence, Identity Theory, Bookmunch.co.uk*), but have been included here because of their high quality. Three interviews have not been published elsewhere and therefore provide exclusive material to scholars: Barnes's 2006 conversation with his Galician translator Xesús Fraga is published here for the first time in English, Margaret Crick's quirky interview full of witty and unexpected questions is here greatly expanded from its original publication, and our own interview conducted in Julian Barnes's north London home in April 2007 was designed to illicit responses to topics left unexplored in previous interviews. We hope readers and scholars will find these interviews of particular value. Not only do they offer insight into Barnes's work, but they also give a sense of his literary personality and show that throughout his career Barnes has expressed with consistency his views about art in general and his own literary work in particular.

This book would not have been possible without the contribution of all the people who have interviewed Julian Barnes, and we thank each of them for facilitating the use of their conversations. Ryan Roberts would like to thank Tricia Hardway for her unflinching support, Barbara Burkhardt for her encouragement, and Lincoln Land Community College for funding travel to Oxford and London in support of his sabbatical research, during which time the final interview of this volume took place. Vanessa Guignery would like to express her profound gratitude to Patrick Rimoux for his constant support throughout this project. Our thanks also go out to Walter Biggins at the University Press of Mississippi and to Seetha Srinivasan, director of the press, for all their assistance and for making this volume possible.

Our final thanks go to Julian Barnes for granting us his "final" interview. We deeply cherish his graciousness, generosity, and friendship.

VG

RR

Notes

1. Barnes, Julian. *Flaubert's Parrot.* London: Jonathan Cape, 1984. 12.
2. Hayman, Ronald. "Julian Barnes in Interview." *Books and Bookmen,* May 1980: 36–37.
3. Freiburg, Rudolf. "'Novels Come out of Life, Not out of Theories': An Interview with Julian Barnes." *Do You Consider Yourself a Postmodern Author?: Interviews with Contemporary English Writers.* Edited by Rudolf Freiburg and Jan Schnitker. Münster: LIT, 1999. 39–66.
4. Ibid.
5. Ibid.
6. "He's Turned Towards Python. (But Not the Dead Flaubert's Parrot Sketch . . .): Interview with Julian Barnes." *Observer,* 30 August 1998: 15.
7. Cook, Bruce. "The World's History and Then Some in 10½ Chapters." *Daily News* (Los Angeles), 7 November 1989.
8. McGrath, Patrick. "Julian Barnes." *Bomb* 21 (Fall 1987): 21–23.
9. Barnes, Julian. "The Past Conditional." *New Yorker* (25 December 2006/1 January 2007): 56–58, 60, 63–64.

Chronology

1946	Julian Barnes born on 19 January in Leicester, England; second son of Albert Leonard and Kaye Barnes, both of them French teachers; one older brother named Jonathan.
1946–56	Moves to Acton, a western suburb of London.
1956–64	Moves to Northwood, a northwestern suburban area known as Metroland which would give its name to Barnes's first novel; commutes via the Metropolitan Line to attend the City of London School; spends summer holidays with family driving through different regions of France.
1964–68	Reads philosophy and then modern languages (French and Russian) at Magdalen College, Oxford, where he takes his B.A. with Honours.
1966–67	Teaches English at a Catholic school in Rennes, France.
1969–72	Lexicographer for the *Oxford English Dictionary Supplement*, in charge of rude words and sports words.
1971–74	Writes a nonfiction work, *A Literary Guide to Oxford*, which remains unpublished.
1972–74	Reads for the bar and qualifies as a barrister in 1974, but has never practiced.
1973–80	Freelance journalist; publishes his first book review for the *Times Educational Supplement* on 25 May 1973. Also writes several pieces under pseudonyms (Lawrence Beesley, Paddy Beesley, Edward Pygge, Marion Lloyd, PC49, and Fat Boy).
1975	First short story, "A Self-Possessed Woman," appears in *The Times Anthology of Ghost Stories*.
1976–78	Publishes satirical pieces as Edward Pygge in the "Greek Street" column of the *New Review*.
1977	Contributing editor of the *New Review* under the direction of Ian Hamilton.

1977–79	Joins the *New Statesman* as assistant literary editor under Martin Amis; meets and makes friends with Christopher Hitchens, Craig Raine, and James Fenton.
1977–81	Television critic at the *New Statesman*.
1979	Marries literary agent Pat Kavanagh to whom most of his fiction is dedicated and whose surname he used as the pseudonym for his detective novels.
1979–82	Deputy literary editor of the *Sunday Times*.
1980	Publishes first novel, *Metroland*; publishes *Duffy*, his first detective novel written under the pseudonym of Dan Kavanagh.
1981	Wins the Somerset Maugham Award for *Metroland*; one of his pen-names, Basil Seal, restaurant critic for the *Tatler*, is nominated Gourmet Writer of the Year; gastronomic tour of China; publishes *Fiddle City* as Dan Kavanagh.
1982	Publishes *Before She Met Me*.
1982–86	Television critic for the *Observer*.
1983	Selected by the Book Marketing Council as one of the twenty "Best of Young British Novelists" along with Martin Amis, Pat Barker, William Boyd, Kazuo Ishiguro, Ian McEwan, Salman Rushdie, Graham Swift, and others.
1984	Publishes *Flaubert's Parrot*, which is shortlisted for the Booker Prize in Great Britain.
1985	Wins the Geoffrey Faber Memorial Prize for *Flaubert's Parrot*; publishes *Putting the Boot In* as Dan Kavanagh.
1986	Wins the Médicis Essay Prize for *Flaubert's Parrot* in France and the E. M. Forster American Academy and Institute of Arts and Letters award for work of distinction; publishes *Staring at the Sun*.
1987	Wins the Gutenberg Prize in France and the Premio Grinzane Carour in Italy; publishes *Going to the Dogs* as Dan Kavanagh.
1988	Translates into English the book by German cartoonist Volker Kriegel, *The Truth about Dogs*; named Chevalier of the Order of Arts and Letters in France.
1989	Publishes *A History of the World in 10½ Chapters*.
1990–94	London correspondent for the *New Yorker*.
1991	Publishes *Talking It Over*.
1992	Wins the Foreign Fémina Prize for *Talking It Over* in France; publishes *The Porcupine*.

1993   Wins the Shakespeare Prize of the FVS Foundation of Hamburg.

1995   Publishes *Letters from London 1990–1995*; teaches a course on creative
        writing in the fall semester at Johns Hopkins University in Baltimore;
        promoted Officer of the Order of Arts and Letters in France.

1996   Publishes *Cross Channel*, his first collection of short stories; Marion
        Vernoux directs French film adaptation of *Talking It Over* under the
        title *Love, etc.*

1998   Publishes *England, England*, which is shortlisted for the Booker
        Prize in Great Britain; Philip Saville directs British film adaptation
        of *Metroland.*

2000   Publishes *Love, etc.*

2002   Publishes *Something to Declare*, a collection of essays about France,
        and *In the Land of Pain*, the English translation of a book by Alphonse
        Daudet; Harry Ransom Center in Austin, Texas, acquires Barnes's ar-
        chive.

2003   Publishes *The Pedant in the Kitchen*, a collection of essays about cook-
        ery originally published in the *Guardian.*

2004   Publishes *The Lemon Table*, his second collection of short stories;
        wins the Austrian State Prize for European Literature; promoted Com-
        mander of the Order of Arts and Letters in France.

2005   Publishes *Arthur & George*, shortlisted for the Man Booker Prize in
        Great Britain.

2005–07 With Hermione Lee, begins hosting a series of BBC Radio 4 pro-
        grams in which Barnes and Lee travel to France to discuss authors such
        as Edith Wharton and Henry James, Rudyard Kipling, and Prosper
        Mérimée.

2008   Publishes *Nothing to Be Frightened Of.*

Conversations with Julian Barnes

Julian Barnes in Interview
Ronald Hayman/1980

From *Books and Bookmen*, May 1980: 36–37. Reprinted by permission of author.

One advantage of reading bad fiction in quantity, as a novel reviewer must, is that he comes to feel more confident about his own work. Another effect that a stint for the *New Statesman* had on Julian Barnes was to make him want to preempt the worst of the available obloquy: "I thought, 'There's only one way I can prepare myself for publication, and that's by writing the worst review I'm likely to get myself.' So I wrote it, and really slanged the book, and in the course of the review said the obvious influences are the following, and then gave lots of names."

He wouldn't tell me the names he'd listed. They may have included an Amis or two, but in fact *Metroland* doesn't obtrude evidence of influences: it's a literary novel, but the literature behind it is well digested. The tone is tangy and individual, especially in the first of the three sections, a maturely sophisticated treatment of premature sophistication in adolescence. In the National Gallery, sometimes using binoculars, Christopher and Toni observe unbeautiful reactions to paintings, and they make notes. "Temple twitch; LHS only" or "Aspiring thorax." They cultivate rootlessness and cynicism, shout ironic encouragement from the sidelines of football fields, compare notes on the boring ineffectuality of adults, compare notes on ventures in piss-taking, indolently lay sardonic plans for the future.

"The difficulty with the first part was that the spirit of it was autobiographical, and the topography was autobiographical, but the actual incidents were invented, and attached to a much more adventurous character than I was at sixteen. But being conscious of the autobiographical element, I looked at it the first two times I wrote it, and thought, 'Is this a novel at all? Why should anyone be interested in it?' That's one of the reasons it's taken so long. Despite its length, it took five or six years, though I had two whole periods of a year when I was too busy to do anything with it.

"In the first version I did of the first part I think I set myself one topic per

3

chapter. I had one chapter where they're doing parents, and one where they're doing sex, and then I thought: 'My God this is much too bald, and if not exactly preachy, at least a bit over-instructive to the reader.' Then I worked at smoothing over the joins and taking bits out—like with pastry. Scenes were all cut up neatly, and then I pushed it all together again, and made it a more plausible shape.

"I didn't think of the hero in the novel's three parts as being three disconnected people. I thought of the development as a structure, an arc. That was there from the beginning. I thought that even if I didn't necessarily know what was going to happen, I wanted a firm structure. I thought of Christopher in the second part as being quite close to Christopher in the first, and of then giving various examples of his skinless contact with experience, which would set up the third part. I'm obviously saying that people develop in ways they don't expect to.

"The third part was the hardest to do and the last to come right, because it was hard, making Christopher's character-change plausible. The first time I did it, I made him amazingly complacent and changed, and it was just wrong for that kind of time-structure. He couldn't have sunk into as deep a rut as I made him fall into. I hope now that it's plausible, in that he's fairly aware of what's happened, and at the same time I hope I haven't made it feel like the unabashedly happy ending one reviewer has congratulated me on writing. When I read that, I thought I might have lightened the tone too much."

Many of his jokes are structural, but he doesn't think while working on a book about keeping the audience amused. "The actual writing bit is masturbatory rather than copulatory. If it makes me laugh at the typewriter, it goes in. It goes in the first time round, anyway. If it doesn't make me laugh the second time round, it comes out. That sounds selfish, but certainly it's the only initial test. There's my typewriter and then there's the wall, and I don't look beyond it. What you're addressing is the page rather than the reader. It's different writing nonfiction. You think how much will your average reader know about that? How far do I pitch it? Whereas as a fiction writer you can pitch it in lots of different places at once. That's one of the attractions."

Before he became a freelance journalist, Julian Barnes worked for three years as a lexicographer on the Supplement to the *Oxford English Dictionary*, and then read abortively for the Bar. "They were both professions connected with words. I was only twenty-two or something when I became a lexicographer. I hadn't abandoned hope of being a writer, and I'm quite relieved that it didn't have much effect, that you can't say, 'This is the writing of a lexicographer.' If it's had an effect on my writing or on my attitude to language, it's the same effect as knowing some law has. It just makes you less jumpy about where the law can get you. If you're trained as a lexicographer, you're maybe just a bit more relaxed about some aspects of language. Working on a dictionary has paradoxically made me adopt a less prescriptive attitude to language."

For about two years he wrote in the *New Review* under the name Edward Pygge. "I suppose it had a psychological effect in that you'd write a piece, and it would appear in public, and people read it, and no one rang you up in the middle of the night and said, 'You're rumbled.' When I started working as a journalist, I used to worry that someone would say, 'Look, you're not a journalist, you're just someone posing as a journalist.'

"Edward Pygge started off with John Fuller and Ian Hamilton and Clive James back in the early days of the *Review*, and I inherited the awesome mantle in something like issue thirty of the *New Review*, and then I did it for about thirteen issues until the 'Greek Street' column closed. I don't know what Ian had read of mine. Some fiction reviews, maybe. He tried me out for one issue, and when he saw the result, he said 'Okay, you can have a go at being Edward Pygge.'"

After taking so long over *Metroland* Julian Barnes took just nine days on the first draft of a thriller which is to be published pseudonymously in July, and three days on revising it. "I think I wondered what it would be like writing as fast as I possibly could in a concentrated way. I went down to the country and shut myself away in a cottage I was lent. I went down there with the opening, the first two chapters and one or two nasty things to happen along the line, and an idea of the hero and the sort of villain I wanted. I wrote for about six or seven hours each day, and in the evening I worked out what was going to happen the next day. To my amazement I found the plot coming—*Metroland*'s not exactly a plotty book, not exactly a novel of action.

"Two or three months earlier James McClure had come to dinner with us and said he'd written each of his first three thrillers in a fortnight. They're quite complex, and they're very well written. Later that night, I was awake at three in the morning and my wife was also awake and I said, 'Two weeks, that's quite a long time really.' It was a sporting challenge as much as anything else.

"Before I went off to write *Duffy* I knew that if I produced something usable I didn't want to publish it under my own name, and that had a very curious liberating effect, and helped me to find the tone in which it's written. When I went through it subsequently, I was surprised how the tone of voice seems to me quite different from the tone of *Metroland*. It's constant. You don't suddenly get a paragraph of *Metroland*. Being shut up with it all the time helped as well, but actually thinking consciously of Dan Kavanagh writing this book helped in a strange way. The only time I felt something similar was when writing the Edward Pygge column, where you definitely didn't want it to come out who you were, because then you wouldn't hear so many stories. Maybe that was liberating in letting you be bitchier than you'd normally want to be under your own byline. Maybe this is liberating in that you could indulge any fantasies of violence you might have. For instance I hate cats, but in a Julian Barnes novel I doubt whether I'd do more than lightly push one off my lap, but give me a pseudonym, and I'll have one barbe-cued by the end of the first chapter."

Escape from Metroland

Caroline Holland/1981

From *Islington Gazette*, 31 July 1981: 16. Reprinted by permission of publisher.

"Julian Barnes: Daunted and Delighted—I can see it all now!" the author joked, as he covered his face in mock horror, imagining the way I would sum up his reaction to winning the much-prized Somerset Maugham Award for his first book *Metroland*.

We were talking in his study in a ground floor flat in St. George's Avenue, Holloway, where he has worked for the last four years.

Many of the awards' previous winners are now famous names, and Julian Barnes recognises that he has got a lot to live up to following the likes of Iris Murdoch, Kingsley Amis, Michael Frayn, and Frederick Raphael.

But the rest of the winners fall into a contrasting category: their names mean nothing—they probably wrote a commendable first novel and have since been forgotten.

So Julian Barnes is aware that his following books—the next is due out in March—will determine which of the two categories he will fall into: fame or oblivion.

At this stage he cannot afford to sit back and feel pleased with himself—not that he would anyway—and he was at pains to stress that he was more surprised than satisfied, more daunted than delighted.

It is an intriguing first novel—it is short, humorous, thought-provoking, sexually explicit, and the characters are carefully drawn. It has been acclaimed as an apologia for the middle-class residents of suburbia and interpreted as the opposite, an aggressive satire—but meant as neither.

The title is the name that Julian Barnes gives to a large area of comfortable suburbia north of London served by the Metropolitan Line.

It is the home of Chris and Toni, two adolescent schoolboys who despise their roots, not quietly and self-consciously, but flagrantly and flamboyantly. The first part of the book contains some wonderful descriptions of their attempts to "épater la bourgeoisie," or shock the establishment.

The middle section deals with the years that Chris (the first-person of the novel) spends in Paris. They are supposed to be his years of adult rebellion, but he doesn't even know the student unrest of 1968 is going on.

When he returns to this country, he already knows the woman who becomes his wife, and she helps him find a job and they settle in, of all places, Metroland. The third and final section describes how Chris comes to terms with compromising his adolescent ideals, and how he drifts apart from Toni who is disgusted with Chris's readiness to accept what he previously rejected.

Reflecting on the irony of returning to Metroland, Chris asks himself: "But isn't part of growing up being able to ride irony without being thrown?" He cannot see his compromise as a cop-out, rather as a hurdle to be jumped on the road to maturity. This sort of rationale is used by many who pass through a rebellious youth, I imagine.

The book is only semi-autobiographical. As a boy, Julian Barnes lived in the suburb of Northwood, Middlesex, which is served by the Metropolitan Line, and he had a close friend called Toni. A few of the incidents and descriptions were taken from real life, but the rest was invention.

And while he and Toni might have been pretentious, rebellious, and interested in sex, as most boys are, he exaggerated their characters greatly.

He wasn't quite sure how his book would be taken, especially by his parents who were sent a copy as soon as it was published.

"I was a bit worried because I thought they might think I was repudiating my childhood, which I wasn't, but it was open to that sort of misinterpretation."

After a few weeks of not hearing from them he went to see them at their home in Oxfordshire—they have moved from "Metroland"—and he waited for them to broach the subject. Quite unexpectedly as they were doing some shopping, his father commented: "Enjoyed your book. Language was a bit lower deck"—and that was it. And his mother made it plain that she too objected to the language, but on the whole their reaction was not unfavourable.

But Toni, who he thought would appreciate the book, didn't like it at all.

"I didn't think he would take offence. I thought he would think it was as distant from him as it was from me, but sadly he hated it, and I haven't seen him since."

He added wryly: "My next book is about sexual jealousy. Goodness knows how that is going to be interpreted!"

Married eighteen months ago, his wife, Pat, works for his literary agent and they live in Dartmouth Park Road, Tufnell Park. He keeps his study in St. George's

Avenue so he can still "go out" to work. There is no question of them ever going to the suburbs either!

"It gives me the shivers when I go back there. I occasionally drive through that sort of area, and I feel ghosts passing overhead. I don't feel roots there, but I don't feel roots anywhere," he said.

He didn't mean the book to be an aggressive satire of the suburbs—although he hasn't made a point of doing any book-signing there!

"It's more about a journey which everyone makes which is from being adventurous to being less adventurous. It's not a put-down of suburbia, it's a useful metaphor for what happens to Chris as he grows up."

Metroland took about six years to write, but his second book took only a year. He has already started on the third which is yet more ambitious and will be written from the point of view of a woman.

"The thing I enjoy most in my life is my work. As Noel Coward said: 'Work is more fun than fun,'" he said.

Writing novels occupies only half of his working hours—for three days a week he is deputy literary editor of the *Sunday Times*.

When he left university, he wasn't sure what to do, although he was obviously a high-flyer. From a state primary school he had gone to the City of London Boys School with a scholarship and then to Magdalen College, Oxford.

After a number of jobs he worked on the supplement to the *Oxford English Dictionary* for three years before deciding to read for the bar.

While doing his legal training he took to writing reviews for a variety of papers and periodicals.

"By the time I had finished, I realised I was getting more enjoyment from writing two hundred words for, say, the *Times Literary Supplement*, than doing a tax case in Bromley Crown Court."

So he went into freelance journalism, until in 1977 he was given a staff job on the *New Statesman* as assistant literary editor. Two years later he went to the *Sunday Times*.

Under the pseudonym Basil Seal—a character invented by Evelyn Waugh who was always available for last-minute dinner parties—he writes a food column for the *Tatler*.

Just recently he submitted some of his work into a "Restaurant Critic of the Year Competition"—and won. For his prize he chose a gastronomic holiday in China.

He never thought of himself as a writer, he rather fell into it. He wrote

Metroland, he says, because he was "getting on" and if he was going to write it was about time he got down to it.

And he did it in the nick of time too, because only writers who were aged under thirty-five on December 31 last year were eligible for the Somerset Maugham Award—and he was thirty-five in January!

"The major obstacle was convincing myself that what I wrote would be of interest to someone," he said.

And it's just as well he got over his inhibitions, too, because *Metroland* is a remarkable book and certainly one of the best pieces of modern fiction I have read in a long time.

Julian Barnes
Patrick McGrath/1987

From *Bomb* 21 (Fall 1987): 21–23. Reprinted by permission of publisher.

Patrick McGrath: Let me begin with something you wrote in *Before She Met Me*. One of your characters propounds the theory that the human brain is made up of three brains: the reptilian, the lower mammalian, and the upper mammalian. He says it's the lower mammalian brain that makes people vote Tory.

Julian Barnes: Sounds pretty accurate to me; I'd still hold to that, yes. It's a wonderful metaphor, actually, which I got from a psychologist called Paul D. MacLean, who wrote: "Speaking allegorically, of these brains within a brain, we might imagine that when the psychiatrist bids the patient to lie on the couch, he's asking him to stretch out alongside a horse and a crocodile." And there are times in your life when you feel that the croc is getting out—which is what the book is about.

McGrath: It's the horse in us that votes Tory, then.

Barnes: It's the horse, is it?

McGrath: Well, the lower mammalian.

Barnes: Yes, the reptilian would vote National Front. I don't know what the American equivalent to that would be.

McGrath: Probably straight Republican ticket. The central figure in that book is a man who's lived in a state of total monogamy for fifteen years, and then quite suddenly leaves his wife for a younger woman. But he can't cope, and things start to go badly wrong.

Barnes: In a way it's a sort of anti-'60s book. It's against the idea that somehow the '60s sorted sex out, that everyone was all fucked up beforehand, Queen Victoria was still in charge—and then along came the Beatles, suddenly everyone started sleeping with everyone else, and that cured the lot. That's a rough plan of English sexual history, as seen by many people. And I just wanted to say, it's not like that; that what is constant is the human heart and human passions. And the change in who does what with whom—that's a superficial change.

McGrath: The idea of adultery is clearly center stage in *Before She Met Me,* but it's very much present in your first novel, too, in *Metroland.*

Barnes: It's funny. There's this idea in *Metroland,* that when you're growing up you wonder about the various things that life is going to contain. And if you were brought up in a reasonably intellectual school, as I was, and with a normally cultured middle-class background, you think there are these things called moral decisions, and that every so often you'll come across one, and you'll say: "Aha! I remember this! This is what I knew was going to happen when I grew up, I'd make moral decisions." And what happens in *Metroland* in the end is that the only moral decisions the central figure, Chris, seems to get to make are sexual decisions—in other words, sex is the area where moral decisions, moral questions, most clearly express themselves; it's only in sexual relationships that you come up against immediate questions of what's right and wrong. I remember once talking to Iris Murdoch at a party, and at the time I think I either didn't have a job, or was dissatisfied with the one I had, and she said: "Oh, you ought to go into the civil service. It's very good for making moral decisions." And I thought, "Perhaps that's where they get made."

McGrath: In your most recent novel, *Staring at the Sun,* you're again dealing with moral decision-making inasmuch as you're concerned with courage. But courage is another of these things that makes a pretty infrequent appearance in our lives, I'd have thought.

Barnes: I remember John Berryman saying in interview that one thing that really upset him was that a man could go through life nowadays without finding out whether or not he was courageous. We do tend to think of courage as a male virtue, as something that happens in war, something that consists of standing and fighting. But there are 85,000 other sorts of courage, some of which come into the book—banal forms of courage—to live alone, for example, social courage. Then, the sort of sexual courage that we see in the relationship of the two women, Jean and Rachel. That's the rough scheme of it, anyway.

McGrath: *Staring at the Sun* is narrated from a woman's point of view. Why did you do that?

Barnes: Pure simple curiosity, basically. Any man, but especially any writer, would give good money to be allowed to be a woman for however long it took to understand it better. There's also the technical interest in writing from a woman's point of view. If you write one book in first-person, and another book in third-person, then one of the things to try is writing from the point of view of the opposite sex.

McGrath: One of the most vivid characters in the book is Rachel, a radical feminist, a lesbian, who attempts the seduction of your central figure, Jean.

Barnes: People think Rachel's a problem, they find her unsympathetic. I don't. I find her rather gutsy. She's drawn from life, to an extent; I did know someone rather like her, though not very well. (It helps when you're drawing people from life not to know them very well. If you're sitting on a bench next to someone and they start telling you their life story, after a while you want to say: "That's enough, I'll do the rest myself. Don't tell me any more or you'll spoil your own life.") I think perhaps if there is a problem with Rachel it's that she's over-portrayed. She's done very realistically, and you're told everything she thinks and stands for. The idea was that there's only so much you can learn in your life. My central figure, Jean, has heroically fought her way out of a second-rate life and made her own life. And then along comes this character of her own sex, Rachel, who has completely outflanked her. Everything that Jean has worked for is completely taken for granted by Rachel, and it was that sense of being outflanked that I was after. And, of course, the business of Jean not having the courage to have an affair with Rachel.

McGrath: That would have been out of character altogether.

Barnes: Yes. But I think sex is much stranger than we think. Somerset Maugham said something about there being nobody who, if his or her sex life were expounded in full truth, would not appear . . . I forget the ending, but, as it were, "a grotesque monster." It seems to me that there's no norm to a sex life. Every sex life is abnormal, anormal. There's a whole spectrum of sexual behavior, and we imagine it somehow pivoting around something called *normality* in the middle. But I think that normality is a black hole. There's nothing there.

McGrath: Let's talk about *Flaubert's Parrot.* Your narrator, Geoffrey, is speaking about an academic called Enid Starkie, and he says: "Dr. Starkie and her kind are cursed from memory: the books they teach and write about can never fade from their brains. They become family. Perhaps this is why some critics develop a faintly patronizing tone towards their subjects. They act as if Flaubert, or Milton, or Wordsworth were some tedious old aunt in a rocking chair, who smelt of stale powder, was only interested in the past, and hadn't said anything new for years. Of course, it's her house, and everybody's living in it rent free: but even so, surely it is, well, you know . . . *time?*"

Barnes: You do often feel when you read academic criticism, not that I do it much, or when you hear academics talking about their books, that they forget that theirs is a secondary activity. They forget that however important a critic is, a first-rate critic is always less important, and less interesting, than a second-rate writer. Their job is, firstly, to explain, but secondly to celebrate rather than diminish.

McGrath: Now, the way you went about undercutting the academics was through Geoffrey's delightful project of remapping the whole field of knowledge that had accrued around Flaubert—so he produces a Flaubert bestiary, the railway spotter's guide to Flaubert, the Flaubert apocrypha. Did you set out deliberately to reorganize a body of knowledge, to illustrate how academic studies are bound by arbitrary conventions?

Barnes: There is a negative, critical side to all this, but I think there's also a positive side. Its main function is not to point out to academics that perhaps there are other ways of approaching Flaubert, but to ask: How can I best pay homage to Flaubert? And because this is the form that's emerged, by its nature it's anti-academic. There's this sort of huge tomb beneath which Flaubert is buried, and people come and look at it—there's an official entrance where you pay one and sixpence, and you get a ticket, you look round the corpse, and then you come out. My plan was to sink shafts in at different angles. So you say, "Well, let's take trains." It would have helped if I'd had it all on computer, I suppose. One could have gone through and got all the references in Flaubert to trains. Some things don't work, but trains work, the bestiary works, and even though it looks rather esoteric—you know, "What do we know about Flaubert and trains?"—if I couldn't produce something with a shape and movement to it *as fiction*, then it couldn't work. There were some things I had to abandon because just nothing came out of them.

McGrath: For example?

Barnes: I had one chapter that I dropped about sex and creativity. When Flaubert's talking about writing, there's an awful lot of sexual metaphors. "Go fuck your inkwell!" is one of his great injunctions to a writer. And when he's writing *Madame Bovary* he says, "I'm having a lot of trouble getting hard," and then, "I think I'm finally going to come!" I was trying to do a chapter on the whole of his life in terms of sexual metaphor, but it sort of didn't quite come off. I showed it to a friend who reads my books before they go to the publisher, and she said, "Well, actually, I'm not sure if it works, but I personally find it offensive"—the idea of the Muse as a woman who has to be fucked flat before a chap can get a book out. "That's rather disgusting," she said.

McGrath: Barthes said he regarded Proust as a sort of mandala.
Barnes: What's a mandala?

McGrath: One of those Eastern designs that are circular and completely symmet-rical, and are supposed to contain all of creation organized in a perfect pattern. I wonder if you feel anything of the sort toward Flaubert?

Barnes: I don't think so. Obviously, he's the writer whose words I most carefully tend to weigh, who I think has spoken the most truth about writing. And it's odd to have a foreign genius for whom you feel a direct love. . . . He's obviously a tricky bastard in some ways, but I find when I'm reading his letters I just want to go and make him a cup of hot chocolate, light his cigarette.

McGrath: Why?
Barnes: Partly because I admire his books greatly. He's a great example of a genius who never wrote the same book twice. Also, in his letters he's so remorse-lessly *intelligent*; he's never dull, he's never banal, he's very funny. There's a phrase in the *Parrot* about relying on the drip feed of another writer's intelligence . . .

McGrath: There's a point in *Metroland* where Chris, who's living in France, be-gins to feel something changing in him, "a resented metamorphosis" he calls it, because he's speaking French all the time. He says, "I found myself more prone to generalization, to labeling and ticketing and docketing and sectioning and ex-plaining and to lucidity—God, yes, to lucidity . . . it wasn't loneliness . . . it wasn't homesickness, it was something to do with being English . . . as if one part of me was being faintly disloyal to another part."
Barnes: That's not bad, that. Not bad for a first book.

McGrath: Is that the French mind for you, labeling and ticketing and docketing and sectioning?
Barnes: Yes, it is. I lived in France for a year when I was twenty-one, and though I spoke French very fluently by the end, I did find that I wasn't really recogniz-ing myself as the same person. It's partly that you're influenced by who you're around, but I think more fundamentally than that, that the language influences the thoughts you can have. Just as you find yourself making French physical ges-tures, because English gestures don't mean anything to them, so you make French mental gestures.

McGrath: This business of the language you use somehow structuring or consti-tuting your reality—do you see this as a first expression of a theme that's repeated through the other novels, that it's the way things are configured in language that determines reality?

Barnes: This is a good line, but I think it's rather for you to develop than me. I think it's quite attractive, but I certainly don't think of things in those terms. You think of each book as a completely separate entity when you're writing it, and you're very flattered, or dismayed, when people say, "Ah, this book picks up this idea from that book." In Holland they asked me about my obsession with suicide. I said, "I'm not obsessed with suicide!" And they said, "Well, there's a suicide in *Before She Met Me*, and there's a suicide in *Flaubert's Parrot*." And I said, "Oh, that's just a coincidence." And then I thought, well, actually, there's quite a lot about suicide in my next book. God, I thought, I better knock it off for a few books. So obviously someone taking an overall view of your work can read your particular themes and obsessions better than you can yourself, and that's something one just has to put up with. Frank Kermode wrote a very friendly review of *Flaubert's Parrot* in which he decided I was obsessed with obsessions. And this phrase got currency, and I found myself being reviewed in this way: "Mr. Barnes is, of course, a writer obsessed with obsessions." And I went around saying, "I AM NOT OBSESSED WITH OBSESSIONS!" I was getting obsessed about being obsessed with obsessions. You go crazy if you think about it too much.

McGrath: To get back to *Flaubert's Parrot*: it was very clear to me that Geoffrey's search for the parrot that stood on Flaubert's desk was a large metaphor for his attempt to figure out why his wife, Ellen, was unfaithful to him. He says, "Ellen's is a true story: perhaps it is even the reason why I am telling you Flaubert's story."

Barnes: It's about the difference between art and life—art is the stuff you finally understand, and life, perhaps, is the stuff you finally can't understand.

McGrath: In one sense, then, the book is about Ellen.

Barnes: Yes. Absolutely. Without the fictional infrastructure it wouldn't exist as a novel, it seems to me. It would be a serious article.

McGrath: But inasmuch as the novel is about Ellen, she's rather a bizarre heroine. She makes only one appearance, and that's comatose on her deathbed. She also has the dubious distinction of having died by her own hand and of having died by her husband's hand.

Barnes: Yes, that's a twist, isn't it? Is that a question?

McGrath: Maybe I should follow it up by wondering if the same could be said of Emma Bovary—that she died by Charles's hand as well as by her own.

Barnes: How come?

McGrath: There's a phrase Artaud uses talking about van Gogh. He says, "Here is a man suicided by society." It occurred to me as a reading of *Madame Bovary* that it is precisely Charles's tedium, his dullness, the whole atmosphere in which he lives, that does her in.

Barnes: But I think that behind Emma Bovary's superficial social and sexual dissatisfactions you can locate a broader despair. I don't know who first coined the term *bovarysme*, but it is the idea that that's the human condition—one of aspirations that will never be satisfied. Geoffrey's Ellen obviously has traits in common with Emma, but a century further on.

McGrath: Was this very much in your mind as you thought about the Ellen character?

Barnes: Yes, I wanted a parallel with Charles and Emma Bovary.

McGrath: So *Flaubert's Parrot* in a sense is *Madame Bovary* from Charles's point of view.

Barnes: Yes, though I think my character, Geoffrey, is smarter than Charles Bovary. He'd have to be, really, to have read all that Flaubert!

McGrath: Well, I hate to keep bringing up parallels and connections between the books—

Barnes: I'm enjoying them, it's just I can't promise instant useful reactions to them.

McGrath: Close to the end of the *Parrot* we come upon Flaubert's notion of the religion of despair, that it's only by gazing into the abyss at our feet that we can grow calm. Geoffrey comes to see that his wife's problem was that she couldn't do this; she could only glance at it sideways, and then her terror would set her off on another of her adulterous sprees. I had a sense that many of the themes handled in *Staring at the Sun* developed from the religion-of-despair idea first articulated in *Flaubert's Parrot*.

Barnes: Well, the first thing to say to that is that I started *Staring at the Sun* before I started *Flaubert's Parrot*; I'd already written about 30,000 words of it. The connection that I see between the two is technical rather than thematic, in that *Flaubert's Parrot* was a book that went off in all directions, and one of the ways of tying it all together was to use repeated phrases and ideas like thin bits of gossamer, to keep it vaguely bound together. That developed in *Staring at the Sun* into actual images, and incidents, and stories, which, as the book continues, take on more depth and significance. At first they're just odd stories, but by the end they become metaphors. That's the connection that I see, but no doubt there are thematic connections as well.

McGrath: I wonder if we can't see the ghost of a parrot flapping through *Staring at the Sun*—in the sense that the metaphor of flight as spirituality, the soul's journey, has been carried on there with all the aeroplane business.
Barnes: I hadn't thought of that at all. I'll give you that one.

McGrath: Oh really?
Barnes: Yes. But all I'm saying is that's not how I work—and I'm not sure that I would work well if I did see things like that. If I thought, "Well, I've had a parrot flying up to heaven, now I'll have an aeroplane flying up to heaven"—my reaction would be, "No, that's a bit obvious, won't do that." So, no, I wasn't reminded of *Parrot*, not at all. Maybe I should have been, but the extent to which you can be a critic of your own books is limited. Fortunately. There is a lot of self-consciousness about writing, but if you had total self-consciousness you'd never get anything done.

McGrath: The quest fails finally in *Flaubert's Parrot*, doesn't it? Geoffrey fails to find the one, true stuffed parrot that stood on Flaubert's desk.
Barnes: I would have thought from our reading of Geoffrey that he would adduce a sort of grim pleasure from the fact that he couldn't find the right parrot. He would be consoled by the fact that there wasn't an easy answer. He would go to Flaubert and find the line that says—this is a rough quote—"The desire to reach conclusions is a sign of human stupidity."

McGrath: His expectations are confounded because he has expected all along to be able to find the one, true answer, like the one, true God, or the one, true political ideology. He learns that you have to accept multiples.
Barnes: That's right. And the immediate parallel is the inability to seize and convey the nature of Flaubert's life.

McGrath: It's a plea for tolerance. I find in all your books the idea that we can never reach a point of certainty, that there's no single truth you can dogmatically adhere to. There will be as many explanations as there are people.
Barnes: That's certainly a Flaubertian line. I suppose I'd go along with it. But you're making it sound as if I don't somehow think that there are right and wrong ways to behave. I think I'm a moralist, but you make me sound like a bit of an old hippy—"You do your thing, man, I'll do mine." Part of a novelist's job obviously is

to understand as wide a variety of people as possible. And you put them in situations where there isn't necessarily an easy answer, and things aren't necessarily resolved. But this doesn't mean you don't have strong personal views about how life should be lived, and what's good and bad behavior, as I certainly do.

McGrath: Simply, then, that the emphasis is on a shift away from the dogmatic.
Barnes: Sure. Dogma has benighted the world, it seems to me. And God, no more than in the twentieth century—category thinking, package thinking.

McGrath: One last thing. Geoffrey says this about people in relationships: "That's the real distinction between people: not between those who have secrets and those who don't, but between those who want to know everything and those who don't. This search is a sign of love, I maintain."
Barnes: I don't know whether I agree with that, but I think it's well put.

McGrath: Beautifully put. I thought of mad, bad, jealous Graham in *Before She Met Me*. The same could have been said of him, but in his case the desire to know everything was a sign of madness, not of love.
Barnes: That's true. Love that gets out of hand can easily turn into madness, it can easily be curdled. The croc gets loose.

The World's History and Then Some in 10½ Chapters

Bruce Cook/1989

From *Daily News* (Los Angeles), 7 November 1989. Reprinted by permission of publisher.

What kind of writer would presume to write *A History of the World in 10½ Chapters*?

The same kind who might set out to write a novel (more or less) about Gustave Flaubert, and then become so taken with the parrot kept by Flaubert that he uses the noisy bird to focus on his subject, and finally names the novel after it— *Flaubert's Parrot*.

It's Julian Barnes, of course—the agent provocateur of avant-garde fiction, England's answer to the post-modernist novel. But, dare mention that and immediately you'll get an argument from him.

"I think each book should try to be something new for you, a challenge," he said. "I can't afford to be too self-conscious about my writing career. I can't say, 'I am a post-modernist,' because, frankly, I don't think of myself that way. My next book is less experimental-looking than *Flaubert's Parrot* and *A History of the World in 10½ Chapters*. The book after it could be a warm-hearted family saga.

"Actually, you see, you don't have all that much choice in it. Form and idea come at the same time. Or, putting it another way, once you have the idea, the form comes right along."

He's quick, witty, not the sort you'd tangle with in intellectual debate, or even social badinage. We were talking together in the Santa Monica publicity office of his publisher. The occasion, of course, was the release of his new sort-of novel *A History of the World in 10½ Chapters*.

The man is the style. It's a quick, witty, clever trot through history and myth with stops along the way on Noah's ark (the real story told by a woodworm); in fourteenth-century France for a trial in which woodworms are prosecuted for harm done to the person of a bishop; the tale of the wreck of the Medusa, complete with an analytical essay of the painting done by Gericault portraying the horror faced in the open sea by the survivors; the search of Mount Ararat for the wreck of Noah's ark; and the last chapter of all, a glimpse of heaven. Those are just a few of the stops along the way.

But each of these is complete in itself. How is this not a book of short stories?

"Well," said Barnes, "it was conceived as a whole and executed as a whole. Things in it thicken and deepen. Such as? Well, there are recurrent voyages in it. Woodworms reappear. And, there are recurrent patterns of human aspirations and failings. I suppose what it boils down to is that if you don't like it, it's a collection of short stories. If you do, it's a novel."

He sighed. "The definition of a novel is pretty much an academic question by now, anyway, isn't it? You know what Randall Jarrell said: 'A novel is a long piece of prose with something wrong with it.' It's such a bother, this business of what is and is not a novel. If I were Czech, and it was *A History of the World in 10½ Chapters* by Julian Barnski, they'd say, 'Well, of course it's a novel.' But, I admit there are things expected of a novel that this one does not provide."

And, yes, it was, he insists, conceived as a whole: "Well, not as a one-idea book. Some come whole in just that way. But, books are like teeth—that is, some have one root and some are molars with three or four. The origin of each book I've done was in the previous one. I had this character in *Flaubert's Parrot*, Geoffrey Braithwaite, a tedious man. It was my idea to make him rewrite the entire Bible. Some of that fed into the first chapter, the Noah one. And I've always been fascinated by the Gericault picture and by the voyage of the Medusa itself. I even thought about doing a book about that once.

"Then, there was the overall watery substance of the voyages, and then a remark I heard, that something was 'as futile as moving deck chairs on the Titanic,' leading me to consider including a deck-chair attendant's account of the Titanic disaster, which, of course, I never wrote."

He added, "In terms of form, this one is closer to *Flaubert's Parrot*. It also deals with one of the questions that obsessed Braithwaite in that book. And that is: How do we seize the past? But, as I say, there's some relationship between that book and this one. There may not be much between them and the next one."

Whatever he writes, he seems now to have established an audience for himself in France, England, and America. This after years of scrambling in London, first as a lexicographer, working on the Oxford English Dictionary, and then as a journalist–assistant literary editor at the *New Statesman* and the *Sunday Times*, then, subsequently, as television critic of the weekly *Observer*.

"I didn't publish my first novel until I was thirty-four," he said, almost apologetically. "It took a long time, seven years. I'd put it away and then pick it up again. At school, I read Cyril Connolly's *Enemies of Promise*, in which he states categorically that 'journalism is the enemy of literature.' It may have been in his case, though not in mine. You do your five hundred words or so in a review, and nobody says you can't write. Journalism got me to take myself seriously as a writer. I still do a bit of it."

He does a bit of something else, too, which he keeps rather quiet. Under the name of Dan Kavanagh, he also writes detective novels about a rather fierce detective named Duffy. He keeps those books quite separate from his "real" novels, even writes them on a separate typewriter. As a result, the Duffy books are about as different from *Flaubert's Parrot* and his latest as they can possibly be. He means to keep it that way. But, Duffy helps pay the rent.

"I don't think that in England you can make a living as a novelist until you're forty and have three or four books under your belt. But, you collect such a lot of bruises along the way! I don't think I'll ever get hardened to bad reviews. After all, you spend three years of your life writing a book, and how long does the critic take to read the book? Four hours, perhaps!

"Yes, I still review—about a dozen books a year, but it doesn't get easier. Writing novels gets a little easier. But, because of the bumps I've taken along the way, writing book reviews actually gets harder."

Into the Lion's Mouth:
A Conversation with Julian Barnes
Michael March/1997

From *The New Presence*, December 1997. http://www.new-presence.cz. Reprinted by permission of publisher.

Michael March: How did you come to writing—when did you start to write?
Julian Barnes: I came to it slowly. Not as a child who insufferably sat under the bedclothes scribbling away. In my teens I wanted to be a good reader because I thought writing is what other people did. I started to write when I was about twenty-two or twenty-three, and I started in a very hesitant and tentative way—trying to compile a nonfiction book, which fortunately never saw the light of day. Shortly thereafter, I started doing bits of journalism, bits of literary criticism and reviews. And while in many cases fiction and journalism are healthy enemies, I found that the most important thing was getting some words out there. The struggle to feel that I had any right, any justification to be a novelist took a long time—which is why I didn't publish *Metroland*, my first novel, until I was thirty-four. My first book took about nine years to write.

March: Do you have any heroes?
Barnes: Yes, of course, I had many heroes. They were the great names of world literature, from Shakespeare to Flaubert to Turgenev to Tolstoy, Voltaire and so forth. They were mainly English, French, and Russian. English being my native language, and French and Russian being the two languages that I studied in school. But there is a huge difference between having literary heroes and having them be helpful to you as a writer. The greater the writer the more daunting it is: the idea that Flaubert's first novel was *Madame Bovary*. Such a hero puts you off the idea that anything you write will ever be worth publishing.

March: Was there an anti-hero who encouraged you?
Barnes: There wasn't one who encouraged me. No, I didn't know any writers; I didn't know any writers until I became a writer. I had two poet friends, Craig

Raine and Christopher Reid. I showed them my first novel, and they told me to put it away in a drawer and forget about it. From which one learns: never show anyone your work; or if you are a novelist, never show it to a poet. So I didn't know any writers before I became a writer. There wasn't an avuncular figure who had already done it and said: you just keep going and it will work out. All the avuncular figures were on my bookshelves.

March: Publication must have been a mystical experience.
Barnes: The promise of publication was something miraculous. Though one of the lessons I learned is that each novel seems to have a time in which it ought to be written. Otherwise, there is something artificial about your address to the book.

March: Which of your novels is closest to your heart?
Barnes: The novel which brought prominence was my third novel—*Flaubert's Parrot*, which was the first one that sold well, won prizes, and was widely translated abroad. In my mind and heart I try not to favor my books. I am grateful to *Flaubert's Parrot* because it helped me. But to be over-grateful seems to be unkind to the others. The ones I feel fondest toward are often the ones people have a tendency to disregard. It's just that I am fed up with people saying, "I really love *Flaubert's Parrot*." And I feel like saying, "Well, what's wrong with the others?"

March: Is there a deep vein between yourself and French literature?
Barnes: It's primary exotic—it's the first foreign country I discovered, it's the other country I know best—geographically, I know France better than I know Britain. Its literature contains as many points of reference for me as English literature—and my books are well received there, so I am very fond of France in return. In most of my books, there is a French element. This is not designed—books always reflect your conscious intentions, as well as your unaware obsessions.

March: Are the French elements philosophical, psychological—fashionable?
Barnes: No, not fashionable—that's the last thing. If I wanted to be fashionable, I certainly wouldn't put French elements into my novels because they displease the British more than they please the British.

March: Are you influenced by Russian literature?
Barnes: It's always hard to say about influences. Most writers I know would probably deny influences. That's a necessary denial, even though it's often false. If you see anything which looks like an influence, you try and rub it out straight away.

The Russia I think of is mainly fictional Russia—it's more of a fantasy emotional relationship, being that I was there only once in 1965.

March: How did your novel *The Porcupine* evolve?
Barnes: In the long term, it came out of the fact that I am a child of the Cold War. I was born in 1946—the whole of my childhood and adult life has been lived in the shadow of the Cold War, even if it's a less fierce and cold shadow than that experienced in Eastern Europe. When I was thirteen or fourteen, I remember vividly my English master sending his wife to the country because of the Cuban Missile Crisis. Obviously, as any normal, sentient human being would, I followed the political history of Eastern Europe as closely as I could. Then, in 1989, I went to Bulgaria for the first time, having been to every other Eastern European country at least once. It was a very emotional experience because they had just got rid of Zhivkov, and there were great shortages of food, electricity, and petrol. They were in a state of exhilaration and a certain amount of fear; and I was deeply moved by their enthusiasm and their irony and their sense that it was possible to renew a country—this sort of tenderizing of your political and national sympathies isn't necessarily something that has anything to do with writing a novel, and I never thought about writing fiction about Eastern Europe. When I returned, I wrote one or two pieces of journalism about my visit. Then, about six months later, I remember waking up in the middle of the night with the classic question: What if? What if a communist leader came to trial—what if, instead of running away or pretending he had cancer or whatever, what if he decided to defend himself by attacking? I was sort of aware that Zhivkov was going to be brought to trial. In fact, he was on trial in the course of my writing the book. I finished the book before his verdict came out. So I wrote it in parallel to those events happening—with help from my newly made friends in Bulgaria.

March: How was *The Porcupine* received in Bulgaria?
Barnes: The reception was very interesting. I went to Sofia for the publication, and I got there just as the verdict was announced. The verdict on Zhivkov was considerably milder than the verdict that I had delivered in my own book. I had been told that a few nights before, in an act which would never take place in Britain, the newsreader at the end of the night's news had held up my book and said: if you want to know what a British writer thinks of the Zhivkov trial, read this book. A great publicity coup for my publishers.

March: *The Porcupine* was first published in Bulgaria.

Barnes: Indeed, it was. It was partly because one of the friends with whom I was collaborating was my translator and publisher. I sent her a first draft and asked for her comments, and her comments were, "I finished the translation; we'll publish in June." I went there, and I was apprehensive, as one would be—I felt I had put my head in a lion's mouth. But the fact that I went there and did put my head into the lion's mouth made it less likely to be bitten off.

He's Turned Towards Python (But Not the Dead Flaubert's Parrot Sketch . . .): Interview with Julian Barnes

Observer/1998

Observer: What is *England, England* about?

Julian Barnes: What's it about? It's about 280 pages. . . . Beyond that, it's about the idea of England, authenticity, the search for truth, the invention of tradition, and the way in which we forget our own history. Towards the end, it's about if and how a nation, like a person, can start again. It plays a public and semi-farcical Grand Project, the building of a replica England on the Isle of Wight, against the private story of a woman, Martha Cochrane, who ends up working for The Project.

Observer: What made you want to write about Englishness?

Barnes: When you start as a novelist, there are various possible projects up ahead on the road. There's "the American novel," for example, which most English novelists seem to fail to find the solution to. And then there's what might roughly be called "the state of England" novel. So you think, "Yeah, at some point, I must do my own country in widescreen." Yet the other thing you learn as you continue through your career is that you have to play subject matter against the sort of writer you are. In my case, as I'm not a documentary writer, it quickly established itself in my mind as an "idea of England" novel rather than a "state of England" novel.

Observer: Was there a moment of inspiration, a trigger?

Barnes: Every time I drive down the M4, there is a wonderful moment of confirmation of the book. Beyond Heathrow there's one of those brown Heritage signposts saying, "Turn off here: to Windsor Castle, Legoland and Royal Ascot." This is one sort of essence of England that the nation is being boiled down to. . . . The way we see ourselves as English people is very different from how we are seen. At a very simple level, we see ourselves as peaceable dispensers of good government, an example to others of the civilised life. People abroad see us as much madder than that, and not just in terms of soccer hooliganism.

The English, and to a lesser extent the British, are considered wild and crazy. If you read Madame De Staël on the English, she writes about a tendency to suicide, a tendency to violence, and the madness brought on by eating too much meat. We haven't been, and aren't seen as, the sort of sobersides that we seem to ourselves. And maybe that's why Lewis Carroll often seems an eccentric sort of Englishman to the English, whereas to the French, say, he seems typical of what seems to them the sort of madcappery that ends up with Monty Python. We think of Python as parodying something essentially English, which is the norm, and they look at Python as an example of the norm.

Observer: This book is très Monty Python.
Barnes: Très Monty Python, yes. In parts.

Observer: You haven't written satire before.
Barnes: I'm awkward with the word "satire." That's why I deliberately used the word "semi-farce" before.

Observer: Apart from "the condition of England" novel are there other novels from the past to which you are alluding?
Barnes: No, I'm not aware of any allusions to previous novels at all.

Observer: Do you admit to influence?
Barnes: Yes and no. The "yes" part is that objectively you know you are living and writing in a cultural continuum, and that anyone looking at your work in fifty or a hundred years will see you as part of a movement, a scheme, a moment, most likely an example of peculiar antiquarianism that has been replaced by post-post-post-post-postmodernism. But in order to work, in order to make something that is individual to yourself and yet a created object out there, you have to persuade yourself that what you are doing is completely original.

At the local level, this means that if you write a sentence which in any way sounds like someone else, you strike it out. Though that doesn't happen very often. On the wider level, it means you persuade yourself that you're completely uninfluenced. The other part of "yes" is that the great writers you admire have an influence on you which is, to use that horrible word, enabling. By creating their own stuff and pushing what they do to the limit and going out on their limb, they don't make you want to crawl along the same branch, but they do free you by saying, "Yeah, you can do that." So obviously to some extent I'm a European writer while being a very English writer. And so I would read Tournier or Calvino and other European writers.

Observer: Who did you read when you were growing up?
Barnes: When I was a schoolboy, I studied French and Russian. So I've got a strong attachment to those cultures: Turgenev, Tolstoy, Chekhov, Voltaire, Flaubert, Montesquieu, Rimbaud, and so on.

Observer: Did you always want to be a writer?
Barnes: No, I didn't. No, no, no, no. I thought that was what other people did. I know there are writers who start scribbling underneath the bedclothes with a torch when they're five. My friend Jay McInerney, when he was only eleven, eight, or probably in the womb, wrote a novel whose first line was "Bring me another Martini, Jeeves," because he felt all butlers were called Jeeves. He'd never read a Wodehouse. He told me that when he was ten or eleven and he wrote this first line, he wanted to be a sophisticated metropolitan novelist. Which of course is what he's become. But I wasn't, at the age of ten, scribbling little notes saying, Flaubert's Dachshund, Flaubert's Vulture, no—Flaubert's Parrot! I didn't know what I wanted to be. As an adolescent, you see the future in terms of your personal and emotional development rather than professional development. In literary terms, I suppose I wanted to be a good reader. I thought that was the highest I'd get.

Observer: In your previous work, you've written about feelings and love. How do you find the transition in *England, England* from that kind of world to the world of satire and politics?
Barnes: Well, that was one of the hardest things, getting the balance and also the point of adhesion between the personal intimate life realistically treated, and the large, semi-farcical story of the island. When I wasn't sure whether it was working or not, I simply extracted from the draft of the book all the sections dealing with Martha's personal life, and then rewrote them as a sort of individual story. Then put them back into the book and made the necessary adjustments. I learnt that from doing *Talking It Over*, when at a certain point I was worried that the woman's voice was being drowned out. I simply took all the pages out and read her story as her story all the way through.

I mean, that's probably one of the advantages of having an old-fashioned type-writer. I suppose you could print out those sections on a computer, but it's good to feel the novel physically coming apart like that and then laying it back in place.

Observer: How much do you plan your fiction?

Barnes: It varies very much from novel to novel. In *Talking It Over,* for example, which involved a lot of intricate interweaving of voices, I tried to plan 100 per cent of the action. As I went on, it was coming out differently, so I ended up having only planned about 80–85 per cent of it. In other novels I just sort of start. But I never start at the beginning. I tend to start at a central moment and often circle round.

Observer: Do you have a favourite book of yours?

Barnes: Of my own? I don't have a favourite. I have different fondnesses. The first one because it was such a struggle. It is a wonderful moment when you first hold a hardback book with your name on the cover. And then the second one you're fond of because it proved you could write another book. (The great fear after writing one book is you are only a one-book writer.) And then the third, *Flaubert's Parrot,* which gave me some sort of visibility, and was also the first to get me known abroad. Then [laughs] there's that one those bastards out there don't like, so you have a particular fondness for it. And so on.

Observer: This is your first novel for six years. Why the delay?

Barnes: I took seven years to write the first one, and then each time, as a sort of defence mechanism, and also out of natural interest and desire, I would always have started the next book by the time the previous one came out. That was just a rule. When I finished *The Porcupine,* that was nearly a twenty–year period when I had always been at work on a novel. I thought, why don't I step back from it for a bit and refresh my thoughts about the novel, what I can do, and what the novel can do? It didn't work. A novelist does his or her thinking about a novel when writing it. The same goes for your thinking about the novel generally.

Observer: What is the purpose of fiction?

Barnes: It's to tell the truth. It's to tell beautiful, exact, and well-constructed lies which enclose hard and shimmering truths.

"Novels Come out of Life, Not out of Theories": An Interview with Julian Barnes

Rudolf Freiburg/1999

From *Do You Consider Yourself a Postmodern Author?: Interviews with Contemporary English Writers*. Edited by Rudolf Freiburg and Jan Schnitker. Münster: LIT, 1999. 39–66. Reprinted by permission of the publisher.

Rudolf Freiburg: Mr. Barnes, in *Flaubert's Parrot,* your meanwhile classic study of the relationship between biography and literature, the narrator leaves no doubt about his contempt for intensive biographical research, and he quite often ponders the question: "Why don't we leave the writer alone?" Now since you have gained international fame, you automatically evoke curiosity as both a person and a writer. I don't want to bother you with questions about your private life but one thing would interest me: could you give us a brief description of a typical working day in your life as a writer?

Julian Barnes: It's an obvious remark to begin with: I'm never not a writer. It seems to me that I am in the happy position of having a job, a vocation, a passion that occupies me twenty-four hours of the day, and everything is grist to the mill. But on a day when I am behaving as people expect writers to behave—that's to say sitting in front of a piece of paper—I suppose that I would get up at about half past eight, I would have breakfast, I would read the newspapers, I would possibly get something else written before I actually start to work. That is to say I might fax a friend or I might write in my diary, something like that as a priming of the pump. And then I would probably sit down at about ten o'clock in the morning, and I would attempt to work—if we're talking about original creative work—until probably about one o'clock with one cup of coffee at eleven o'clock. I would then break for lunch and I would not go back to original creative work for the rest of the day. The afternoon would be spent either doing that dreadful part of the writer's life—managing your career, answering letters, answering questionnaires—or doing journalism. Or possibly, if the brain was working well again—and the brain doesn't usually work very well again until about five o'clock—then I would start correcting at that point or rereading.

Freiburg: Your books display an impressive amount of knowledge and scholarship. Do you sometimes hire research assistants?
Barnes: No. I have only had a researcher on one book and that was on *A History of the World in 10½ Chapters* where I did use someone to research things that I couldn't be bothered with finding out myself, like, how you travelled from England to Turkey in the 1840s—things like that. And that was o.k. but on the whole, I think, a writer of the sort of books that I write should do his own research. The detail that is in them is the result of my own passion for whatever subject I'm writing about.

Freiburg: So research could be creative, too, in that respect.
Barnes: Research *can* be creative, yes! I mean I certainly don't believe in research except when you're writing. Popular novelists research banking for two years and then they write a novel in three months. But I don't know what I need until I start writing the novel, and I also think there's a danger of over-researching, there's a danger of putting all your research into the book.

Freiburg: A sort of "factography" that does not interest anyone anymore, perhaps. If you look at the history of the English novel, you sometimes come across cases in which people try to influence authors: Richardson is a good example; when he wrote *Pamela* and *Clarissa*, he received quite a lot of letters that said, "Why didn't you change the fate of that particular character?" or, 'Why didn't you consider a much happier ending for *Clarissa*?" Has that happened to you? Do you sometimes get suggestions from readers?
Barnes: Not suggestions, though I sometimes get disagreements from readers because they don't think something would have happened or they think a character would have behaved in a different way. I like that, because it means that the book has created its own reality in the readers' mind. And I quite like it when people disagree about the endings of my books. Several of my books end in a deliberately ambiguous or a neutral way. And so, to take an example: *Talking It Over,* English readers think that Gillian's ruse will succeed, that the marriage will continue, that Oliver will be cross for a few days, that Stuart will be purged, and that the Oliver-Gillian marriage will in some way be saved. French readers say, "Well of course she will leave him, won't she? She wouldn't stay with a man like that!" And I say, "O.K., I'm sorry, I invented her, so I think I ought to know." And they

say, "No, no, you are quite wrong, she would leave him." And I say, "But in England you see, we tend to marry twice at the most," and they say, "No, no, no, she will be off . . ." and so on. But I like all that [laughs].

Freiburg: Let me stick to the problem of reception for another moment. On the one hand there is the "normal" reader, on the other hand there is the professional critic. Do you take criticism into consideration?

Barnes: I've never taken it into consideration when writing. I've never had a review—this sounds arrogant—but I've never had a review which has told me something about the book that I didn't know already. I think that I am like most writers; I read criticism for its praise and I'm pleased by praise and displeased by blame, and this in a way is rather juvenile. I think finally now I've passed the age of fifty, I've outgrown this juvenility in that when my last book *England, England* came out, I read the first English review, which happily was by our most intelligent critic—John Carey—and happily he'd liked the book very much, and happily he understood the book very well. And I thought there's no point reading any more because this man understands it and likes it. And all the others will be worse—they may praise more but after a while that gets a bit disgusting, and so I just haven't read any reviews since. I thought that maybe when the novel came out in America it would be different. The first American review, in the *New York Times*, was faxed through to me—my wife and I came back one evening, and I went into my office and I saw what was clearly—I could tell from the type face—a *New York Times* review, and I reacted like a sort of teenage girl who finds a mouse in her bedroom. I said, "There's something nasty in here; come and take it away!" I couldn't take it out of the fax machine! And, you know, it's only one book, but I think that this will be my attitude from now on. Criticism doesn't help you practically as a writer, so all you get is an emotional lifting-up or an emotional lowering-down. Really you ought to be mature enough not to need the praise after a certain point.

Freiburg: You just gave me a key word: maturity. In your first novel, *Metroland*, you told the story of two friends, Christopher and Toni. In this story of adolescence you describe growing up as a process of disillusion.

Barnes: Yes. It's the story of two boys who begin seemingly on a parallel course and seemingly in accord about everything and then their lives diverge. And again, as I was saying, by the time you get to the third part of the book, the ending is ambiguous, or balanced, or unclear so that on the one hand Chris, who is the main character, either has—depending how you look at him—become mature, sensible, wise, or has completely sold out and tuned all his values to those of wider society; whereas Toni—according to your choice—is either a ridiculously immature poser as he always had been, or someone who has stuck by his ideals and still believes in art and value and truth in the way he did when they were fifteen or sixteen.

Freiburg: Do the slogans Toni and Chris are so fond of, that is *épater la bourgeoisie* and *écraser l'infâme*, still make sense to you?

Barnes: I think the *bourgeoisie* exists as strongly as it ever did. More and more so! I think, Europe is nothing if it is not *bourgeois*. Whether they are as *épatable* anymore is difficult to say, because the artistic and the rebellious always underestimate the wiliness and the resilience of the *bourgeoisie* and their ability to survive all manner of insults and patronizing assaults. I think it's become harder. If you think about the artistic works that shock, it's hard to imagine the equivalent of the *Rite of Spring* happening in classical music today. It may be that the *bourgeoisie* has become less shockable or it may be that artists have temporarily mislaid the soft spot, the target. But I do see it as a continuing disjunction or disparity between different ways of living—sure.

Freiburg: You just mentioned "different ways of living"; one form of unfulfilled living, which I sometimes try to explain to my students, taking your books—and *Metroland* in particular—as examples, is linked to the idea of "living death," the paradoxical notion that one can be dead and alive at the very same moment. I don't want to reveal myself as a staunch believer in intentionality, but was the paradox of "life as death" an idea that you cherished when you wrote that book? In the sense that one can be buried in one's career, in one's habits, or in a marriage? Do you consider existentialism as a cure for this paradoxical form of life or non-life?

Barnes: The phrase the "living dead" is, I think, in a way a much more German expression than an English expression, and similarly a concept. No, it was more the idea of someone setting out on a journey seemingly in one direction and then ending up back where he started. It was about the compromises that people make in a way without realizing that they're doing so. And making compromises, you know, with the best of intentions, maybe because they love someone, because they want to provide home for a child, because they need to earn money. Christopher is not a bad guy in any way. When you're fifteen, sixteen, eighteen, or whatever, you do believe in a sort of debased version of existentialism, that you can shrug off all your genetic and familial inheritance, that your task as an individual existing in his or her own right in the modern world—without any necessity of surviving a totalitarian religion or totalitarian politics—that your task as such an individual is to become free, discover what you are, and what your capabilities are, and to construct your own life, invent your own life in some way which accords with your essence. That's very much how I was at sixteen, eighteen, longer, that's very much how Chris is. And then in the book—though it's not really emphasized, I don't think, very strongly—the fallacy, or if not the fallacy, the fallibility, the susceptibility to attack of this position, the susceptibility to being ground down is what comes through. I'll just give you a bit of autobiography: I was very much like that when I was in my late teens, early twenties, and had a difficult and distant relationship with my parents, and then later a sort of distantly accepting relationship—a very English relationship—with them. But since they died—my father died five years ago, my mother two years ago—I somehow have become more aware of their power, or the power of what their genes are over me, than when they existed. It's as if when they were there physically in front of me, I could say, "I'm not like you!" and now they've disappeared, I feel as if there are wires running through me still from the generations past and I think, "My ability to be free and discover some particular individual essence, was not entirely a foolish hope but it was bound around by all sorts of governing conditions laid down by my ancestors."

Freiburg: You've just talked about "loss," and in my view it is precisely the idea of loss that permeates your writing. When I read your books, I'm delighted by the exquisite sense of humour that they display, but I also feel a very strong vein of elegy. In *Talking It Over, Metroland,* and also in *Flaubert's Parrot* you talk about a state that has been irretrievably lost, friendship that one took for granted, a love in Paris, the loss of a wife, and the loss seems to instill a kind of sharpened consciousness and elegiac feeling. Would you agree?

Barnes: Yes, I think there is probably a pervasive melancholy in a lot of what I write. I think that this partly comes from the objective assessment of the human condition, the inevitability of extinction—and also from an objective look at how many people's lives turn out and how rarely achievement matches intention. And I recognize such pessimism in the sorts of English writer whom I like and admire. People often ask me, "What novelists do you admire or are you influenced by?" and I am always rather unable to help; I mean I can give them a list of novelists I greatly admire, but to what extent they have influenced me or to what extent they accord with my own sensibility and taste I'm not really sure. Whereas, I think, if the question were, "Which English poets do you admire?" then the first three I would come up with would be Thomas Hardy, A. E. Housman, and Philip Larkin, all of whom, in their different ways, despite being quite witty and funny writers, are deeply pessimistic and deeply melancholic. So I would say that they were people who I felt closer to than say Evelyn Waugh, Graham Greene, Ford Madox Ford, whom I admire very greatly as novelists.

Freiburg: The "pervasive melancholy" sheds some light on human happiness. When I read your books, I had to think of Jonathan Swift's famous definition of happiness. In his *Tale of a Tub* he presents the definition, "a perpetual possession of being well deceived." I don't know whether you came across it? Would you subscribe to such a sceptical notion of human happiness?
Barnes: [laughs] Tell me the quote again exactly!

Freiburg: Happiness is nothing but "a perpetual possession of being well deceived," a definition which I personally like very much.
Barnes: No, I don't think I would. In a way, I wish there were different words than "happiness." The key words which we build into the fabric of our lives—a lot of them have become worn or accreted with barnacles and stuff like that; so we could do with a couple of fresh words. I don't think when I have been at my happiest I have been at my most deluded. I think the delusion is that happiness once achieved will necessarily continue. I think that that's the delusion. Most people are most happy when they are most in love, and I don't think that being in love is a delusion. I think it may be a delusion that the person you're in love with will continue to enchant you, or will continue to behave in the way that made you love them, or that you will continue to behave in the way that made them love you. But these are delusions about the longevity of happiness rather than the state itself. But maybe Swift would agree with this qualification.

Freiburg: In *Talking It Over* I especially admire Ollie because of his use of words, his command of language, and I got the impression that you endow him with an unforgettable blend of different registers. Ollie is a master of four-letter words, but then again he impresses his friends with a language reminiscent of "Johnsonese." Was that a deliberate intention: to yoke these heterogeneous styles together?
Barnes: Yes, Oliver is of all my characters probably the most self-constructed [laughs]. As words are his prime mode of expression rather than anything like having a job he is very self-constructed in his language, and obviously it's a pleasure to the writer himself to have such a character who can just range far and wide and mix high style and low style. Maybe Ben Jonson as much as Samuel Johnson, or Ben Jonson and Samuel Johnson together.

Freiburg: In *Talking It Over* you show one story from different perspectives, which is an extraordinarily efficient device. In postmodernism theoreticians discuss the idea of the "concurrence of theory and literature" or the "concurrence of theory and creativity." That means that theory mirrors literature, and that literature to a certain degree also mirrors theory. Would you agree that one might interpret your novel in terms of—let us say—Foucault's theory of discourse?

Barnes: *Well*—I once got into trouble in Italy where I was at a British Council evening—I don't know how many years ago but it was certainly after *Flaubert's Parrot*, possibly after *History of the World*—and so the whole question of postmodernism came up, and the question of literary theory. And someone from the audience was asking the question and I said, "Well actually, you know, I haven't read any literary theory," and everyone laughed—because they knew this was the British sense of humour—but then I said, "No, actually I really haven't, you see," and they suddenly began to realize that I was serious and a terrible chill fell over the audience because many of them had worked in universities and devoted several years of their lives to theory and liked to fit my novels into some constructed grid. But at the risk of offending you in turn, I would say that I have never read any literary theory. I've read a few pages of Derrida, I've occasionally been sent theses on my work where there would be a paragraph of quotation from me, in which my purposes seemed to me self-evident and self-explanatory; and then two pages of a sort of Derridaish prose which seemed to me to make the whole thing much less clear than it was in the first place [laughs]. To answer your question straightforwardly: in my case there is no continuing dialogue between writing fiction and literary theory. I'm deliberately unaware of literary theory. Novels come out of life, not out of theories about either life or literature, it seems to me; I am very English in that respect. I think that when literary theory drives literature, the danger is you get something as fundamentally arid as the *nouveau roman*. But, you know, I admit that the writer doesn't always know what he's up to. I think I know more than most critics, but I know that there are things that you're not aware of as a writer. I'm also aware that you can be influenced at second hand, and you can be influenced by things that are in the air, but it would strike me as a very strange and counterproductive way to begin a novel not with, "X met Y in the supermarket while they were both buying avocado pears," but instead with, "In the tenth book of dialogues by Jean-Michel Whoever, the proposition is put forward that . . ."

Freiburg: You said literature begins with life, and I think you will agree that "memory" serves as the link between life and the production of literature.

Memory in my view again is one of the keywords in your books. As a writer do
you prefer a good or a bad memory?

Barnes: Phew!—That's a very good question! The trouble is you don't have a
choice. You're stuck with the sort of memory you've got, which is usually very
precise in some areas and hopeless in other areas and constantly—as I increasingly
begin to realize—constantly interfered with by your own rewriting of your own
past. We all think that it's other people who rewrite their past but that we are the
arbiters of truth, and if you're a writer, you think that more than anyone else because you're helping construct the record of human existence and therefore you
think, "My memory is the true one, those of other people change." But I remember quite recently a friend and I—a very old friend of mine whom I have known
thirty, thirty-five years or so—were talking about a mutual acquaintance and I
had been saying something disparaging—and she said, "But don't you remember
you really fancied her thirty years ago?" And I said, "No I didn't." She said, "Yes,
you did!," and cited me an instance and I realized, "Yes of course!" And it wasn't as
if this person in the meantime had entered my thoughts much or that I had some
particular reason for trying to wipe her off the record. It's as if some adjusting
mechanism is going on all the time which you're unaware of, which is fitting your
past and adjusting it to some version of how you've turned out, which you weren't
even aware needed a propaganda department to justify. So in that respect I think
I probably have the same memory as everyone else—that is, a good and a bad
memory. The advantage of having a bad memory is that you forget where you
learnt things or where you heard things, and therefore you can integrate them more
easily into your fiction. I have a friend who's a film critic, who has an astonishing
memory for film mainly, but also for other things. Occasionally I would tease him
and say, "I can't remember who was the second principal carpenter on *Un homme
et une femme*, and he will run the credits to himself in his head—you'll see him—
then he'll reverse them and say, you know, "Producer, director, best boy, grip, light-
ing, props, camera," and then he'll tell you. I would think to have such a memory
curses you creatively. I think it's a wonderful gift to have as a critic and indeed most
literary critics that I know and am friends with have a far better memory of great
books than I do. It's obviously in part because they teach them at regular intervals
and so have regular refresher courses, but even so I think that their basic ability
to remember details and structure of a novel is probably better than mine. And
that again is not necessarily unhelpful to a novelist. There's bound to be a certain
burden of the past, a certain oppressiveness of great writing. So if you don't remember too well, then it's not sitting on your shoulder quite so heavily.

Freiburg: Are you familiar with or have you ever read about Bacon's doctrine of the faculties of the mind, *ratio, memoria*, and *imaginatio*?
Barnes: Francis Bacon?

Freiburg: Yes, Sir Francis Bacon. He—and others before and after him—sees parallels between the faculties of the mind and the fields of human knowledge. Thus *memoria* corresponds to history, *ratio* to philosophy, and *imaginatio* to poetry or literature. And then he says, "Get rid of imagination as it doesn't serve a purpose." Could one say that treating the world as you sometimes do in your books, one can observe an infiltration of memory by imagination—and will this also lead to—I hope my question isn't getting too complicated—would this also lead to the infiltration of history by imagination?
Barnes: Gosh! "I don't know" is the answer. I don't really understand Bacon's terms and why he thinks the imagination is a danger to poetry.

Freiburg: He thinks that you perceive the world and that all the sensorial data are stored in your memory. Rationality is there to compare the data in your mind with the outward world. The role of imagination, however, is to mix these things up so it creates a blend, a *mélange*; it's a made-up world, you might say, and in this way it's not true anymore. The old debate going back to Plato of course.
Barnes: I see. So he wanted poetry to be more like prose [laughs] or more like the newspapers!

Freiburg: Exactly—more like the newspapers [laughs].
Barnes: Yes. Well, I'd have to disagree with that obviously. Of course fiction is untrue but it's untrue in a way that ends up telling greater truth than any other information system—if that's what we like to call it—that exists. That always seems to me very straightforward, that you write fiction in order to tell the truth. People find this paradoxical, but it isn't. It's also the reverse of politicians, who tell facts in order to tell lies [laughs].

Freiburg: Let us talk about the mind for another minute. Before you begin with the story of *Before She Met Me* you present a humorous but also grotesque motto; you say: "Speaking metaphorically of these brains within a brain, we might imagine that when the psychiatrist bids the patient to lie on the couch, he is asking him to stretch out alongside a horse and a crocodile." Does that basic view of human beings explain the sudden metamorphosis of ordinary people into maniacs and of everyday life into tragedy in some of your books?
Barnes: That was a line which I originally found quoted by Arthur Koestler. He

gave me the source which is a psychiatrist called Paul D. MacLean, and at the time it absolutely fitted the novel that I was then writing, which is about a civilized man who finds that the horse and the crocodile have not gone away. I don't think it's contentious to say that some sort of pattern, some sort of model like that is the only way we can make sense of a lot of the events of our recent history, how things which begin optimistically can turn into complete tragedy; how cultured nations can resort to *barbarie*, barbarity; how seemingly benign new forms of government like communism can turn into terrible dictatorships. You could say it's inherent in the nature of those systems, but I think the disparity in the human individual makeup is also a factor in it. People are capable of holding in their heads the notion that they are doing good for mankind—let's take the Soviet model—that they are doing good for mankind and helping to perfect human society while at the same time killing large percentages of it. Now you would think that you have to be a sort of deep psychotic in order to believe this, whereas in fact a lot of people who clearly *did* believe this were intelligent, politically aware, highly motivated, patriotic. People who on the one hand, you could say, because of political and historical reality had been reduced to a state of paranoia and therefore viciousness, but had also been so reduced by their basic psychology. You're German, I'm British—I was born in 1946—I was brought up, as we all were, with a notion that in the thirties and forties we saw the decline of a great cultured nation into barbarism and that we the British would never have behaved like that. And the further comparison with the French: that the French, when invaded by the Germans, collaborated to a degree that was shameful and of course we—the British—would never have behaved like that. Well, we can't test the first analogy, but the second analogy was very, very clearly tested during the German invasion of the Channel Islands. The British there, who, as people often are who live on small islands and are very attached to the mother country—like the Falkland islanders, are more British than the British, behaved exactly like the French. And so, from that you may deduce that it's just historical or geographical accident that because we happen to be an island, we happen to have been kept away from some of the things that would otherwise have shown us in our true colours.

Freiburg: Do you see parallels between this collective behaviour of a group of people or a nation and the individual behaviour of a man like Graham in *Before She Met Me*, a kind of everyman, who turns into someone suffering from an obsession. Would you accept the idea that there is banality in evilness and evilness in banality?

Barnes: *Well, I'm not really sure,* you see. I know that this is what we're meant to believe nowadays. We're meant to believe that evil is banal, we're meant to be snobbish about evil. But I would have thought that if anything, there was a sort of banality of saintliness. When you were a kid, before your moral system was really in place, bad things always seemed much more glamorous than good things. The bad guys always wore much more stylish uniforms than the good guys [laughs], they often had the best lines, as the Devil does. These are my instinctive, on-the-spot- responses to this. Is it Hannah Arendt who's coined the phrase?—Someone like that. I think it's almost a way of comforting ourselves and being snobbish about it. Evil is very attractive, and sexy, and endlessly fascinating. You know, it's like drugs; the reason people take drugs is because they like doing it, because it excites them and they feel better, and they feel they're more alive. And to be told by magistrates and judges that they're just spaced-out zombies and that drugs are very boring and banal is not a way to stop them using them if that's what we want to do.

Freiburg: Does that theological context of evilness, I mean theodicy, the problem of the legitimacy of evilness in the world or the question of the existence of God in face of all that evil that terrorizes the world, interest you?
Barnes: Well, God comes into my novels because so many people believe in God. God comes into *A History of the World* a lot because there has been a lot of God in the history of the world. But in my novels of contemporary life—*Metroland, Before She Met Me, Talking It Over,* the one I'm writing at the moment—I don't think God comes in at all because God for the characters that I'm interested in doesn't exist anymore, as for most British people. I've never had a religious period in my life, I wasn't brought up in a religious family, there was no sort of weakening at school. My brother, who's a philosopher, is severely down on God. I have a sense—uhm, how can I put it?—I don't believe in God but I miss him is how I would put it because ...

Freiburg: That's a fine phrase I think!
Barnes: [laughs] ... because I think that His absence makes life less grand. There is a chapter in *A History of the World in 10½ Chapters,* as you will know, about medieval animal trials. Most people who look at animal trials tend to think that if in medieval times they gave judicial trial to a pig for eating the face of man who was lying in a ditch in a drunken stupor, that this was a sign of how incredibly primitive and stupid the Middle Ages were. It seems to me that it's a sign of how wonderfully larger and more extended the sense of what life was in those days,

and that when the pig was executed by an official hangman, it was actually elevating the status of the pig rather than anything else. It was putting it into the order of God's creation, it was giving it a conscience, you could say, whereas now the horizon has lowered. God is not in his sky and we treat pigs worse now than they did in the Middle Ages.

Freiburg: I heard an interesting answer yesterday at the Cambridge Seminar on the Contemporary British Writer. Salman Rushdie said that for a writer only dead religions are interesting because then you can use the mythology to describe society, nationality, culture, and so on. But let me ask you a question that worries me as a university teacher. I can imagine almost no class in our contemporary university where the postmodern idea of history is introduced without going back to at least one of your books, *Flaubert's Parrot, A History of the World, The Porcupine*. You are exhaustively quoted in the *Oxford Dictionary of Quotations*, for instance, with the phrase, "History just burps, and we taste again that raw-onion sandwich it swallowed centuries ago." There are critical articles that quote your definition of history as "merely another literary genre," and the general critical view would be that you treat history as a "narration" and this of course is an idea closely associated with the name of Hayden White. My question is, did you develop these ideas on your own when you formed your characters and planned your plot, or was there a theoretical influence on your work?
Barnes: Well—I'm afraid the answer is the same as it was before. I've never heard of Hayden White, I'm afraid, and no—all my ideas come as I write. I'm in that respect a very pragmatic British novelist. Appetite comes with eating and ideas come with writing. I never start my novels wanting to prove something; I never start my novels with any sort of thesis. I think it's usually a mistake. I've very frequently done what novelists do and put epigraphs at the start of my novels. When you're writing a book you often find something which is just so apt and so suitable that you can't bear not to use it. So *Talking It Over* is prefaced by a wonderful Russian saying which I found in Shostakovich's memoirs: "He lies like an eyewitness," which is absolutely perfect for the novel. The only danger of putting it there rather than into the body of the novel is that it might make people think that you are writing a novel in order to illustrate that point of view and you aren't really. As you write the novel that point of view becomes clearer, and then you discover the epigraph and then you put it at the front of the book. So I'm aware that my novels are sometimes discussed happily and gratifyingly in history lessons as well as literature lessons, but I don't regard them as being part of an ongoing debate which I'm keeping up with.

Freiburg: Only perhaps in the sense that "it is in the air," as you said before.
Barnes: Yes.

Freiburg: The next question is a very important one especially from a German point of view. Sometimes when I explain the idea that history is a narration, or that history does not really make sense, that you have to interpret it, also that you construct it and reconstruct it, I get applauded from the "wrong" faction [laughs]—I don't mean my students of course, there we are safe, but it happened to me that I discussed this vision of history at a conference and an extremely staunch conservative said, "Yes, that's exactly what we also think." Has that ever happened to you, that you were acclaimed by people, radical thinkers, who misused your ideas?
Barnes: Well—you see I don't go on platforms and debate subjects. I don't go to conferences. Occasionally I go to literary festivals, I will read my work in public and I'll talk to my readers but I don't—partly because of lack of time and partly because of lack in inclination—I don't put myself in a position where I am, say, debating what history's about or something like that. On the other hand—to answer your question from a different direction—Flaubert said something like, "success is always off the mark—it was the farcical parts of *Madame Bovary* that people liked." And you are so often surprised by what people praise you for, but as long as they are praising you for something that actually is in one of your books that's fine, because it's about that moment of contact and that moment of exchange of truth between writer and reader. It may be the case that what you think of as a sort of banality, strikes someone as wonderfully fresh and what you think of as the most important insight of a book, someone either pays no attention to or knew already. So as long as it is actually your own book that they're praising that's fine. I was talking a couple of days ago to Kazuo Ishiguro, who said he'd once had a whole conversation with someone who on the one hand was referring *to his books* and referring to them by their titles, but referred to *him*—both to his face and *to Ishiguro's wife*—as Timothy all the way, thinking he was Timothy Mo [laughs]. Now this is disturbing for a writer as you can imagine. So as long as they don't think you are someone else, that's alright.

Freiburg: The brilliant story that you published in *Cross Channel*, "Experiment" ends with the metaphor of tasting wine, you remember . . .
Barnes: Hmm . . . yes.

Freiburg: . . . and in the end you say: "If a wine tastes to you like a young Australian Chardonnay, then that in a sense is what it is. The label may subsequently declare it to be an expensive burgundy, but if it hasn't been that in your mouth, then that is what it can never really become." Would you say that history is also a matter of taste?

Barnes: Well, the way history is remembered and therefore to a certain extent the way history is written about is a matter of taste, but I certainly don't believe that all tastes are equal, or that taste is any substitute for truth. I'm Orwellian in this respect, in that I think that 100 percent truth is unreclaimable and unknowable, but that we must maintain the superiority of a 67 percent over a 64 percent of truth.

Freiburg: "Taste" in French and in France—as you know much better than I do— is quite often linked to the expression, *je ne sais quoi*, and that again is associated with the idea of the *exagium, essai*, the essay, in the sense that the essayist wants to give a sample of his world view or attitudes. We just talked about getting acclaim for the right thing. Would you like to be praised for being a brilliant essayist for example in *Flaubert's Parrot*?

Barnes: Well, I have had acclaim for being an essayist in that the novel won the *Prix Médicis Essai*, though when people tell me that this proves that *Flaubert's Parrot* is an essay, I have to explain that "*essai*" in French is different from "essay" in English; that "essay" in English is strictly nonfictional, whereas "*essai*" in French is a much broader term—it's not quite *jeu d'esprit*, but it can be something broadly imaginative. I confess to being slightly sensitive about this because sometimes being called an essayist is a way of putting you down or denying the sort of novelist you are. My novels vary greatly from one to another, but when people talk about *History of the World* and *Flaubert's Parrot* in particular there is a line of criticism which seeks to deny that they are *really* novels. Actually I'm less sensitive about this than I used to be because it seems to have gone away a little and now the books are mainly discussed as novels.

Freiburg: When I asked this question I thought of Montaigne's essayism, and also of Adorno's idea that there is an heretic element in writing essays. And if you mention the question of literary values, in my personal view the essay ranks far above the novel.

Barnes: *Well, I don't know!* I can't think of *Flaubert's Parrot* as anything except a novel. I think if you withdrew the fictional infrastructure, it would just sort of collapse. It wouldn't be worth reading. You can just read it for the information and the opinions, but I think that if you give it a full reading, you *have* to see and feel why this man Geoffrey Braithwaite is telling you all these things he is, and the whole impetus of the novel is aiming towards the chapter called "Pure Story" and that without it, the elements of the book would still be there, but it would be like taking the tentpole out of a tent—that the fabric would still be there, but it wouldn't look like a tent, it would just be a load of fabric lying on the ground.

Freiburg: Does the word palimpsest still play an important role for you in the present debate? Palimpsest in the sense that you present one story and then there is another layer of narration beneath it like in *Talking It Over*, where you reanimate the pretext of *Jules et Jim* or as in *Before She Met Me* where you—as one critical article informed me—construct intertextual links with Nabokov's *Lolita*?
Barnes: Now that's a new one!

Freiburg: It's in a German dictionary on English literature.
Barnes: I think that is grotesque!

Freiburg: But in *Flaubert's Parrot* you make use of *Madame Bovary* . . .
Barnes: Yes . . . yes that's certainly true. I don't think of it as a continuing, a necessary element in my work. Obviously *Flaubert's Parrot*, yes. In fact I always resist the idea that *Talking It Over* is a homage to or a reworking of *Jules et Jim*. When it comes in, it's a sort of necessary joke, it's a passing illusion, it's how things are, it's how things feel at the start of the novel and how they feel at the start of *Jules et Jim* and because it's a cultural reference point, one of the three friends obviously has to make the reference. But it was more a sort of wink, it was more saying to the reader, "Bit *Jules et Jimmy*, isn't it?" But when someone says, "But does anyone remember what happens after they go bicycling?" of course people generally don't remember that.

Freiburg: And do you like the term palimpsest in this context?
Barnes: Well, no—not really! I mean a palimpsest is a manuscript that's been written over several times, isn't it? And bits of the previous writing show through. No, I think when I do use previous sources or reference points, I want them to be in the same focus as what I'm writing about; I want the world of Flaubert's novels to be as clear as the text that it appears in.

Freiburg: Let us shift our attention to *The Porcupine* which I admire very much.
Barnes: Good!

Freiburg: If you follow critics, *The Porcupine* could be looked upon as a political novel. Some say that it is an adaptation of Bulgarian history, also a farce, but in my view it's especially a satire. The question which I have is connected with the problems we discussed before. We talked about the loss of divinity, or the loss of belief in God, implying the loss of many values and norms. Do you think that it is still possible to write satire with the intention of attacking someone, or of correcting a blemish or deficiency?

Barnes: No, I don't believe in that traditional interpretation of satire—I've always had trouble with it [laughs]. It seems to me that the official purpose of satire is to chastise the mighty and to correct the powerful, but the mighty and powerful are remarkably unaffected by this. I can't think of a great pope or cardinal or king who has actually been reduced to humility by satire. What usually happens is that the satirist has his head cut off [laughs]. No?—Actually the purpose of satire or the real function of satire is to console the dispossessed, is to mock the mighty for the consolation of the weak and the poor. And this seems to me a different purpose, once you're aware of it, and a legitimate purpose, and a good purpose, but I don't really see myself either in *The Porcupine* or in *England, England*, which has also been described as satire, as actually writing satire. I think *England, England* is farcical rather than satirical. I don't have the illusion that Rupert Murdoch is going to read *England, England* and behave differently. And I would also call the book a political novel rather than a satire. It seems to me also that satire exaggerates, whereas in *The Porcupine* I tried to draw the figure of Petkanov as realistically as possible. It's a political novel about that old but still true problem: the weakness of liberalism confronted by the certainty of a system that believes it has all the answers. And this is still the case even when liberalism has triumphed. It's still the case that though the dictator, the man with an answer for everything, is put on trial and found guilty, in a way he's the victor. So I think of it as a novel about those themes. I'm not really sure who—if it's described as a satire—who is thought to be satirized, because it takes all its personnel seriously.

Freiburg: Satire in my opinion is based on the existence of norms. It is almost impossible nowadays to believe in norms. There is a sort of pluralism that influences normative thinking, leave alone the essayistic scepticism that prevents any solid belief in dogmatic truth, so that it becomes more and more difficult to write satire.

Barnes: I think that's true. But I can imagine satire on let's say the European Parliament, the European Commission, things like that, Brussels, the regulations. I'm not planning such a book, but I think when people seem to believe that they're behaving in a completely normal logical way, whereas in fact to a person who sees more clearly, they're behaving in a deeply irrational or completely foolish or stylized or whatever way, then that's a genuine invitation to satire. Somehow the idea that all those commissioners resigned and yet all commissioners carried on working—this is the stuff of satire, isn't it? That is also the problem, though, that the world produces its own competing satire, by itself. You know about Tom Lehrer? He gave up satire the day Kissinger got the *Nobel Prize* [laughs]. Yes, he said, "It is impossible, I can't do satire anymore, the world has got there before me."

Freiburg: Theoreticians again differentiate between satire as genre and satire as a mode of writing. You do not write satire according to the first definition but there definitely are a lot of satirical elements in your books. One technique which I could detect is what we call *meiosis* or the principle of semantic gravity. You present a figure as a well-respected man or even sublime character, as someone who cherishes lofty notions, and then you contrast that with down-to-earth behaviour. For example you talk about a philosophical system and then suddenly the word "pee" turns up, or somebody is outed as a sexual maniac or even a sexual pervert. Is that a consciously employed technique that you've learnt from eighteenth-century models or does it come naturally?

Barnes: I think the answer is: it's partly how I am and it's partly how English literature is. Shakespeare is our great writer and Shakespeare is nothing if not a mixer of genres, and a mixer of forms of rhetoric, and a mixer of prose and poetry, and a mixer of high and low, and a mixer of farce and tragedy. So it's always been there in our literary culture; some of it is obviously personal to the writer and some of it is deeply intrinsic to the culture. It's very interesting to read Voltaire on Shakespeare and see what a sort of utter barbarian he really regards him as: a genius but completely undisciplined [laughs]. Racine is very rarely put on in England, but there were two Racine plays put on in London last summer with Diana Rigg—including Ted Hughes's translation of *Phèdre*—and I went twice and it was very interesting to see the depth of incredulity in the average British theatregoer that this was thought of as theatre, or tragedy. And at that moment I understood the depth of incredulity amongst the French when first faced with Shakespeare.

Freiburg: I see. In *Metroland* you coined a fine phase, "riding irony without being thrown," which I would like to use as a starting point for my next question. I have never seen such deft handling of irony since I read eighteenth-century literature, so I would like to bestow the title of "an ironical gentleman all over" on you, a title that was once given to Daniel Defoe. But then, Defoe and Swift wrote quite famous ironies that were misunderstood: *The Shortest Way of the Dissenters* and *The Modest Proposal.* Have you ever experienced your irony misfiring?

Barnes: Oh yes! Yes, yes. There's a line in the second chapter of *A History of the World in 10½ Chapters,* which says that "the definition of irony is what people miss," it's something like that. I'm aware of being misread and misunderstood, but no more than most writers. There was an English political commentator called Bernard Levin, who reviewed my very first novel *Metroland,* which as I said earlier I regard as poised and ambiguous in its conclusion, and he reviewed it as in terms of, "Thank God: someone is at last standing up for the suburbs and speaking out for the virtues of suburban life" [laughs], and I thought, "Hang on!" . . . But then, you know, lots of people who read books—and even review books— don't understand certain essential things about literature. They think that you get to the last chapter and the author tells you what to think. Some people think that because *The Porcupine* ends with a woman standing in the rain holding a photograph of Lenin, that this means I'm a Leninist and that I believe that he's going to come back, his ideas are going to come back, they should come back. But you know, this sort of misreading is inevitable.

Freiburg: Irony and satire dare to break taboos. I think that's what they live on. I was rather surprised that you already mentioned the grave of Lady Di as another tourist attraction in *England, England.* Was this sentenced as a break of taboos by your English reviewers when the book came out or did they accept it?

Barnes: I only read one review, as I said; I've no idea what they said.

Freiburg: But how far would you go in breaking taboos? I would characterize your kind of writing as Horatian rather than Juvenalian, but then suddenly such a breaking of taboos occurs. Would you be so courageous as to break holy taboos?

Barnes: Well, I think there are two parts to that question. The first is that when you are writing you follow the momentum of the book and therefore when you put Lady Di's grave on the Isle of Wight, you don't think, "This is a breaking of a taboo," you think, "What else would Sir Jack have there that I have missed?" She's just been dead for two years, so she died while three-quarters of the book was written probably. So it was at a fairly late stage that the question of whether or not she should appear in the book came up and then I realized, "Yes of course, but I'll just tuck her in there." Shakespeare's grave and Princess Di's—as if it was no more strange that Sir Jack got her grave there than that he had got Shakespeare's grave there. It's deliberately thrown away, so it's not clear whether he actually bought the body in the grave or whether it's just a replica.

And then part two is when the book is about to turn from an idea in your head on pieces of paper to something out there in the public, you may look at it more differently and you may consider whether it might give offence and stuff like that, and sometimes it's brought to your attention because every novel is read for libel nowadays. I had a three-page libel report on *The Porcupine* which says that there were four people in the world who might sue. They were Gorbachev, the Queen, Nancy Reagan, and Frank Sinatra, and the lawyers could not recommend that the insurers insured the novel against libel. So the publishers had to make the decision of publishing it without libel insurance. And I said, "Great! Just think what would happen if we got sued by the Queen! That [laughs] would be great!" So it's about that point that you're obliged to think about it. On the other hand—to answer the second part of your question, the end of your question—I don't see that you could now set off innocently to write a blasphemous novel about Islam— given what's happened. You couldn't do that unknowingly anymore. I don't think being blasphemous in itself is of particular interest to me, or thinking, "What will offend people most deeply—let's go for that." If I did end up doing something blasphemous it would simply be because I've been following where the book was taking me.

Freiburg: Like in the parody of the prayer, "Alfalfa," which is a very mild form of blasphemy in *England, England*?
Barnes: Yes, yes.

Freiburg: The gist of *England, England* is of course the play between the original and the copy, and if you look at your books in terms of structure, you see a similar notion in *A History of the World in 10½ Chapters* where you discuss the dichotomy between history and its icon. History is illustrated by the icon, but then suddenly the icon assumes an autonomous state, becomes completely independent of its origin. I could observe the same procedure here in *England, England*. You've got the original, then there is the replica—or as postmodernists again would say the "*simulacrum*"—and after a certain time the replica gains autonomy. You may have come across A. N. Whitehead's famous quotation that the European philosophical tradition can be interpreted as a series of footnotes to Plato [laughs]. Are there traces of Platonic philosophy in *England, England*?
Barnes: I don't really know because I've read very little Plato. But you know, Plato and Platonism are obviously so bedded in European civilization that the question of secondary influence might be there, but again that's not my starting point, as I said earlier. I mean there is indeed a reference to Plato in *England, England* but

it's a schoolroom reference, it's what we all remember of being told about Plato, rather than tipping off the reader that Plato is the palimpsest behind this particular novel.

Freiburg: But I think the satire is very clear concerning the French academic.
Barnes: Yes. That is a satirical chapter I would agree, though not with the direct intention that someone like Baudrillard would mend his ways [laughs].

Freiburg: Can you help us with the objects he buys?
Barnes: Yes. Oh yes. He's a fisherman, he's a certain sort of anglophile. The British make the best fishing equipment according to some people—I'm not a fisherman—but I can't now quite remember what he does buy—he buys some waders doesn't he?

Freiburg: "Waders from Farlow, flies from House of Hardy, and aged Caerphilly from Paxton and Whitfield."
Barnes: It's just the idea of him being one of these international academics who flits into one place and then just does a little perfect piece of shopping and then flits off to the next place . . .

Freiburg: To Frankfurt!
Barnes: Does he go to Frankfurt?

Freiburg: Yes he does [laughs]. In *England, England* you make this interesting list of what could be called the quintessences of England.
Barnes: Yes.

Freiburg: May I ask you to give five or six quintessences of Germany?
Barnes: Oh! Yes, I can do that. *Lederhosen*, Beckenbauer—I've got to reach the exact obvious ones—but . . . uhm . . . thinking what would be . . . well, no, let's think in tourists' terms—we'll take out Beckenbauer; let's think if we're having a "Deutschland Deutschland Theme Park," it would have to be *Lederhosen*, it would have to be *Bier*, uhm . . . I will come back to this question. We'll come back to this question in the end.

Freiburg: Do you know some contemporary German literature?
Barnes: Well, not what's going on in the younger generation because of partly the slowness with which things are translated and partly reading slowly myself. So I think most English writers are stuck probably at the Grass-Böll-generation and then will have read a few novels here and there which they will then proudly cite

to you [laughs]. What was that one I read quite recently, which I thought was very good, though of course that was probably written at least ten years ago—a novel called *The Wall Jumper*, by Peter Schneider?

Freiburg: I think it was turned into a film.
Barnes: Oh really!

Freiburg: We know you as a novelist, also as an essayist with all the restrictions that we talked about. Will we be able to read a drama by Julian Barnes? And will there be poems?
Barnes: No, I will not turn into a poet. I did write some poetry when I was in my early twenties—it wasn't any good. There's a long history of novelists thinking that they will be good dramatists and turning out to be bad dramatists: Henry James, Flaubert, Graham Greene. My ideas come to me in the form of the novel rather than the form of the drama. I still have a lot of things I want to explore in the novel form and the longer that you go on doing that, then the less likely you are to be able to write a play. In the nineteenth century, novelists envied the theatre, partly because it was seemingly more glamorous and you met actresses, but also because it could bring in a lot of money. And indeed drama still brings in more money than fiction. And you still get to meet actresses. But I think that in the twentieth century it's probably been replaced by the film script. Faulkner, Fitzgerald, and so on went to Hollywood. And that in a way is a slightly less threatening alternative career. I've written a couple of screen-plays which never got past first draft, but the very fact that you're not entirely responsible, that lots of other people are going to mess it up for you and rewrite it probably means it's less stressful for a novelist to turn into a script writer rather than a dramatist.

Freiburg: Thank you very much for the interview.
Barnes: Uhm ... we have to think of five quintessences of Germany. What is that natural phenomenon that you get at the top of mountains—I think that is German—it might turn out to be Swiss. You stand on the top of a mountain at sunrise and your shadow is projected onto a bank of clouds? Do you remember that phenomenon? I don't know where I first read about that, but it seemed it's one of those sort of natural phenomena that only occur in either South Germany or Switzerland and it's a German name, it has something of "Caspar David Friedrich," it's that sort of atmosphere. *Alpengluhen*? Uhm ... I'm not doing very well am I?

Freiburg: Yes, you are [laughs]! But it's hard to name the most important clichés.
Barnes: Yes. And it's the marketable clichés as well. That's the other thing. I mean the quick answer is *Bier*, *Wurst*, uhm . . .

Freiburg: *Bratwurst.*
Barnes: Yes, *Lederhosen*, *Sauerkraut*, and the World Cup—which Germany hasn't been quite so good at winning lately.

Freiburg: Yeah, that's right [laughs].
Barnes: Which was a great relief to the rest of us. Probably the Black Forest or something like that, or the Rhine maiden, who sang from the rocks on the Rhine and lured men to their destruction? Something like Lorelei—she would be there. Uhm . . . the Berlin Wall . . .

Freiburg: That's more than five . . .
Barnes: Yes, so that's . . . you pick any five.

Freiburg: Thank you again.

"History in Question(s)":
An Interview with Julian Barnes

Vanessa Guignery/2000

From *Sources* (Orléans, France) 8 (Spring 2000): 59–72. Reprinted by permission of the publisher (Éditions Paradigme).

Vanessa Guignery: In this interview, I would like to focus on the topics of history and the knowledge of the past as dealt with in your novels. As you know, many contemporary theorists and historians such as Hayden White and Paul Ricœur have tried to point out the similarities between fictional discourse and historiography, and it seems that you yourself are interested in this subject. First, I have picked up three definitions of history in your novels and I would like you to elaborate on these definitions. The first one comes from *Flaubert's Parrot*, where the narrator writes that one is often tempted to "declare that history is merely another literary genre" (90); could you comment on that?

Julian Barnes: I suppose one of the things I meant there was that most of the evidence of history, most of the evidence of lives of people who have lived and what they did and what happened to them, has disappeared, that what we think of as historical evidence is a very, very tiny fragment of all the total evidence that was there during the lifetime of most of humanity. And therefore, inevitably there is bias; there are one or two sorts of bias. Either you only write the history for which there is evidence, or, if you try to write more than that, if you try to write a more complete history, then you have to fictionalise or imagine. And so, to that extent, history, if it attempts to be more than a description of documents, a description of artefacts, has to be a sort of literary genre. But often the greatest historians write narrative as well as the best novelists.

Guignery: Can you relate this to the definition of biography in *Flaubert's Parrot*? The narrator draws a parallel between biography and one possible definition of a net as being "a collection of holes tied together with string" (38).

Barnes: Yes, that is increasingly what I feel about biography. I have very mixed feelings about biography, partly because I am so wary of its certainties. A biography makes too much sense of a life, it seems to me. Biographies in a way ought to be more boring. Biographies make people's lives more interesting than they probably were. They seem to make a person's life a series of dramatic high-lights, and often that is a narrative necessity for the biographer, because you have to concentrate certain strands and certain moments. I read a very good biogra-phy of Virginia Woolf by Hermione Lee not long ago; part of it is done in themes, and so there is a section on Virginia Woolf's madness, which is brilliantly done. And you think about it intensely when you are reading that section, but then you are inclined to forget it. There ought to be a running head at the top of each page saying "she was worried about going mad this day as well." And so, you know, a true biography ought to have a full account of a very boring day in the character's life as well.

Guignery: Is that why you chose not to write a biography about Flaubert? You felt that maybe the genre was not appropriate.
Barnes: I think the genre was inappropriate to *me*, as a writer. Also I would have *not* wanted to do all the boring bits. The boring bits of being a biographer, it seems to me, are doing the family for a start. I hate it when those biographies start with, "His great-great-grandfather was born in. . . ." And then doing the child-hood. I know it's important, but I just can't be bothered about it.

Guignery: But, at the same time, you conducted a lot of research for *Flaubert's Parrot.*
Barnes: I did a lot of research, yes, that's true. But . . . it's a mixture of principles and self-indulgence, you see. It's why it comes out as a novel. It's a mixture of not really approving of the biographical format and also being a novelist in any case, and then also wanting to write about what you really want to write about.

Guignery: The second definition of history is to be found in *A History of the World in 10½ Chapters;* in "Parenthesis" you define it as "soothing fabulation" (242). Is this related to what you've just said about the similarities between his-tory and fiction?
Barnes: Yes. "Fabulation" comes into the story of the woman who is cast adrift, and it's a medical term for what you do when a lot of your brain has been de-stroyed either by a stroke or by alcoholism, or that sort of thing. And—it's rather gratifying for a novelist—the human mind can't exist without the illusion of a full story. So it fabulates and it convinces itself that the fabulation is as true and

concrete as what it "really" knows. Then it coherently links the real and the totally
imagined in a plausible narrative.

Guignery: And do you think the same process applies to history?

Barnes: Well, historians will probably find this extremely patronizing of me, I
don't know. But it seems to me that it is often the case. You can think of this complicity between the reader of history and the historian: the reader of history
wants to be told the whole story, wants to understand all the motivations, wants
to know exactly what happened. And historians ought to say more often, "I don't
know, I don't know why, I don't know why he did that, it was completely out of
character. We'll never understand it. All the evidence has been lost." Well, some of
them do, but . . .

Guignery: The third definition is from *England, England,* and this is Dr. Max,
the Official Historian, saying, "History, to put it bluntly, is a hunk" (148). [Barnes
laughs] If we compare this to the preceding quotes, you bring something new
here. What is your comment on that?

Barnes: "History is a hunk." Well, we don't know much about Dr. Max, but he is
probably gay and he is very provocative and waspish. His line, which is not particularly original, is that there is still a sort of masculine bias for history. It's still
mainly about the bloke-ish things. It's the history of power and battles. In a way,
this is inevitable, because for most of history in most of cultures, the reins of
power have been wielded by men, and what comes down to us are the lives and
achievements of men. But when you have such an overwhelming majority of influence, you forget—I am not saying anything unusual—you forget the silent 50
per cent. So, he is trying to object to that.

Guignery: In *A History of the World in 10½ Chapters,* you write for eight chapters
about history, and then at the end of "Parenthesis," you confess that "objective
truth is not obtainable" (245), but that we should nevertheless believe that part of
it is, otherwise we would fall into "beguiling relativity" (245). Why did you feel
the need to state that at this point in the novel?

Barnes: I suppose the point at which "Parenthesis" comes is the point at which
I've given a series of alternative narrations, dislocated in time and place, and it
seems to me as a writer, at that point, that it is time to say something on my own
part, on my own behalf. And at such a point, the reader would be quite justified
in saying to the writer, "Well, what do *you* think about it?" So, that part is mainly

about love and truth, but it's also against part of what the book has already been doing, which is undermining traditional history. It's saying, "It's no good just lying back and saying, 'Well, we'll never work it out,' and it's no good saying, 'Of course, we understand history, all we have to do is apply the following theories or the following scientific principles or Marxist ideology, whatever.' What we should do eventually is believe that truth is obtainable. History may not be 56 per cent true or 100 per cent true, but the only way to proceed from 55 to 56 is to believe that you can get to a hundred."

Guignery: In the first chapter of *A History of the World in 10½ Chapters*, you revise sacred history, and revising history is something that many contemporary writers do. Some critics tend to say that the writers who revise history might be considered as revisionists. So when you write about the necessity of believing that part of objective truth is obtainable, is this a way of escaping the risk of being accused of revisionism?

Barnes: No, that part of "Parenthesis" is certainly not written out of the fear of what critics might say, or anything like that. If you take something like the story of Noah's ark (even if it didn't exist, you'd have biblical versions), what the woodworm's version is saying is, "Actually, a lot of that is all bullshit, and this is what really happened." But, saying what "really" happened from the point of view of a woodworm is still a very partial truth. Even if you put the two together and you strained them for as much truth as possible, you'd probably end up with only about 37 per cent truth. So, it's not incompatible, but it's backtracking a bit, and saying, "That's what I think."

Guignery: In *A History of the World in 10½ Chapters*, Marx's line on history is quoted twice: "History repeats itself, the first time as tragedy, the second time as farce" (175, 241). It initially appears in the first of "Three Simple Stories" in which the narrator meets Lawrence Beesley who survived the tragedy of the *Titanic*. Is that narrator an earlier version of yourself? Have you actually met Lawrence Beesley?

Barnes: Yes, that's true. That simple story is completely true, that's about me.

Guignery: So, at the end of this story, the narrator tells us about the shooting of the film *A Night to Remember* dealing with the tragedy of the *Titanic*, and he relates an anecdote. Apparently, Beesley wanted to be among the extras on board the replica of the *Titanic* even though he was not allowed to, and when the director spotted Beesley, he told him to disembark . . .

Barnes: Yes, the first time you go down with the *Titanic*, it's for real, and the second time you go down, you are ordered off it before it sinks in the film. Yes, exactly. That seemed a perfect illustration.

Guignery: And then, in "Parenthesis," you repeat that quotation by Marx, but you add: "No, that's too grand, too considered a process. History just burps" (241). In both cases, it seems that you speak in your own name, that you are the narrator. So, what is your opinion on that?

Barnes: Gosh! That's a real examination you're giving me! I think I go for the "Parenthesis" narrator. I think history does repeat itself, but never according to such simple rules, first time as tragedy, second time as farce. Mostly it repeats itself first time as tragedy and second time as tragedy, or, alternatively, first time as farce and second time as farce. There is no artist with a sense of dramatic form in charge of history.

Guignery: But apart from this, you do believe that history repeats itself, don't you? Don't you feel this is rather a static view of history?

Barnes: It's not a static view of history, but it's not a linear view of history either. It's rather like my view of literary history. When you start off, you're taught there are giants of literary history, but really in terms of technique and everything, there is linear progress throughout literary history. But the more I read the less I believe that. You read someone like Turgenev, and you think that his narrative strategies are as sophisticated as those of anyone writing today. It's as if all writers stand at different points on a great circle and we relate across it at different angles towards different writers. But the great writers of the past are always your contemporaries.

Guignery: But at the same time, it seems that with each new novel, you want to experiment with new narrative forms.

Barnes: Yes, of course, it's one of my key motivations. I think form is terribly neglected in the contemporary British novel. But I'm aware always of my predecessors. Take for example *A Hero of Our Time* by Lermontov. It's a wonderful book. It's his only novel, and it was my favourite book when I was about sixteen or seventeen, the time when Russian melancholy is absolutely in tune with your soul, when you suddenly realize you're Russian. It's a novel, but it looks like short stories. In the first story, the hero is just glimpsed and a coach goes by—that's a tiny part of the story. Then in each story he has slightly larger parts, so he gets nearer to you, through this series of stories, and you realize that he is binding the whole thing together. It's a wonderful narrative ploy and that seems postmodernist or whatever you like to call it. And it gets exactly the same response. Idiots say, "Oh, it's not really a novel." So, similarly with history, the idea that we've been making constant, inevitable, grand progress seems to me not really likely, not really plausible.

Guignery: In "Three Simple Stories" in *A History of the World in 10 ½ Chapters*, the third one relates the tragedy of the *St. Louis*. At the beginning, the narrator makes discordant comments when he keeps adding the phrase, "which is normal." Apart from this, the narration seems quite neutral (I hesitate to use the term "objective"), with an accumulation of dates and facts. Why did you choose this mode of narration, which is close to the historical account of the case? Why didn't you fictionalise it?

Barnes: I think because it was so terrible. It's a terrible story which didn't need amplification. It didn't need being "written." It needed holding back from. And so at the beginning, you anticipate a reaction of "Gosh, how extraordinary!" and you kill it with "No, that's normal, that was normal, this was normal for the time." So you establish that these terrible circumstances are normal, and then you let it go and it gets worse. I think I would have also felt, if I had fictionalised it, that I was unfairly playing with people's lives. I think when you get near areas like the Holocaust, unless you are particularly a special witness of them, like, say, Primo Levi, then I think you have to be very, very careful about using them in any way. They're almost sacred subjects.

Guignery: In *A History of the World in 10 ½ Chapters* and *Cross Channel*, you often start with historical events: the *Santa Euphemia* in chapter two of *A History of the World in 10 ½ Chapters* reminds one of the *Achille Lauro*, the trial of insects in chapter three is based on similar trials. Why were you so keen at that point on starting with historical facts?

Barnes: I suppose that was the only basis there was. If I was going back as far as the Ark and I was looking for themes and motifs that tied in with one another, I think I would have been lost without historical bases, I would have foundered without having historical bases. First of all, obviously, you use Genesis because that is something everyone knows, that's an easy point of access—it's the Book. But, further than that, I think I just needed a support. I mean for instance, the two women who go to Mount Ararat in the mid-nineteenth century, they didn't exist, I made them up; but in terms of what the journey was, I obviously relied on historical documents, travels of the time. Any story or telling that takes place in history, you have to locate in a particular time or in a particular civilisation. I think it's also the case that when you write fiction, even if part of it is tied to history, it's no different from when you're writing completely imaginary fiction. It all has to come from somewhere, it all has to have some basis. You never purely invent, every book has to come out of something that you've heard or seen or experienced or read about or whatever. So, somehow the idea of plunging into a nonspecific historical area wouldn't strike a spark. If I said or thought, "Well, let's do seventh-century Peru," and I didn't know anything about it at all, it wouldn't actually get my imagination, my narration going.

Guignery: Another subject you seem to be interested in is the problem of forgetting one's history. You introduced that subject particularly in "Evermore" in *Cross Channel*, where Miss Moss fears that the WWI cemeteries might be ploughed up. You also developed that theme in *England, England*, except that it seems there that history is preserved but in an extremely simplified way, and for purely touristic and therefore economic purposes. What can you say about that subject?
Barnes: "Evermore" is about the fear that things will be forgotten, but of course history will be forgotten just as people will be forgotten. And *England, England* is more about the creation of false truths about a country, and these coarse icons that are made to stand in for real things. After I had written it, I came across a wonderful quotation from Renan: "Getting its history wrong is part of being a nation." It would have made a perfect epigraph for the book. Getting its history wrong is also part of creating a nation. You have to build up those myths of liberation, myths of fighting the oppressor, myths of bravery. Often they have a certain percentage of truth in them, so they're easy myths to build up. But then being a nation as well as becoming a nation also depends on the continuation of those myths, which you see in all countries; well, I think you probably see it more in Britain than you do in France, but you have your myths as well.

Guignery: And do you think that historians and maybe novelists are there to preserve those myths, that history, that identity?
Barnes: I think we are more apt to point out that they are myths rather than to build them up. I mean there are obviously people working on both sides of this. There are still writers (historians and novelists) who are building up national myths, while the rest are trying to knock them down. We need to be able to hold more than one idea in our head at a time. We need to understand that Henry V was a great English king and a brilliant strategist at Agincourt, and also a complete bastard who helped end the rules of chilvalry by massacring his French prisoners.

Guignery: In *England, England*, you develop the idea of creation, fakery, and the dichotomy between the replica and the original. Why did you choose to deal with this theme in terms of the replica of monuments and typical English sites, and not, for example, in terms of copies of paintings, which would have led to the theme of plagiarism?

Barnes: It's about what are the main national, recognizable symbols of my country. It comes out of the survey done by Jeff of the fifty quintessences of England. It's rather ruled by that. It's also ruled by practical thinking about how such an island venture might happen and what they would put there. I mean, I could have treated the idea of the fake and the replica differently, but it would have been a different book. *England, England* is a letter to my own country at the turn of the millenium. It seems to me that, increasingly, countries are caricaturing themselves and are using a very air-brushed version of certain aspects of their own history. It's not new, but it's certainly being done more extremely and with more commercial efficiency now than before. And the whole replica thing is all over the place, replicas of Venice and a half-size Eiffel tower in Las Vegas. Why go to Paris when you can see it in Las Vegas?

Guignery: In *England, England*, the French intellectual says that "we prefer the replica to the original" (53). Do you think that the same process takes place in art, that we keep the work of art, the replica, and forget the real thing, i.e. the original thing, the original event? I'm thinking in particular of Géricault's painting *The Raft of the Medusa*; in *A History of the World in 10½ Chapters*, you write yourself that the painting, the work of art, has survived, but the narrative has been forgotten. In *Flaubert's Parrot*, you also show that what we remember is the paper parrot of *Un Cœur simple*, Loulou, and not the original parrot that served as a model for Loulou. So, do you think this is usually the case, that is, the replica remains and not the original?

Barnes: I don't know. I think it depends on the individual case. It's certainly true that great works of art often transcend and replace the original story. So art can make us forget history, or forget accurate history. It's very hard to imagine the real history of the American West for anyone of a generation who grew up seeing westerns. I think that's almost completely obliterated. I think it is almost impossible to have any sort of virgin awareness of what the West was like anymore—except to remember to be suspicious of heroes. Custer was like Henry V—he massacred defenceless women and children. Westerns don't mention that. Shakespeare, even when celebrating Henry V, doesn't forget the fact that he killed prisoners.

Guignery: This reminds me of what Dr. Max says in *England, England*: "There is no authentic moment of beginning, of purity [. . .] There is no prime moment" (132).

Barnes: Very often we can't remember that moment, can we? Or we make one up. The great religions make one up always. They always make up a particular moment when it all began, whereas we know that, for instance, Christ was just one of any number of similar prophets around at the time and he just happened to get lucky historically, to be taken up. In *England, England*, the point is not quite that we prefer the replica to the original, but that we prefer the convenient replica to the inconvenient original. So, you go to see Michelangelo's David in Florence and now you look at it and you have seen it, and then they tell you that it's actually a replica because the old one was getting polluted. The old one has been cleaned up and is now in a museum. And you think, "Well, I probably won't be able to spot the difference, I've seen it now." And in a way you have. And if it's a very good replica, most people won't have any better aesthetic reaction to it. And part of it seems to me completely OK. You can now by laser technology completely replicate the Elgin Marbles quite cheaply, so that to the naked eye they are completely the same as the "real" Marbles of the British Museum. Indeed, the British government offered the Greek government these replicas instead of the Marbles, and they said they want the original, thanks very much, they don't want these ones. But, if you put them side by side, you wouldn't know the difference at all. And this may become a good thing in a way. If great sculptures can be cheaply reproduced like that and also great paintings, we could all have great paintings on our walls, which we wouldn't be able to distinguish from the real ones apart from knowing that they were not real. Even an art historian couldn't tell the difference looking at them. We could all have great paintings. And it would be democratic, wouldn't it? If they are any good. At the moment you can get almost anything up on the Internet except that the visual quality is not very good. And it's interesting to note that your first thinking is that if that was the case, that we all have a Mona Lisa, this would make the Mona Lisa less valuable, less fetishized. But on the other hand, just because a book has gone into five thousand editions rather than two, it makes the first edition more valuable rather than less. So it's wrong to hope that all these Monets in Japanese banks have become less valuable; they've also become more valuable, because even more people would have the picture but know that it wasn't the original.

Guignery: In the third part of *England, England*, Martha Cochrane goes back to the original country: Anglia. Is this a way of going back to the past?

Barnes: Martha goes back to Anglia, which is different from Old England, because Anglia is the result of Old England collapsing and going back to a pre-industrial, agricultural, pre-technology England. The third part is really about two things. It's partly about finishing off Martha's story, and it's also about the question of to what extent a country can begin again, and what that beginning again means. I think that third part tends to be a bit misread by people as being what I personally approve of, or it's the book's answer to the questions raised previously. And I don't think it's the answer at all. After all, Martha is pretty bored by Anglia. Anyway, I don't write those books in which I, the author, tell you at the end of the book, "This is my advice, folks!" But people are used to that sort of book, and they think that the end of a book is usually the author telling what to think. This is an old-fashioned way of reading books and there's nothing I can do about it if that's what people do to mine. But the third part is meant to be the slow movement of the book, and it's meant to be rather opaque and rather ambiguous. And it's not meant to be like the first part, though it obviously has a structural balance with the first part: for instance, the ridiculous little fair that they get going is a version of the Agricultural Fair in Part One. What I try to do is ask the question, "Say everything collapses somewhere, and then you start again, what does such starting again consist of for a country? And is it the same answer as before?" But there isn't, as Dr. Max says, an original, a moment of beginning. Every time you dig down in a famous building, St. Paul's Cathedral or whatever, you get to another building underneath and then another one underneath and then another one. . . . And it's the same with countries. And so even if an industrialized western nation went into complete freefall and everything by which we currently identify that industrial democratic state collapsed, and then they started again, there's no such thing as a clean slate, you always start with little bits of remembered or rediscovered stuff. So, for instance, the schoolteacher teaches them wrestling with an open encyclopedia in his hands. And there's also that dreadful mixture of tunes that the band plays at the Fête. But even so, the Fête is a great success, and as someone says, it seems already to have become a tradition, where you might have thought, "My God, what a terrible and awful mishmash of stuff!" But that's how things like that are established. That's how we make our new traditions.

Guignery: And in Anglia, the idea of the fake remains through Jez Harris, this character who keeps inventing stories about the people living there. So, this third movement does not mean going back to authenticity.

Barnes: Yes, everyone except Martha has changed their name and their profession and their location, and almost all of them are not from the country anyway. In many ways, it's a completely fake village. It's a bogus village reinventing itself. We create something from fragments and bits of memory, national memory, and we stick it together with a very rough glue and then once it's been there for a certain time, like a year, we think this is real, this is authentic, and then we celebrate it. It's fabulation all over again—convincing ourselves of a coherence between things that are largely true and things that are wholly imagined.

Julian Barnes:
The Art of Fiction CLXV

Shusha Guppy/2000

From *The Paris Review* 157 (Winter 2000–2001): 54–84. Reprinted by permission of the author.

Shusha Guppy: You are very European, which is unusual for an English writer, but also very English, especially to a foreigner. In France, for example, they think of you as quintessentially English. Where do you place yourself?

Julian Barnes: I think you are right. In Britain I'm sometimes regarded as a suspiciously Europeanized writer, who has this rather dubious French influence. But if you try that line in Europe, especially in France, they say, "Oh, no! You're so English!" I think I'm probably anchored somewhere in the Channel.

Guppy: Sartre wrote an essay called *Qu'est-ce que la littérature?* What is literature for you?

Barnes: There are many answers to that question. The shortest is that it's the best way of telling the truth; it's a process of producing grand, beautiful, well-ordered lies that tell more truth than any assemblage of facts. Beyond that, literature is many things, such as delight in, and play with, language; also, a curiously intimate way of communicating with people whom you will never meet. And being a writer gives you a sense of historical community, which I feel rather weakly as a normal social being living in early twenty-first-century Britain. For example, I don't feel any particular ties with the world of Queen Victoria, or the participants of the Civil War or the Wars of the Roses, but I do feel a very particular tie to various writers and artists who are contemporaneous with those periods and events.

Guppy: What do you mean by "telling the truth"?

Barnes: I think a great book—leaving aside other qualities such as narrative power, characterization, style, and so on—is a book that describes the world in a way that has not been done before; and that is recognized by those who read it as telling new truths—about society or the way in which emotional lives are led, or both—such truths having not been previously available, certainly not from official records or government documents, or from journalism or television. For example, even people who condemned *Madame Bovary*, who thought that it ought to be banned, recognized the *truth* of the portrait of that sort of woman, in that sort of society, which they had never encountered before in literature. That is why the novel was so dangerous. I do think that there is this central, groundbreaking veracity in literature, which is part of its grandeur. Obviously it varies according to the society. In an oppressive society the truth-telling nature of literature is of a different order, and sometimes valued more highly than other elements in a work of art.

Guppy: Literature, then, can take a lot of forms—essays, poetry, fiction, journalism, all of which endeavor to tell the truth. You already were a very good essayist and journalist before you started to write fiction. Why did you choose fiction?
Barnes: Well, to be honest I think I tell less truth when I write journalism than when I write fiction. I practice both those media, and I enjoy both, but, to put it crudely, when you are writing journalism your task is to simplify the world and render it comprehensible in one reading; whereas when you are writing fiction your task is to reflect the fullest complications of the world, to say things that are not as straightforward as might be understood from reading my journalism and to produce something that you hope will reveal further layers of truth on a second reading.

Guppy: Did you want to be a writer at an early age?
Barnes: Not at all. It is an abnormal thing to want to be an artist, to practice an art. It is comparatively normal to practice an interpretative art. But to actually make things up is not something that, well, usually runs in families or is the recommendation of a career master.

Guppy: Yet England has produced some of the greatest writers, and perhaps the greatest literature, of the world.
Barnes: That is a separate truth. But there is nothing when you are growing up, even as a reasonably well-educated person, to suggest that you have an authority to be more than, say, a reader, an interpreter, a consumer of art—not a producer of it. When I became a passionate reader in my teens I thought writing was something that other people did. In the same way, when I was four or five I wanted to be an engine driver, but I knew that this was something other people did. I come from a family of schoolteachers—both my parents were teachers—so there were

books in our house, the Word was respected, but there was no notion that one should ever aspire to write, not even a textbook. My mother once had a letter published in the London *Evening Standard*, and that was the maximum literary output in our family.

Guppy: What about the Amises, the Waughs . . . ?
Barnes: They are self-evident abnormalities, like Fanny and Anthony Trollope. Writers are not like royal pastry chefs, handing down their talent and their badge of office from generation to generation.

Guppy: You say that you read voraciously; whom did you read?
Barnes: When I was fourteen or fifteen I was just beginning to read in French, but the first time I read *Madame Bovary* it was certainly in English—the consequence of our English teacher giving us a reading list that consisted mainly of the classics of European literature, many of which I had never heard of. At the time we were obliged once a week to put on army uniform and play at soldiers in something called the Combined Cadet Force. I have a vivid memory of pulling out *Crime and Punishment* along with my sandwiches on a field day; it felt properly subversive. This was the time when I did the basic spade work of my reading. I suppose it would consist of the great Russians, the French, the English. So it would be Tolstoy, Dostoyevsky, Pushkin, Goncharov, Lermontov, Turgenev; and Voltaire, Montaigne, Flaubert, Baudelaire, Verlaine, Rimbaud. In English I read more modern fiction—Evelyn Waugh, Graham Greene, Aldous Huxley. T. S. Eliot, of course, Hardy, Hopkins, Donne.

Guppy: What about the English classic novelists—George Eliot, Jane Austen, Dickens?
Barnes: They came later. I didn't read English at university, and still haven't read the full canon. George Eliot came a bit later, and Austen has always been a bit hit-or-miss with me, I must say. *Middlemarch* is probably the greatest English novel.

Guppy: So when did you think, "Maybe I can be on the other side and write those books that others would like to read?"
Barnes: I think in my early twenties. I was working on the *Oxford English Dictionary*, and I was very bored. So I tried to write, and did produce a literary guidebook to Oxford, an account of every writer who had passed through the city and university. Happily it was never published, though it was bought. After I had done that, when I was twenty-five, I started trying to write a novel, but it was a long and greatly interrupted process, full of doubt and demoralization, which fi-

nally turned into my first novel, *Metroland*, published when I was thirty-four. So it was an eight- or nine-year process, and of course I shelved the book for long periods of time. I had absolutely no confidence in it. Nor was I convinced of myself. I didn't see that I had any right to be a novelist.

Guppy: Any contributions to the *OED*?

Barnes: I was an editorial assistant on that four-volume supplement, writing definitions and researching the history of words, looking for early usages. So I spent three professional years with the language post-1880, in letters C to G. I doubt it shows through in my fiction.

Guppy: As an undergraduate at Oxford you wrote essays, like everyone else. Did any tutor detect a special talent in you and try to encourage it?

Barnes: Special talent? I don't think I had one that was detectable. When I had a viva for my finals one of the examiners, who was a rather stern Pascal scholar at Christ Church called Krailsheimer, said to me—looking at my papers—"What do you want to do after you've got your degree?" and I said, "Well, I thought I might become one of you." I said that partly because my brother had got a First and had gone on to become a philosophy don; also because I had no real notion about what to do. Krailsheimer toyed with my papers again and said, "Have you thought about journalism?" which was of course the most contemptuous thing he could have said—from his point of view. He doubtless suspected a glibness inappropriate for a serious scholar. In the end I got a Second and had no chance of staying on at Oxford anyway.

Guppy: Why did you get a Second?

Barnes: I didn't work hard enough. I changed subject twice. I started with French and Russian, then changed to PPP (Philosophy/Politics/Psychology) and then changed back to read French. It was hardly a glittering academic progress.

Guppy: Do you think that one year in PPP has marked your mode of thinking, and therefore your work, in any way?

Barnes: Not really. You see, I wasn't very good at it. I chose PPP because I thought reading literature was a bit frivolous. I had been well taught at school, and I decided I didn't need to go on doing French and refining my French prose and my views on Racine for another three years. I felt I needed something to get my teeth into, and I thought philosophy and psychology were proper subjects. Of course they are, but I didn't seem to be the right student for them; I don't have that sort of mind. All those genes went to my brother. And I was frustrated to keep finding that philosophy seemed to consist of telling you one week why the philosophy you had studied the previous week was entirely wrong.

Guppy: Yet there is a good deal of philosophy, and of course psychology, in some great writers. Schopenhauer said that he learned more psychology from Dostoyevsky than from all the books he had read on the subject.
Barnes: Quite. And that is why the novel is not likely to die. There is no substitute, at least so far, that can handle psychological complexity and inwardness and reflection in the way that the novel can. The cinema's talents are quite other.

We have a great friend who is a clinical psychiatrist in Sydney; he's always maintained that Shakespeare's descriptions of madness were absolutely perfect accounts from a clinical point of view.

Guppy: So you chose novel writing as a profession.
Barnes: Oh, I didn't *choose* it as a profession—I didn't have the vanity to choose it. I can perhaps now state that I am at last a novelist, and think of myself as a novelist, and can afford to do journalism when it pleases me. But I was never one of those insufferable children who at the age of seven is writing stories under the bedclothes, or one of those cocky young wordsmiths who imagine the world awaits their prose. I spent a long time acquiring enough confidence to imagine that I could be some sort of novelist.

Guppy: *Metroland* was clearly autobiographical, as most first attempts are. Did you set out to do it in that way?
Barnes: I'm not sure. Certainly the first third of the book is close to my own adolescence: the topography and the psychology especially. Then I began to invent, and I realized that I could. The second and third parts are largely invented. When the book was published in France about five years ago, one of the most gratifying moments was being taken by a French television team to somewhere in northern Paris. They sat me on a park bench—I think it was Parc de Montsouris, at least it was somewhere unfamiliar. So I asked them, "Why are you interviewing me here?" and they said, "Because just over there, according to your book, is where you lost your virginity." Very French! "But I made it up," I said, and they were very shocked. That was quite nice, because it meant that what had begun in largely autobiographical mode had shifted into the invented without anyone noticing it.

Guppy: What did you hope to accomplish with this shift into invention? What did you want to convey in that novel?
Barnes: *Metroland* was about defeat. I wanted to write about youthful aspiration

coming to a compromised end. I wanted to write a novel that was un-Balzacian, in that, instead of ending with the hero looking down from a hill onto a city that he knows, or at least believes, he is going to take, it ended with the non-hero *not* having taken the city, and accepting the city's terms.

The central metaphor works like this: Metroland was a residential area laid out in the wake of the London underground system, which was developed at the end of the nineteenth century. The idea then was that there would be a Channel tunnel, and pan-European trains would run from Manchester and Birmingham, pick up passengers in London and continue through to the great cities of the Continent. So this London suburb where I grew up was conceived in the hope, the anticipation, of great horizons, great journeys. But in fact that never came to pass. Such is the background metaphor of disappointment for the life of Chris, the hero, and of others, too.

Guppy: By the way, not many of Balzac's heroes are like Rastignac and "take the city."

Barnes: But they think they are going to. They are allowed to stand on the hill and look down on the city.

Guppy: Balzac is not one of your heroes. There seems to be this choice between Balzac and Flaubert, rather like that between Tolstoy and Dostoyevsky. Alain Robbe-Grillet dislikes Balzac, because he thinks that his world is too ordered, cohesive; whereas Flaubert's work reflects the chaotic, unpredictable nature of the world. Do you feel the same?

Barnes: If the world has to be divided between Balzacians and Flaubertians, then I belong to the latter. Partly because there is more art in Flaubert. Balzac is in some ways a premodern novelist. *Madame Bovary* is the first truly modern novel, by which I mean the first through-composed novel. In the nineteenth century, many novels, especially in England, were published as they were written, in serial parts in magazines; novelists wrote with the printer's boy tugging their sleeve for copy. The equivalent English novel to *Madame Bovary* would be *Middlemarch*, which in terms of structure and composition is more primitive—partly, I believe, because of its serial composition. I'm sure that in terms of the description of society Balzac is Flaubert's equal. But, in terms of artistic control—the control of narrative voice and the use of style indirect libre—Flaubert shows a new line and says, "Now we are starting again." And if *Madame Bovary* is the start of the modern novel, then his unfinished novel *Bouvard et Pécuchet*, which was published posthumously in 1881, is the start of the modernist novel. It is interesting that, according to Cyril Connolly, *Bouvard et Pécuchet* was Joyce's favorite novel. I asked Richard Ellmann about this, and he said it was probably the case, even if there was no documentary proof. *Bouvard et Pécuchet*—a novel about two earnest, illusion-filled clerks who try to understand the whole of human striving and the whole of human knowledge, who are defeated and then go back to being copyists—is extraordinarily modern. And the second part of the book, the thought of simply giving the reader an accumulated heap of rubbish that the two heroes decide to copy down, is a phenomenally advanced idea for 1880; it is amazingly bold.

Guppy: What about other novels, like *Salammbô*, which Flaubert himself didn't like?

Barnes: Oh, he did! But he said a lot of contradictory things about his work, as we all do. For instance, he said he wanted to buy up every copy of *Madame Bovary* and destroy it because he thought that it had overshadowed the rest of his work. In fact *Salammbô* was a great success—it was a social success as well as a literary success. I think the *Trois Contes* are among the greatest short stories ever written. *L'Education sentimentale* is fascinating but possibly a hundred pages too long. *Salammbô* is what it is: a jeweled contraption that draws you in, and which you have to accept on its own terms. There is no point, as a reader, trying to compromise. Then there are the letters, which are instructively marvelous.

Guppy: The correspondence with George Sand, especially. Nobody reads George Sand now, but in those letters she comes across as wise and compassionate and lucid.

Barnes: I'm sure she was. When you read that correspondence, you often feel that Flaubert is right, but that George Sand is nicer. Sometimes she is also right—it depends partly on your temperament. I'm more convinced by Flaubert's aesthetic arguments; on human psychology I think the match ends in a tie.

Guppy: The correspondence with Louise Colet is very illuminating, too. There is this courageous woman who holds a salon with no money, who is so hard up that she has to dry the tea leaves used at one reception to serve at the next, yet keeps soldiering on; while Flaubert, who has a much easier life, constantly whines and is full of complaints and self-pity.

Barnes: Flaubert was a great artist, George Sand a very good novelist, and Louise Colet a minor poet. He reflects incessantly about art. The strange thing about the exchange with Louise Colet is that Flaubert is instructing her, page after page, on the grandeur and intricacy of art. Yet he is an unpublished novelist, and she is the star of the Paris salons, who has affairs with famous artists and so forth. In that sense, among many, Flaubert is not at all like me: I certainly would not have had the nerve to instruct Louise Colet before I had published a novel.

Guppy: Going back to your own work: after *Metroland* and the good reviews it received, were you more confident?

Barnes: Seeing the book in physical form and reading some good reviews was reassuring. But then, such is my nature—and I assume I share this with lots of other writers—I thought, "What if I only have one book in me?" So the second novel is always harder, though in my case it was at least quicker. I still find myself thinking, "Well, I may have written seven or eight or nine novels, but can I do it again the next time?" But I'm convinced that a high anxiety level is the novelist's normal condition.

Guppy: Of course, some novelists have produced only one great book— *Dr. Zhivago, The Leopard*. In fact, should one be a sort of jobbing novelist and produce lots of books at regular intervals? Why shouldn't one great book suffice?

Barnes: Absolutely right. No reason at all why one should go on writing just for the sake of it. I think it is very important to stop when you haven't got anything to say. But novelists sometimes stop for the wrong reasons—Barbara Pym gave up because she was discouraged by her publisher, who said that her books had become flat. I'm not much of an E. M. Forster fan, but he stopped when he thought he had nothing more to say. That is admirable. Perhaps he should have stopped even earlier. But is any novelist going to recognize the moment when he or she has nothing more to say? It is a brave thing to admit. And since as a professional writer you are full of anxiety anyway, you could easily misread the signs. But I'm with you about the quality of the two novels you mention, especially Lampedusa's *The Leopard*, which is a key book. Pasternak was always known as a poet, who then wrote one novel, which became a cause célèbre, but Lampedusa was thought of as this irrelevant Sicilian aristocrat who gave English courses and ate pastries; then he came up with this masterpiece, which was only published posthumously.

I think you hope, broadly, that your best work will survive, but how you produce your best work is perhaps a mystery—even to you. There are writers who are enormously prolific, like John Updike, whom I revere, and who has produced fifty, sixty books. The Rabbit quartet is clearly one of the great postwar American novels. But you can't say to him, "Look, would you please write the Rabbit quartet and leave it at that." Some writers are like cacti—every seven years here comes a glorious flower; then there's another seven years of hibernation. Others can't work like that; temperamentally they *have* to be writing.

Guppy: Then there are various literary genres that produce a crop of writers and books and then fade. For example, magic realism, which has worked well in South America and in third-world countries generally. It has fared less well in the West and seems to be fading away.

Barnes: Yes. But magic realism is part of a much longer and wider tradition—think of Bulgakov. And he—I may be wrong—seems to come out of Russian painting as much as anything else. It's a complex imaginative tradition that existed long before the label was applied. The argument against magic realism, to put it crudely, is that if anything can happen, then why does it matter if this happens rather than that happens? Some people think it's a justification for indulging in hallucinatory fantasy. But that is bad magic realism. Those who write good books in the genre know that magic realism has to have structure and logic and cohesion just as much as normal realism or anything else. The quality of product varies as in any other genre.

Guppy: The new fashionable form is to take an historical character or event and build a fictional edifice around it. For example, Penelope Fitzgerald's *The Blue Flower*, which is based on the life of Novalis, or last year's Prix Goncourt, *La Bataille*, based on Napoleon's battle of Eyleu. Maybe you started it with *Flaubert's Parrot*?

Barnes: Or maybe Flaubert started it with *Salammbô*? Or Walter Scott. Penelope Fitzgerald is an excellent novelist. I think she won the Booker for the wrong book, and her last four novels, which are her best, are still underrated. But, to answer your question, I didn't fictionalize Flaubert. I tried to be as truthful about him as I could.

The novel based on a true historical event is certainly one current literary trend at the moment. But it's not especially new. John Banville was writing about Kepler years ago. More recently Peter Ackroyd has written about Chatterton, Hawksmoor, and Blake. Blake Morrison has just published a novel about Gutenberg. I think this is partly a question of filling a vacuum. Much history writing strikes the general reader as theoretical and overly academic. Historians like Simon Schama, who believe in the fictional virtues of narrative, character, style, and so on, are rarities. Straight narrative biography is also very popular. That is probably where most nonfiction readers tend to go at the moment; so the biographical novelist hangs about the street corner, hoping to seduce a few clients away from the straight and narrow.

Guppy: Yet the traditional historical novel—Mary Renault's *The King Must Die*, to give a quality example—is looked down upon as being rather lowbrow.

Barnes: I suppose because the old historical novel, which tried to re-create mimetically the life and times of a character, was essentially conservative, whereas the new historical novel goes into the past with deliberate awareness of what has happened since, and tries to make a more obvious connection to the reader of today.

Guppy: Would you say that you belong to the straight realist tradition?

Barnes: I've always found labels rather pointless and irritating—and, in any case, we seem to have run out of them in the wake of postmodernism. A critic once called me a "pre-postmodernist": neither lucid nor helpful in my view. The novel is essentially a realist form, even when interpreted in the most phantasmagoric manner. A novel can't be abstract, like music. Perhaps if the novel becomes obsessed with theory (see the *nouveau roman*) or linguistic play (see *Finnegans Wake*) it may cease to be realistic; but then it also ceases to be interesting.

Guppy: Which brings us to the question of form. You once said that you try to make every work different. Once you have broken the mold of the traditional narrative, it seems to me that you have to keep changing—you can't go on, say, finding new historical characters and events to build stories around.

Barnes: You could. I remember at school, in the sixties, we were being taught Ted Hughes by our English master, who was a bright young man just down from Cambridge. (He was the one who gave me the reading list.) He said, "Of course everyone's worried about what happens when Ted Hughes runs out of animals." We thought it was the wittiest thing we had ever heard. But of course Ted Hughes never did run out of animals; he may have run out of other things, but not animals. If people want to go on writing about historical figures, they can always find some.

Guppy: But don't people always like to try something new?

Barnes: It doesn't work quite like that. I don't feel constrained by what I have written in the past. I don't feel, to put it crudely, that because I've written *Flaubert's Parrot* I have to write "Tolstoy's Gerbil." I'm not shut in a box of my own devising. When I wrote *The Porcupine*, I deliberately used a traditional narrative because I felt that any sort of tricksiness would distract from the story I was trying to tell. A novel only really begins for a writer when he finds the form to match the story. Of course you could play around and say, "I wonder what new forms I can find for a novel," but that's an empty question until that proper idea comes along, and those crossing wires of form and content spark. For instance, *Talking It Over* was distantly based on a story that I'd been told five or six years previously. But it was no more than an anecdote, a possibility, an idea for an idea, until I apprehended the intimate form necessary for this intimate story.

Guppy: What about *England, England*, which is a political novel about a tycoon? How did you find the form for that?
Barnes: The tycoon was based to some extent on Robert Maxwell, the press baron, who was a grotesque rogue. *England, England* is my idea-of-England novel. That and *Porcupine* are my two novels which overtly treat political matters.

Guppy: What do you mean by "my idea-of-England novel"? Can you differentiate it from the state-of-England novel, of which there have been a few infelicitous examples lately?
Barnes: England as a functioning economy is comparatively rich and healthy; many elements of society are comparatively happy. That may be the state of England; but, whether it is or not, what is the idea of England? What has become of it? The English are not very self-conscious the way the French are, so I wanted to consider the idea of England as the millennium turned. England as an idea has become somewhat degraded, and I was interested in what would happen if you pushed that, fictionally, to an extreme. You take some of the tendencies that are implicit in contemporary Britain, like the complete dominance of the free market, the tendency of the country to sell itself and parody itself for the consumption of others, the increasing dependence on tourist dollars; then you add in one of my favorite historical notions, the invention of tradition. You take all this and push it as far as it can go and set it in the future. It's a garish, farcical, extremist version of what the country seems to be getting like now. But that's one advantage of fiction: you can speed up time.

Guppy: Perhaps because of your preoccupation with form, some critics have compared you to Nabokov and Calvino, writers who have played with form to invent their own prose space. Were they among your influences?
Barnes: Influence is hard to define. I've read most Nabokov and some Calvino. I can say two things: first, that you tend to deny influence. In order to write the

novel I'm committed to, I have to pretend that it's not only separate from every-thing I've written before, but also separate from anything anyone in the history of the universe has written. This is a grotesque delusion and a crass vanity, but also a creative necessity. The second thing is that when asked about influence, a writer tends to give a reading list and then it's pick-and-mix time as to whoever the reader or the critic decides has influenced you. That's understandable. But it also seems to me that you can be influenced by a book you haven't read, by the idea of something you've merely heard of. You can be influenced at second hand, or even be influenced by a writer you don't admire, if they're doing something sufficiently bold. For example, I have read novels and thought, "This doesn't really work," or, "This is actually a bit boring"; but maybe its ferocity of attack, or au-dacity of form, suggests that such a thing—or a variant of it—could work.

Guppy: But there is always one writer, a grand progenitor, who really does mark you. For you it was Flaubert. Were you conscious of his impact?

Barnes: Yet I don't write Flaubertian novels. It is the safest thing to have a pro-genitor who is not just foreign and dead, but preferably long dead. I admire his work absolutely and read his correspondence as if it were written to me person-ally and posted only yesterday. His concerns with what the novel can do, and how it can do it, with the interrelationship between art and society, are timeless; he poses all the main aesthetic and professional questions and answers them loudly. I agree with many of his answers. But when, as a twenty-first-century English nov-elist, I sit down in front of my IBM 196c, I don't allude in any direct or conscious way to a great nineteenth-century Frenchman who wrote with a goose quill. The novel, like the technology, has moved on. Besides, Flaubert wrote like Flaubert—what would be the use of anyone else doing so?

Guppy: Apart from Flaubert, were there others, closer to our time, whose books you thought on reading them, "Ah! That's it! That's the stuff!"?

Barnes: Not exactly. What I think when I read a great novel, for example Ford Madox Ford's *The Good Soldier*, which I think is one of the great novels of the twentieth century, a great English novel—although Americans admire it, too—when I read something like that, I do, to a certain extent, absorb various technical things, for example about how far one can push an unreliable narrator. But the main lesson would be a general one: to take the idea you have for a novel and push it with passion, sometimes to the point of recklessness, regardless of what people are going to say—that is the way to do your best work. So *The Good Soldier* would be a parallel example rather than anything you might set out to copy. Anyway, again, what would be the point? Ford's done it already. The true influence of a great novel is to say to a subsequent novelist: Go thou and do otherwise.

Guppy: What about American literature? You have already mentioned Updike. Did you read them early on? I mean particularly the greats—Melville, Hawthorne, et cetera.
Barnes: Sure. Hawthorne particularly, then Fitzgerald, Hemingway, James, Wharton—I'm a great admirer of hers—and Cheever, Updike, Roth, Lorrie Moore, who I think is the best short-story writer in America since Carver. But American novelists are so different from English novelists. They really are. No point trying to write like them. I sometimes think Updike is as good as the American novel can get, especially, as I said, in the Rabbit books.

Guppy: How exactly are American novelists different from English novelists?
Barnes: Language, primarily; also vernacular (as opposed to academic) form; democracy of personnel; nowness. On top of this, contemporary American literature can't not be affected (as was British Victorian literature) by coming from a world-dominant nation—though also one noted for historical amnesia and where only a small percentage of citizens own passports. Its virtues and vices are inevitably linked. The best American fiction displays scope, audacity, and linguistic vigor; the worst suffers from solipsism, parochiality, and dull elephantiasis.

Guppy: What about contemporaries, both continental and English?
Barnes: It is difficult with your contemporaries; you know them, and/or you know too much about them. The other thing is that past the age of fifty, you realize that you last read some of those great writers mentioned earlier when you were seventeen or eighteen, and you want—and need—to reread them. So when faced with the latest fashionable novel of several hundred pages, I think, "Have I read all of Turgenev?" And if I have, then why not reread *Fathers and Sons*? Now I am in a rereading stage. In France not much seems to be happening. Michel Tournier still seems to me their greatest living novelist. No one else comes to mind. But I wouldn't claim to be keeping up as much as I should.

Guppy: People say nothing much is happening in France, but French novels aren't any more trivial than what is published here. And intellectually France is still very influential, particularly in philosophy and critical theory. It has conquered American universities, from Levi-Strauss to Derrida.
Barnes: That's true. A lot of their literature's energy has gone into theory and

psychology; but apart from Tournier they haven't really produced anything substantial since the death of Camus. I thought Camus's posthumous *Le Premier Homme* made you realize what's been missing in the French novel. Recently there was *The Elementary Particles* by Michel Houellebecq. It is a rough, insolent book, deeply unpleasant in many ways, but definitely touched with some sort of genius.

Guppy: What about up-and-coming novelists? If you believe the reviews, we seem to have a huge number of first-rate budding novelists. Foreigners envy the health of the English novel.

Barnes: In England I can't think of anybody in the next generation following mine whom I look at with particular envy. Short-story writers, perhaps. In Britain, Helen Simpson; in America, Lorrie Moore—I've mentioned before, a terrific talent. My own generation is as talented as you can get: Ishiguro, Ian McEwan, and others. But I would say that, wouldn't I? I suppose I'm slightly impatient with the lack of ambition in the next generation coming along. I don't hold it against them wanting to make money—novelists have spent a long time not making any money—and I don't resent any twenty-five-year-old who gets offered a hundred thousand pounds for a first novel and takes it. What I do resent is that they mostly turn out something entirely conventional, like the story of a bunch of twenty-somethings living in a flat together, the ups and downs of their emotional lives, all narrated in a way that will easily and immediately transfer into film. It is not very interesting. Show me more ambition! Show me some interest in form! Show me why this stuff is best dealt with in novel form. Oh yes, and please show me some awe at the work of the great novelists of the past. Still, I was greatly cheered by Zadie Smith's recent first novel, *White Teeth*, which had both high ambition and bristling talent.

Guppy: Your own book *Talking It Over*, about a triangular love affair, was made into a movie; was it good?

Barnes: It was made into a French film called *Love, etc.* with Charlotte Gainsbourg and Charles Berling. It lasted one week at the Curzon Cinema. Yes, it was rather good. It was a proper film in its own right, rather than a dutiful book adaptation.

Guppy: *Talking It Over* was in the form of a few characters talking to camera, so to speak, taking it in turn, letting the story emerge that way. Nearly ten years and several books later you have gone back and taken up the story again, with the same central characters. And you've used the title of the film, *Love etc.* The end of the story leaves the reader wondering what will happen next. It seems to be the second panel of a triptych. Will there be a third panel?

Barnes: I don't know. I never thought I'd write a continuation of *Talking It Over*. You're right that *Love, etc.* ends with several of the characters at a point of crisis, which must be resolved one way or the other very soon. Obviously, I could sit down tomorrow and work out those resolutions. But that would only take me a few chapters into a new novel. What happens after that? I have to allow my characters additional years of life so that they can provide me with the material; that's what it feels like at the moment, anyway.

Guppy: How do you create your characters? Are they roughly based on people you know or encounter? Or do you invent them from scratch? How do they develop in the course of the narrative?

Barnes: Very few of my characters are based on people I've known. It is too constricting. A couple are based—distantly—on people I've never met: Petkanov in *The Porcupine* is clearly related in some way to Todor Zhivkov, former boss of Bulgaria, and Sir Jack Pitman in *England, England* to Robert Maxwell. But I never dreamed of researching Maxwell: that wouldn't have helped my novel at all. At most you take a trait here, a trait there anyway. Maybe minor characters—who are only a trait here and a trait there in the first place—can be taken wholly from life; but I'm not aware of doing so. Creation of character is, like much of fiction writing, a mixture of subjective feel and objective control. Nabokov boasted that he whipped his characters like galley slaves; popular novelists sometimes boast (as if it proved them artists) that such-and-such a character "ran away with them" or "took on a life of his/her own." I'm of neither school: I keep my characters on a loose rein, but a rein nonetheless.

Guppy: You are very good at women characters—they seem true. How does a man get into the skin of a woman?

Barnes: I have a Handelsman cartoon on my wall of a mother reading a bedtime story to her little daughter, who's clutching a teddy bear. The book in the mother's hand is *Madame Bovary*, and she's saying, "The surprising thing is that Flaubert, who was a man, actually got it." Writers of either gender ought to be able to do the opposite sex—that's one basic test of competence, after all. Russian male writers—think of Turgenev, Chekhov—seem exceptionally good at women. I don't know how, as a writer, you understand the opposite sex except in the same way as you seek to understand any other sort of person you are not, whether you are separated from them by age, race, creed, color, or sex. You pay the closest attention you can, you look, you listen, you ask, you imagine. But that's what you do—what you should do—as a normal member of society anyway.

Guppy: Jealousy seems to be an important theme in your work: for example, in *Before She Met Me*, in *Talking It Over*, and in *Love, etc.* Is this part of the French influence also? Jealousy is a great theme in French literature—from Racine's tragedies to airport novels.

Barnes: I don't think my preoccupation with jealousy is French or French influenced. I frequently write about love, and therefore about jealousy. It's part of the deal; it's what comes with love, for most people, in most societies. Of course, it's also dramatic, and therefore novelistically attractive, because it's frequently irrational, unfair, boundless, obsessing, and horrible for all parties. It's the moment when something deeply primitive breaks the surface of our supposedly grown-up lives—the crocodile's snout in the lily pond. Irresistible.

Guppy: You are one of the few writers who are genuinely interested in sports. What do you play? How keen are you in following these sports?

Barnes: As a boy I captained my school rugby team until the age of about fifteen. I've also played soccer, cricket, tennis, snooker (if you call it a sport), squash, badminton, table tennis, and a bit of golf. I was the school's under-twelve, under-six-stone boxing champion. That was a mixture of luck and calculation. I'd never boxed before, but noticed the day before registration closed that no one else had entered this category, so I'd get a walkover. Unfortunately, someone else had the same brilliant idea at roughly the same time, so we were obliged to fight. He was marginally more scared than I was. That was my first and last bout. I still follow most sports—it would be easier to list the sports I don't follow, like formation swimming and carpet bowls; though late at night, glass in hand, televised carpet bowls can prove strangely attractive. As for participation, nowadays I prefer to go walking: daylong tramps in Britain, weeklong tramps in France and Italy. The only rule is, the luggage has to be sent on ahead. You can't enjoy the landscape if you're weighed down like a Sherpa. As for writers and sport, male writers anyway, I think they are more interconnected than you allow. Think of Hemingway—boxing, bullfighting; Jarrell and Nabokov—tennis; Updike—golf; Stoppard and Pinter—cricket. For a start.

Guppy: In *Cross Channel*, the old man in the story "Tunnel" says that in order to be a writer you need in some sense to decline life. Do you think you have to choose between literature and life?

Barnes: No, I don't think we do or can. "Perfection of the life, or of the work"—that's always struck me as Yeatsian posing. Of course artists make sacrifices—so do politicians, cheesemakers, parents. But art comes out of life: how can the artist continue to exist without a constant re-immersion in the normality of living? There's a question of how far you plunge. Flaubert said that an artist should wade into life as into the sea but only up to the belly button. Others swim so far out that they forget their primary intention of being artists. Self-evidently, being a writer involves spending a lot of time on your own, and being a novelist demands longer periods of isolation than does being a poet or a playwright. The creative to-and-fro of the collaborative arts has to happen internally for a novelist. But at the same time it's to fiction that we regularly and gratefully turn for the truest picture of life, isn't it?

Guppy: How do you work? Are you disciplined? Do you keep regular hours?
Barnes: I'm disciplined over a long stretch. That is to say, I know when I start a novel that it will work best if I write it in eighteen months, or two or three years, depending how complicated it is, and nowadays I usually hit that rough target date. I'm disciplined by the pleasure that the work gives me; I look forward to doing it. I also know that I work best at certain hours, normally between ten in the morning and one in the afternoon. Those are the hours when my mental capacity is at its fullest. Other times of the day will be fine for revising, or writing journalism, or paying bills. I work seven days a week; I don't think in terms of normal office hours—or rather, normal office hours for me include the weekends. Weekends are a good working time because people think you've gone away and don't disturb you. So is Christmas. Everyone's out shopping and no one phones. I always work on Christmas morning—it's a ritual.

Guppy: Is writing easy for you? Perelman said that there are two kinds of writers: those to whom it comes easily and those for whom every word is a drop of blood being sucked out. He put himself in the second category. What is it like for you?
Barnes: I'm not very sympathetic to the bloodsucking complaint, because no one ever asked a writer to be a writer. I've heard people say, "Oh it's so lonely!" Well, if you don't like the solitude, don't do it. Most writers when they complain are just showboating in my opinion. Of course it's hard work—so it should be. But would you swap it for child-minding hyperactive twins, for instance?

Guppy: One can like the result but not necessarily the process, don't you think?
Barnes: I think you *should* like the process. I would imagine that a great pianist

would enjoy practicing because, after you've technically mastered the instrument, practicing is about testing interpretation and nuance and everything else. Of course, the satisfaction, the pleasure of writing varies; the pleasure of the first draft is quite different from that of revision.

Guppy: The first draft is fraught with difficulty. It's like giving birth, very painful, but after that taking care of and playing with the baby is full of joy.
Barnes: Ah! But sometimes it isn't a baby, it's something hideous and malformed; it doesn't look like a baby at all. I tend to write quickly when I'm on the first draft, and then just revise and revise.

Guppy: So you rewrite a lot?
Barnes: All the time. That's when the real work begins. The pleasure of the first draft lies in deceiving yourself that it is quite close to the real thing. The pleasure of the subsequent drafts lies partly in realizing that you haven't been gulled by the first draft. Also in realizing that quite substantial things can be changed, changed even quite late in the day, that the book can always be improved. Even after it's published, for that matter. This is partly why I'm against word processors, because they tend to make things look finished sooner than they are. I believe in a certain amount of physical labor; novel-writing should feel like a version—however distant—of traditional work.

Guppy: So you write by hand?
Barnes: I wrote *Love, etc.* by hand. But normally I type on an IBM 196c, then hand correct again and again until it's virtually illegible, then clean type it, then hand correct again and again. And so on.

Guppy: When do you let go? What makes you feel it is ready?
Barnes: When I find that the changes I'm making are dis-improving my text as much as improving it. Then I know it's time to wave good-bye.

Guppy: What do you use your computer for, then?
Barnes: I use it for E-mail and shopping.

Guppy: What are your plans for the future?
Barnes: I'm not going to tell you! I'm a bit superstitious. Actually it is not so much superstitious as practical. The last piece of journalism I wrote was for the *New Yorker* about the Tour de France. Much of it was about drug use in professional cycling. I did a lot of research, and I found myself—unusually for me—talking about the research to people. When I came to write the piece I was a bit

flat. I found it very difficult to write. I'd come back from having talked to, say, a Dutch sociologist of cycling about the history of drug taking back in the 1890s, and I'd spill it all out to everyone I met—because it's quite fascinating—and then I'd sit down to write it, and I'd think, "Is this really so interesting?" That was confirmation of a lesson I'd learned long ago but momentarily forgotten: Don't talk it all away. It's a matter of self-preservation. I'm retentive by nature anyway. But there will be other books, don't worry.

Julian Barnes, Etc.

Robert Birnbaum/2000

From *Identity Theory*, 8 March 2000. http://www.identitytheory.com/people/ birnbaum8.html. Reprinted by permission of the author.

Robert Birnbaum: In publicizing your talk with your friend Jay McInerney, the *New York Observer* referred to him as "having parlayed a best-seller into a career of writing about wine." Is that the kind of thing that disturbs you when people write about writers? Or are you fair game for that?

Julian Barnes: No, I don't think one is fair game for it. We're not politicians, after all. No, it's not the sort of thing I like. Either about myself or about my friends. We're not running for office. Also, in Jay's case it's rubbish to say he's switched from being a novelist. It's always been his passion, and he's just written a little book of articles about it. But then, he made the fatal mistake of having a hugely successful first novel . . . as a young man. That will, therefore, take him five or six books published to work through.

Birnbaum: He and Brett Ellis are both treated with the same high disregard.

Barnes: Yes, for slightly different reasons. Brett Ellis is regarded as a possibly dangerous and corrupt human being because of what he writes. Whereas Jay is regarded as a metropolitan slicker and therefore not worth taking seriously. In dealing with writers, as in most things in America, all tendencies are exaggerated. We get some of it in Britain, but then success is not as great as success in America.

Birnbaum: You do say in *Love, etc.* that "America is the exaggeration of everywhere else."

Barnes: Well Stuart says that. I sort of agree.

Birnbaum: The wonderful thing about writing a book in which a handful of characters express a very wide range of observations and opinions is that they will all be ascribed to you, as contradictory as some might be . . .

Barnes: That's true. There is a little page and a half in which Gillian, who has now been married ten years to Oliver, makes a resigned complaint about marital sex. I've noticed that people occasionally come up to me and look me in the eye and say, "Marital sex," knowingly and with complicity. I want to say, "Hang on. I'd just like to point out I am not a forty-year-old female art restorer. Actually, I'm not married to Oliver." [laughs]

Birnbaum: Some characters' observations and remarks you can clearly say are particular to a character. But more general observations like the one about America, you leave the particular speaker or character . . .
Barnes: Well, if you read that passage to me I would probably agree with some of what Stuart said. If there is any one thing that I am conscious of saying, with my voice chiming with Stuart's, is the myth of America as the land without irony. Some of my best friends are ironists. The most ironic writer in the world is probably Gore Vidal. So what do they know . . .

Birnbaum: He's so non-American.
Barnes: It's probably not mainstream American, but the notion that irony somehow got dropped off the back of all the [ocean] liners that crossed the Atlantic is just ridiculous. Jewish irony for a start. It's a great tradition.

Birnbaum: I wonder if the critique of Jewish writing uses the word "irony." It is, but a different word is used . . .
Barnes: Yes, there's probably a Yiddish word, I don't know.

Birnbaum: Maybe it's "schtick"?
Barnes: You couldn't not say that Woody Allen doesn't deal in irony. Does he not? His humor is pretty Jewish. On the whole the beauty of this form, for a novelist, is that you disappear as a writer. You as a controlling narrator. You leave the reader alone with views of the characters. And the reader makes up his or her own mind.

Birnbaum: That seems to be an abiding concern of yours. I read an article on you where a quote from *Flaubert's Parrot* was resurrected asking why people focus on the writer and not the writing? I understand the claims about the burden of celebrity. It seems to be a very human and appropriate thing to want to know how people go about their lives doing various things, the baseball player, the surgeon, the explorer. . . . That's not what you reject, otherwise would we even be sitting here together?
Barnes: [Chuckles] No. I have, obviously, a divided position on it. As a writer, I want my books to be read as something separate from myself. I produce them

as crafted objects out there. To which the reader may respond in whatever way he or she wishes. As a reader of an impressive book I have a natural human curiosity about who made it. On the other hand I think I know enough—have seen enough of the dealings of modern biography to be very protective of my own life and of those around me. There is a danger that celebrity, even the small celebrity of being a writer, joins you on to a different way of behaving and a different way of being behaved to. And, as I said, we are not running for office. You don't like me, I don't mind. You don't like my books, I don't mind.

Birnbaum: You really don't mind if people don't like your books?
Barnes: I prefer people to like them, of course. For everyone who likes my books there will be someone who doesn't. Fine, read someone else. Sorry I didn't convince you. But that's it, you know.

Birnbaum: I take that to mean if some people didn't like your books, okay. If nobody liked your books, you would be very troubled.
Barnes: I would not be here [laughs]. I would be deeply troubled, of course. There is nothing nicer—when you come to America for a week or two weeks—what happens (which happens maybe once in four or five years in England) is someone comes up to you and shakes you by the hand and says, "I really like your stuff." Which might become repetitive if I was American, and lived in America. I remember walking around Ann Arbor with Jay McInerney when *Bright Lights, Big City* was being made into a movie. People were popping out from behind the hedges and shouting, "Michael J. Fox" and stuff like that. Whereas in England, it's a different culture. They keep their distance. You occasionally notice on the London Underground, they cop you with one eye. They know who you are, but that's enough. Obviously, I like that, but it's nice to get the contrast here for a week or two.

Birnbaum: Once again you note the truism of two cultures separated by a common language. Happily, I made regular use of my dictionary in reading *Love, etc.,* and a word that came up was Oliver's repeated use of "crepuscular" . . . which primarily refers to twilight. But it seems that Oliver weighs it with more negativity.
Barnes: Oliver tends to move it away from its merely pictorial sense of the falling shades of evening . . . towards shades of darkness.

Birnbaum: In the *American Heritage Dictionary* there is reference to night crawlers, things that come out from under the rocks . . .

Barnes: He's not quite using it in that sense. *Crépuscule* is French for evening, twilight. Oliver, now having reached his forties and his life clearly not taking off, is already beginning to feel a bit of chill of an evening that might not be too far away.

Birnbaum: What is redemptive about him?
Barnes: I don't know if redemptive isn't too big a word for some characters in some novels. He is a character I know irritates a lot of people immediately. One of the interesting things in this novel and in *Talking It Over* is that because there is no author there mediating it, because there is no third-person narrator introducing Oliver as a character, readers tend to respond much more quickly to the characters in the book. And they come to judgment much more quickly. Because the membrane between readers and characters is so thinned, that if it works, is like meeting real people. So people say, "I really hated Oliver. And then towards the end I got rather touched by his plight." This is a bonus that I hadn't exactly counted on when I started working with the technique. If it was a third-person narrator, people would probably think Oliver was pretentious and irritating. But he must be here for a purpose because he has been introduced to us and I'll wait and see . . .

Birnbaum: Are you saying that you couldn't do as well writing about him as he does for himself?
Barnes: No. Because these characters are so close to you as a reader, instantly, you respond to them as you would if you met a guy like Oliver in a bookstore. And he was using fancy long words and looked a bit shabby and you thought he was pretentious. And you think, "I don't want to have anything to do with this guy." That is something you have to conquer as the writer. So, what's redemptive about him is even when he is irritating he knows stuff and tells you stuff. Even when he's showing off. For example, in the first chapter he plays that game, you know, name me six famous Belgians. And then he gives you the answer. On the one hand you might think, "You show-off." On the other hand you might find it interesting. You might be entertained by him to a certain point. And then as the book goes on, I hope his plight as it develops . . . I hope it moves you. That's all I can say.

Birnbaum: By himself, it might be easier to see Oliver as a sympathetic character. But juxtaposed to Stuart his former best friend and the first husband of his wife. Well . . . Stuart seems to have grown up. Perhaps even admirably. Not an outstanding individual, not world historical but he has moved from point A to point

B in his life. Which is a respectable thing and perhaps the most you can expect from most people, that there's some growth and that they have learned things.
Barnes: So the fact that Oliver patronizes him irritates you? [laughs]

Birnbaum: Yes, yes. And there is this Rashoman aspect here in the way that you have constructed the story.
Barnes: Yes, that is another aspect which I hope makes it, I hope, immediately, like life. There is no human interaction let alone emotional involvement that doesn't usually come with two versions.

Birnbaum: At least.
Barnes: At least, yes.

Birnbaum: You have Stuart saying, "Trust invites betrayal." It seems that trust may be a sufficient condition and a necessary condition?
Barnes: Stuart is saying that because in the first book he has been deeply and emotionally trashed and betrayed by the two people he most loved, his best friend and his wife. So that's why he comes to that particular conclusion. Depending on whose version you believe, the boot is on the other foot in this book, as Stuart is then trusted by both of them, and Stuart also betrays trust in taking his revenge. I agree with you, it's a necessary condition for betrayal but not a necessary consequence. You can't be betrayed by the street-crossing person. If Russia had attacked the U.S. with nuclear weapons, it wouldn't have been a betrayal. It would have been an expected consequence.

Birnbaum: The issue of the truth value we assign to fact and fiction is, I think, becoming more interesting and regularly challenged. One of your characters states, "The story of our lives is never autobiography, it's a novel."
Barnes: Fiction is the supreme fiction. And everybody's autobiography is a fiction but not the supreme fiction. I work as a novelist, and I also work as a journalist. And I am very conscious of the essential difference of the two skills. When I write a piece of journalism, I want it to be completely understood at first reading as all journalism should be. In order to do that, you, of necessity, elucidate and simplify. And so the world appears more comprehensible. When I metaphorically move to the other part of my desk and write fiction, I am aware that my task is to represent complication and the fullness of the world. And to write the book, while certainly comprehensible and I hope enjoyable on first reading, would leave something in the reader's mind to invite them back. I do keep this distinction firmly in mind. It's easy, if you are doing both, for them to coalesce in some ways.

Birnbaum: Some would hold that journalism frequently involves manipulating facts and images to get to a preconceived conclusion . . .

Barnes: As a journalist, I deal in checkable fact, and I will produce an appealing assemblage of facts which will lead to a conclusion which either I will draw or will be clearly implicit. It's quite opposite with a novel where you are not dealing in facts but dealing in truth. And at the same time you are not leading the reader to a particular conclusion. Especially in this book [*Love, etc.*], you are leading the reader to a place where he or she can make up their own mind. So they are fundamentally different paths through the forest.

Birnbaum: What is the urgency about identifying things as true or the truth?

Barnes: It's deep within most of us. The places where the truth comes from are now less various than they used to be. Especially with the decline of the truth of religion as generally not believed anymore. The truths offered by the state seem much less reliable than they used to. And the truths of journalism are a bit hit-and-miss, as we know. And also often hugely influenced by established and corporate money. That seems to me to leave us with the truths of art. To which I cling to as someone who lives by the arts in both senses.

Birnbaum: What do you make of reality TV? *Survivor, Temptation Island, Big Brother, Real World* . . .

Barnes: It has its alarming side. Because the people in that house [*Big Brother*], which wasn't a real house, became celebrities afterwards. The nastiest one, Nasty Nick and everyone hated him and it was picked up by the tabloids. . . . Whereupon he hires a press agent and does his image over and shows he is not really as nasty as all that. He writes his autobiography . . . it's five minutes of fame or whatever it was taken to an extraordinary degree. The only nice human thing I know about these shows is that when they did *Big Brother* in Spain, the ten Spaniards said, "We like one another very much. We're not going to vote out anybody. We're going to stay here." Nice to see some national difference still. Whereas in competitive Northern Britain they are voting each other out of the house straight away.

Birnbaum: I wonder if my discomfort with this newest version of TV crapola is generational. That is, is there a developmental stage where one rejects innovation and novelty out of hand, that one is out of step with progress? Or is this stuff inherently junk?

Barnes: There is also a discomfort because they seem to be, they are so well presented as reality and yet you know they are deeply manipulative. So you know it must be the case that the director has gone in and said, "Nasty Nick, do you think we could do that again? That bit where you said, 'You're a real bitch.'" It's a much sharpened sense of the manipulativeness of TV. A heightened manipulativeness, I think that's what we respond to with unease. I don't view it as a sign of cultural decline.

Birnbaum: I have given up viewing everything as the end of civilization . . . it appears to be still standing. Good books are still being published and good movies are still being made. It is still somewhat frightening because there is so much that seems worthless. The volume of the shit stream seems to be greater than the trickle of wonderful things.

Barnes: I think that's true. The English writer Kingsley Amis on some other subject famously said that more will mean worse. It's certainly the case in television. At the moment English television, which has four terrestrial channels, is still pretty good and there are enough good shows being pumped out. As soon as you get up to twenty, thirty, forty cable stations—apart from anything else you then channel hop. That has a distinct effect on your concentration levels.

Birnbaum: What did we do before we had remote controls?

Barnes: There weren't so many channels. And we decided to go sit and watch a particular program on the whole, didn't we? Now we more tend to think, "Oh, shall we watch some television?" And then see if there is anything interesting on.

Birnbaum: Earlier you talked about your purpose in writing novels to pose some questions and perhaps answer some . . . do questions about your intentions for yet another sequel come up often?

Barnes: I'm asked that a lot, already. A thing I was not asked about the first one which came out ten years ago. And therefore I was blissfully unaware for eight years that I was going to write a sequel. But having decided to and then having deliberately made the ending as open-ended as I could with as many questions left to the reader as possible. And indeed having the characters asking the reader what they would do, I feel I should probably go back to this narrative. Though not immediately because the characters have to live enough life to be interesting. I could easily go back to London and start writing the first two or three chapters.

Birnbaum: Or you could bag it. Though if I were a betting man, I would prepare myself some years hence to read about Gillian, Stuart, and Oliver . . .

Barnes: If I were a betting man, I would say yes. But I know what my next two or three books are probably going to be. I think it would be quite nice to wait seven, eight, ten years.

Birnbaum: Was it the case that as time passed . . . did you reread the book? Or was the fate of these young characters in *Talking It Over* a lingering notion?
Barnes: No, it wasn't always lingering. Usually when I finish a book it is absolutely finished and gone from me. And that's how I felt about this one when I finished it. It doesn't invite a continuation. Lots of people asked me about it over the years, and also they disagreed about it. I think it was their disagreement about what would happen to the marriage of Oliver and Gillian—finding myself arguing about things I hadn't thought of. Though that wasn't enough in itself. I think what came back to me was the pleasure and the stimulation of using this author-less form of just not being there—obviously running the whole, but not being an obvious force in the book. I thought there was more that I could do with this form than I did in the first book. I also thought of various ways of pushing, thinning even further that membrane between reader and characters. There is a bit where Gillian addresses the reader on the assumption that the reader is in bed reading the book and thinking that maybe he or she will have sex after they finish this chapter . . .

Birnbaum: In the way TV shows like *It's Gary Shandling's Show* removed the fourth wall and spoke directly to the audience . . . did you reread *Talking It Over*?
Barnes: Absolutely.

Birnbaum: I take it you don't normally do that [reread], so how was that?
Barnes: I was rereading it with a particular purpose. I reread it for exactly what I needed. I gutted it. It would have been unhelpful for me to assess it as a book. I gutted it for the lives of these people . . .

Birnbaum: Looking for continuity?
Barnes: Sure, I was the continuity girl. And reminding myself of the way they spoke, some of their prejudices I had forgotten, some of the ways they expressed emotion, and so on. Also, looking at it for questions that I left unanswered. And looking at it to see who I wanted to keep and who I wanted to leave. I nearly killed off Madame Wyatt, Gillian's mother, which would have been a serious mistake. When I was making up my mind, I remembered something Evelyn Waugh said about P. G. Wodehouse. He said, "Part of Wodehouse's genius as a writer was that he never killed off a single character." I thought Madame Wyatt as the older

and outside seemingly emotionally wise woman would be too good to waste. . . .
She provokes a different sort of thinking.

Birnbaum: There is a bittersweetness about her point of view . . . her continental
complexity. Is it possible that every ten years of your life you may go back to this
group?

Barnes: No, I think not. I really think a third one will do it. In the first book they
were at the end of their twenties just turning thirty. Life was still fresh. Life still
had its hopes. In this book they just turned forty. They are each aware in a different way that it's—not exactly last-chance time—but it's a time at which certain
key things if they go one way or another are going to affect the rest of their lives.
You live in a country that's much more optimistic that mine—believes in constant
renewal, constant redemption, and so on.

Birnbaum: Reengineering . . .

Barnes: . . . which we tend not to do so much in Europe. In your forties, that's
when things are going up or down that's how they are going to continue. It's time
to call for the bill.

Birnbaum: I saw an interview with Billy Bob Thornton and his closing remark
was, "It's never too late." Isn't the fascinating possibility with Oliver that he ulti-
mately does redeem himself albeit much later in life than anyone might expect?

Barnes: He might get a streak of luck, but luck also runs out. It's true that in your
country people think nothing of . . . whenever I see those U-Haul trucks going
across the country I think of them as a metaphor for America and Americans' attitude toward life. There are times when you pack all your emotional and moral
baggage into them and you move off to another part of the country. Instead of
being an academic you become a realtor or you become a judge. This couldn't
happen in England or most of Europe. Or maybe it would happen once. Just as
people get divorced much less in Britain where the idea of tearing up your life and
going off in a completely different direction several times is almost inconceivable
to most British people.

Birnbaum: Because?

Barnes: (long pause) We're more conservative. It's not in the . . . even though
we have become more Americanized in the last twenty years and attitudes have
changed radically and it's much more of a winner-take-all devil-take-the-hind-
most society than it was when I was growing up. One part of Americanization
that hasn't happened is this belief in endless renewal.

Birnbaum: Is this an alternative view or definition of freedom? Is this about freedom?

Barnes: It's about freedom and optimism. It could almost be written into your constitution: "Everyone has the right to change their career and their emotional and moral status several times." Everyone has the right to be forgiven. That's another thing that is deeply American. You love forgiving people. You love executing them as well. You love killing them and you love forgiving them.

Birnbaum: Is it because people are better taken care of in social democratic countries?

Barnes: It's not the case in Britain. It's been the case in social democratic Europe that increasingly working hours have been shortened and retirement age has been brought forward and so on. I don't think it's anticipation of retirement that stops people changing their job. It's deeply engrained in the culture that at a certain point between ten—preferably as early as possible—and twenty-five you will decide what you want to do and so it's an affirmation of your personhood. Therefore it's a denial of self, and it would amount to a crisis of some sort and an admission of defeat [to change careers]. I also agree with Stuart when he goes to America and remakes his life and talks about it mainly in terms of his marriage. In Britain you would say my marriage failed. In America you might say my marriage ended. That's maybe about forgiveness as well. And there is the tyranny of orthodoxy that continues. There is an assumption that the end of a marriage means a failure of some sort. Whereas it doesn't necessarily at all.

Birnbaum: Stuart refers to marriage as the most difficult human enterprise.

Barnes: Does he? I can't remember that. But I'm sure you're right. They talk about it so much . . . well it is a very difficult . . .

Birnbaum: Stuart calls it "the ultimate challenge."

Barnes: It is. I don't want to sound like a marital soothsayer. It is easy to have sex and easy to fall in love, and it's hard to keep it fresh. Raymond Chandler wrote a letter to a friend of his who was getting married which was full of advice. At the end it said, "Always remember that marriage is like a newspaper, it has to be made fresh every damned day of every damned year." That's very difficult and it demands . . . apart from basic questions of love and sex . . . it demands tenderness, thoughtfulness, and giving of space and also knowing what you want and respecting what the other person wants and so on and so forth. Also, it necessitates a continuing interest in the other person. One of the wisest things that great

Ford Madox Ford said at some point, "You marry to continue the conversation." Which I thought was brilliant. . . . I think they do change, but as long as there are still conversations. The way I visualize it, or would dramatize it, is when you meet someone and fall in love with them, it's as if you are at opposite sides of the restaurant looking at one another, feeding on one another as well as the dinner and looking at one another. As you go on, you end up at one of those tables where you are sitting side by side, looking out at the world. But you are talking to one another about the world, and you have a whole bank of shared assumptions from previous conversations. So it does change, but the conversation must go on.

Birnbaum: *Love, etc.* is a slender volume that deals with big issues and ideas.
Barnes: Well I hope so. What I'm doing . . . I am trying to tell a story which encloses and describes the way people love and are friends nowadays. And what that involves and the dangers and attractions are. I wouldn't dream of telling any but my very closest friends if they begged and bribed me for advice, I wouldn't tell anyone what to do. I'm not that sort of writer.

Birnbaum: Are *Talking It Over* and *Love, etc.* your most personal works? They seem to be so heartfelt and require authorial identification with the characters . . .
Barnes: I'm glad you said that. I have a reputation of being a chilly ironist or something like that. "It's not true, it's not true," he cried.

Birnbaum: Perhaps when you have such a well-developed and specific vocabulary, it might frighten people away from the heart of the matter.
Barnes: I'm not backtracking. But these books are not more personal than *Flaubert's Parrot*, in fact. I'm as fascinated by the emotional and sexual life of people as I am by Flaubert. But this book is no more autobiographical than the Flaubert book is.

Birnbaum: I wasn't suggesting . . .
Barnes: The assumption often is that if you write a book about a deposed communist leader—we know that's not autobiographical—the one about a love triangle or whatever terrible phrase the publisher uses, that's probably really about him.

Birnbaum: Well, there is involvement and there is emotional attachment. Some things can be more of a rational exercise or an emotional outpouring . . .
Barnes: Well yes, but I think there is a lot of emotion in ideas. You can write a book—maybe I didn't succeed—I hope that you can write a book about the dialogue and the struggle between a hard line communist ex-dictator and a

compromised liberal prosecutor which will not just be an exchange of idea and opinion but actually involve the emotions. So that you want one to win and to win in the right way. And you are upset when the one who wins, wins in the wrong way. When we talk about a novel provoking emotions, we tend to think of the emotions that have to do with our own amatory life. I think that books can be emotionally exciting in many different ways.

Birnbaum: How much has what you have written determined what your future projects are? That is, because you have done this or that you avoid this or that?
Barnes: I try to put everything I have written in the past behind me. That's why I never read assessments or theses about me. I don't want to know what my books have in common. They are single jobs that I work on each time.

Birnbaum: What does the word "oeuvre" suggest?
Barnes: It suggests I'm dead, is one of the problems. There are lots of different dangers in any artistic pursuit and vainglory is one of them. Thinking of yourself as constructing an oeuvre is dangerous. I don't even think of myself as having a career which has a particular structure to it. I just write one book after the other. And I forget the previous ones, and I let everyone else get on with it.

Birnbaum: You did allude to what you are doing next . . .
Barnes: The next main thing is a collection of stories, a second collection of short stories themed in a similar way. And also a collection of essays I've put together over the years on French subjects.

Birnbaum: Recently I have talked to a number of essayists who feel, perhaps self-interestedly, that this is a particular time when the essay will flourish. As a practitioner of almost all literary forms what's your take on the stature of the essay?
Barnes: I like the essay or the long piece of journalism, rather. What I don't see—and it would be very good if it did expand because there's good space out there for long investigative pieces—nowadays the pieces we used to read growing up, their function has been slightly superseded by television documentaries. And then you get the news story in the papers based on the TV documentary. Investigative journalism ought to retake some of that ground. And alongside of that the reflective essay could perhaps make a comeback. Because the general tendency in the thirty years that I've practiced journalism is for the pieces to get shorter, paragraphs to get shorter, pictures to get bigger, attention span to decrease. I find when I publish long pieces—I did one last year about the Tour de France and drug use in the last century—readers really will stick with a piece.

Birnbaum: Doesn't it sell readers short to assume that they won't? There are readers and there are readers . . .

Barnes: Yes, there are readers and there are readers, but magazine editors and proprietors . . . it may be that the old essayistic style, its time had come. The classic complaint about the *New Yorker*, there were too many pieces about the timber industry, which were interesting in themselves, but had absolutely nothing to do with what was happening in the world in the last five years. Of course, they did *Hiroshima* and stuff like that. Yea, I would certainly welcome that . . .

Interviews: Julian Barnes

Peter Wild/2002

From *Bookmunch.co.uk*, 3 June 2002. http://www.bookmunch.co.uk/iv01_002. htm. Reprinted with permission of the author.

Peter Wild: Reading *In the Land of Pain* I was struck by just how much more than a translation the book is, what with the introduction and the endnote and the footnotes. It came to seem that this was very much a labour of love. Curious that a book about "illness, dying, and death" should provoke such strong feelings. What was it that fascinated you enough to want to translate, and has that particular itch been scratched or can we expect to see a rather darker Julian Barnes novel at some point in the future?

Julian Barnes: Well, it goes back quite a long way. I first read it when I was researching for my novel *Flaubert's Parrot*. I thought that it was a remarkable book—its honesty and its directness and its lack of either sentimentality or self-dramatisation. Flaubert said at one point that it's only by looking down at the black pit at our feet that we can remain calm (i.e. you're more likely to panic if you don't look at it, and the only way to look at it is to look at it with a straightforward stare). That's what Daudet does. I don't think I've translated it now because I've suddenly got gloomier and started becoming obsessed by death. I've always been obsessed with death. It's been a constant thing. I think I just reread it and thought, "Hang on, another twenty years has passed and this book has never been translated into English." And then once I started, it became clear that just a translation was not going to be adequate. You needed a lot of notes and a certain amount of background material. I actually enjoyed the pleasures of scholarship perhaps for the first time and, as a result, spent far more time on it than probably justified in publishing terms. But I had a lot of fun with it, if fun is the right word. Serious pleasure at any rate.

Wild: Translation seems to arouse very strong feelings. On the one hand you have Shelley's famous quote about the violet and the crucible (". . . it were as wise to cast a violet into a crucible that you might discover the formal principles of its

colour and odour, as seek to transfuse from one language into another the creations of a poet"), or Dante ("Nothing which is harmonized by the bond of the
Muses can be changed from its own language without having all its sweetness destroyed"). At the other extreme you have someone like, say, Borges ("Perhaps . . .
the translator's work is more subtle, more civilized than that of the writer: the
translator clearly comes after the writer. Translation is a more advanced stage of
civilization"). What are your feelings on the art of translation?

Barnes: Having been translated myself quite a lot I know that you always lose
something. It's always a question of minimizing your losses. You're bound to lose
maybe 5 percent, maybe more—depends on the writer, depends on the translator.
I think that's inevitable. I still think that works in translation are obviously well
worth reading. I still think that the person who can only read English can get a lot
out of foreign literature. I don't think that the translator is higher than the writer.
I think that the translator can be a parallel writer. It's an odd mixture of creativity and subservience at the same time. Every so often you have to rein yourself
back, as a translator, from being too obviously there on the page. I think it was
okay for me because I knew I was going to be there on the page in all of the footnotes. I did feel, when I was translating Daudet's own words, I did feel a strong
sense of service. I felt that it was my duty to represent this man as closely as possible in tone and weight of words to what he wrote.

Wild: In a *Salon* interview round about the time of *Cross Channel*, you said, "If
you read something in translation, you should feel as if there isn't any barrier between you and the author . . ."

Barnes: I suppose that this is a rather different kind of translation, because it can
only really work with a lot of annotation. After all, he didn't write it to be read by
a reader. I suppose I want the reader to hear Daudet's voice as clearly as possible
in the text, and then hear my voice, helping to explain what his voice is saying, in
the notes.

Wild: Would you like to see Daudet receive more interest on the back of your
translation?

Barnes: I don't really know. He has had a strange posthumous reputation in that
he's known for his lighter and comic work, and he did write one or two novels
that are quite serious although very much of their time. I think it's really up to
publishers. The torch I have carried has always been for this particular book
rather than Daudet as a generally undervalued writer. He was well valued in
his time. I don't think that, apart from this book, there's a hidden masterpiece

waiting to be unearthed. If you've read all Flaubert, and you've read quite a lot of Zola, and you've read some Goncourt novels, then Daudet is worth reading.

Wild: Are there any other books that you are tempted to translate in the future?
Barnes: Not at the moment, no. This took longer than I thought it would. I mean, it was extremely pleasant work—well, unpleasant sometimes, but always fascinating. I haven't really got a list of things that need translating. I wouldn't be interested in re-translating something. Every so often someone says, "Will [you] do a new translation of *Madame Bovary*?" Well, yes, if I didn't have any of my own books to write and I could put five years aside. Something may come along in the future, but at the moment this is not a new career path.

Wild: The central character of *The Porcupine* was inspired by Bulgaria's deposed Communist dictator, Todor Zhivkov, and the book was first published in Bulgarian. Did you write the Bulgarian version or did the translated version exist prior to your own?
Barnes: I have a few Bulgarian friends, one of whom was particularly helpful with the book and who happens to be my Bulgarian publisher and translator. I sent her a late draft of *The Porcupine* and didn't hear from her for a while and then about six weeks later I got a letter that said, "I have now finished the translation." I said, "Hang on. Look, I sent you this for comment, not translation." She said, "No, no, we'll do it soon. It will be very good to have it out at the time that Zhivkov is to be put on trial," as indeed it was. Because I had this close affection with my friend, publisher, translator, she wanted to get it out as soon as possible. And it takes nine months to produce a book in England, and I just thought it would be a rather good bibliographical note. It makes it a curiosity. Some people think it is one of my jokes.

Wild: Has the problem with Professor Mark Hogarth [academic who registered the names of many writers—including Julian Barnes, Ian McEwan, Martin Amis, Jeanette Winterson—and demanded financial compensation to return them] been resolved?
Barnes: Yes, it has. Eventually there was an action by the Society of Authors on behalf of me, and I think three or four other writers, and we certainly got our domain names back. I don't know what happened with the other people whose name he stole. I think, as I understand it, that it was not possible to bring a class action on behalf of everyone and each case does not naturally set a precedent, which is sort of strange and not very good law it seems to me. It was something I felt very strongly about, because as a writer your name is one thing that you're

really close to. I'm not saying that anyone isn't close to their name, it's just that your name is associated so closely with what you do and the idea of somebody setting up a website without my permission to sell books for a profit or whatever the original plans were . . .

Wild: I think he wanted one third of the money earned from the sales of books in that particular year.
Barnes: He asked me for something like—it sounded less at first—three percent of the cover price of every book sold throughout the world that year, as if you could work it out yourself. It works out, given that average royalty is ten percent, that he was asking for a third, in effect, of one's income. I'm afraid that rather hardens me and my position. I now have a website at www.julianbarnes.com.

Wild: I read an interview a few years ago in which you said you were slightly hesitant regarding all of this new technology . . .
Barnes: Did I say that? I'm up to speed on email and shopping on the web. I don't write on my computer yet. I don't know whether I'm going to. I work on an electric typewriter and that is still going strong. I have this website which I occasionally visit. The guy that runs it is very diligent. Sometimes if I want to know what I'm doing in the next few months, I look at my website.

Wild: I was wondering how you felt about all of this talk surrounding the Man Booker Prize. Do you think it would be a good or bad thing to introduce American books into the mix?
Barnes: I'm against [introducing American authors]. I think that the prize has been defined as a prize for British and Commonwealth writers. I don't expect to be put in for a prize for American books. I don't see why they should be put in for ours. I think it's an exaggeration by Ian McEwan to say that Philip Roth would have won the prize four times in a row. I judged the Guardian First Book Award a bit ago—two years ago when Zadie Smith won it—and in the final five or six books I think that she was the only British author. There were four American books, maybe, and one Canadian book. It seems to me sort of ridiculous that a first book award run by a British newspaper—the one thing you think it should do is encourage local talent. It's not quite the same with the Booker, which is obviously for more . . . finished writers. I think that it would lose its individuality.

Wild: Do you think that it is inevitable?
Barnes: I think the thing will be corporate-lead won't it? It will become much less of a book prize and more of an advertisement.

Wild: I think you can already see that in the choice of people selected as judges, people like David Baddiel.

Barnes: That's right. For a start, they don't need five judges. I think they'd get on much better with three. And I think that the judges should be much more literary. One year it was judged by Cyril Connolly, Mary McCarthy, and George Steiner. Now we're getting clowns from politics chairing the judges. Without mentioning any names.

Wild: What are you reading at the moment? What have you read recently that is worth recommending?

Barnes: Funny that we've been talking about translation, really. At the moment, I'm reading what is in fact a very poor translation, but it's the only one ever of the German writer Fontane's late great novel *Der Stechlin*. I was told this was his late, great novel by my German publisher when I was over there earlier this year. I got a copy and I'm ploughing through, but it is one of the most toiling translations that I have ever come across. It is like looking through a window that hasn't been cleaned in years and is full of cobwebs. It's terrible, but I'm ploughing on because I admire Fontane greatly.

Wild: Are you one of these people who can stop reading a book if it's terrible or must you plough on to the end regardless?

Barnes: No, I do stop if I don't like it. This I'm not going to stop because I know that—even peering through this dim glass—I can see something. The last Fontane I read was a short novel called *L'Adultera*, which is a sort of lighter version of *Effi Briest*, which is a great masterpiece—one of the great nineteenth-century novels. I'd urge people to read *Effi Briest* if they haven't already.

Wild: What are you working on at the moment? Can we expect a new novel in a year, or two years?

Barnes: You can expect a novel in two years. I've started scratching around, but I haven't made a proper start yet.

Wild: What is your favourite part of the writing process?

Barnes: I think that the favourite point is when you are about a quarter of the way into the first draft and you think—yes. Yes, there is a novel here, and yes, I have got a pretty rough idea of where it's going and how long it will be and how long it will take, and I've got this rich and wonderful period of work ahead of me. Then you get to the end of the first draft and that's when the real work has to begin.

Julian Barnes in Conversation

Vanessa Guignery/2002

From *Cercles* 4 (2002): 255–69. Reprinted by permission of publisher.

Nicole Terrien: I do not really know how to introduce Mr. Barnes to all his readers: I guess the questions will be enough to provide a kind of quest for self-definition of Julian Barnes as a writer. Perhaps you could introduce yourself?

Julian Barnes: If you like: I am Julian Barnes. I wrote this book [shows *Flaubert's Parrot*], which is the proof—it's got my photograph somewhere! I'd just like to thank Professor Capet for organising this Conference with such amiability and efficiency. I would say as a preliminary remark that it makes me feel slightly awkward in two respects.

The first is that it makes me think of one of those Polycarp dinners that Flaubert was given towards the end of his life on the feast day of Polycarp, his chosen patron saint, when they would serve him dishes named after his work: so it would be *Potage Bovary*, followed by *Poulet Homais, Salade au Cœur Simple*, and *Glace Salammbô*—there are about three or four other dishes on that particular menu, and I must say I half-expected Professor Capet to have ordered roast parrot when we had dinner last night. At one of these banquets, there was a moment when Flaubert's friends decided to crown him; they had a laurel crown ready, and someone came forward, placed it on his head, but it had been made too big, so it slipped down around his neck. And he said, "I feel like a tombstone"—Well, I feel like half a tombstone today: that's the first ground for awkwardness.

The second is a more practical ground: which is that *Flaubert's Parrot* is a novel, which it's very appropriate to talk about here, evidently, because it was here that the novel began—but it began here exactly twenty years and two months ago, and was finished seventeen and a half or eighteen years ago, and therefore *you*, in asking any questions of me, will have the advantage on me that I will have forgotten quite a lot of it. This is, I'm afraid, one of the necessary happenings when you are a novelist—that writing a new novel necessitates the almost total forgetting of the previous one. And since *Flaubert's Parrot*, I have written half a dozen novels or so. So, some of my answers may be more "creative" than truthful!

Vanessa Guignery: Thank you, Julian. First, I'd like to thank Julian Barnes very warmly for being here today, because he very rarely attends academic meetings, so we should really be grateful to him for accepting to be here today. One of the reasons why he accepted to come has certainly to do with place: this symposium takes place in Rouen, the Flaubertian city, the city which Geoffrey Braithwaite visits in the first and last chapters of *Flaubert's Parrot*, the city where he sees the first stuffed parrot at the Hôtel-Dieu before discovering the second one in Croisset. My first question has to do with the genesis of the book: could you tell us how the idea for the book came up to you?

Barnes: Yes, I can!—I can answer this one!!! I think it's true that most of my books have two starting-points, or two different sorts of genesis. There is a long-standing, long-delayed, and usually unrecognised beginning, an obsession with a particular subject or theme, which usually I am conscious of, but I am not aware that it is necessarily going to turn into the subject for a novel; and then, at a certain point, usually there is a moment of ignition at which the notion that this interest—this mere human interest—might turn into a literary endeavour comes in focus. So, to begin with, I read French at school and University; I was given *Madame Bovary* to read by the English master—not a French master—when I was about fifteen. I read it expecting that it was going to be a hot book because it was about a married Frenchwoman—so, obviously an erotic novel. I think that when I read it on that front at fifteen, I was very disappointed, but the older I get, the more it seems like an erotic novel to me. And then I did a special paper on Flaubert when I was at University, and continued to read him. I published one novel, two novels—I had always wanted to do something about Flaubert, but I knew I did not want to write any sort of biography or any sort of work of criticism.

Then at a certain point which I had forgotten until I consulted my travel notebook—I keep one, as Flaubert kept them—for September 1981, for a trip to Normandy and the Loire—I had forgotten that the incident which sparked off *Flaubert's Parrot* came out of a commission I had, which was to write a book about French writers' houses—it was going to be a guide to every French writer or artist whose house was publicly available for visit, and I think I even signed a contract for this book. And on this particular trip—it was theoretically a holiday but it included visiting in the following order: Michelet's château at Vascœuil, Monet's garden, Voltaire's patron's château at Sully, Alain-Fournier's birthplace,

Balzac's château at Saché, and Anatole France's house at Tours (where I remember being taken round by Anatole France's grandson, who introduced his wife by saying, "This is my third wife." I did not make any comment, but he said, "No, no, I must explain: my first wife decided that she preferred other company to mine; my second wife died; and so, this is my third wife, but I am not a man who runs after women." That was going to go in the book that was never written). From there Corneille's house, Flaubert's birthplace, Flaubert's *pavillon*, and Maupassant's birthplace. So I was researching hard, as you can see.

This was September 1981, twenty years and two months ago, and I had not looked at this notebook since. These are the three relevant entries which I then wrote. After a sort of rather dismissive account of how Corneille's house consisted of almost nothing that had anything to do with Corneille (I hope that's not offensive to anyone), it goes on: "Flaubert's statue, place des Carmes, looking rather loftily upwards with a sticking out moustache disdaining the game of *boules* being played beneath him" (end of entry). Next entry: "Avenue Gustave-Flaubert, containing an *Imprimerie Flaubert* and a snack-bar/restaurant called *Le Flaubert*. Round the corner to the musée Flaubert: mixed surgical instruments, medical texts, and Flaubertiana. A copy of the magazine containing his first published item, pictures of his family, the room he was actually born in (Louis Quinze fireplace), and most memorably, the bright-green perky-eyed parrot which was lent to him when he was writing *Un Cœur simple*, and which irritated him at the same time, as giving him an inner sense of parrothood." Line space, next entry:

"Croisset, the high point of pilgrimage. In Flaubert's day, a village outside Rouen. His broad house as seen in an amateur picture above the Seine, backdropped by green. Now Croisset is part of the docks area. Huge gantries loom alongside, and rails for cranes to run along. The Seine looks commercial, and there is a bar, *Le Flaubert*." Then there is various stuff about the house, and an inventory of the museum, which I shall spare you—it ends with "The handkerchief with which he mopped his brow before he died, and a very ordinary tumbler, from which he took a drink a few instants before he died. Then, crouched on top of one of the display cabinets—what did we see, but *ANOTHER PARROT* (capital letters and underlined as in the notebook). Also bright green, also according to the *gardienne*, and also a label hung on its perch, the authentic parrot borrowed by Gustave Flaubert when he wrote *Un Cœur simple*!! I ask the *gardienne* if I can take it down to photograph it. She concurs, even suggests I take off the glass case. I do, and it strikes me as slightly less authentic than the other one, mainly because it seems benign—and Flaubert wrote of how irritating the other one was to have on his desk. As I am looking for somewhere to photograph it, the sun comes out—this is on a cloudy, grouchy, rainy morning—and slants across the display cabinet. I put it there and take two sun-lit photos, then, as I pick the parrot up to replace it, the sun goes in. It felt like a benign intervention by Gustave Flaubert, signalling thanks for my presence, or indicating that this was indeed the true parrot."

So you can see, I think, the start of the novel very clearly in those passages. I did not know of course then, when I took these notes, or for a while afterwards that this was the beginning of a novel. I thought that this was an interesting coincidence, a provocative ambiguity. I thought briefly, "Should I write an article in a scholarly magazine about this?" Then I thought, "That's not the sort of thing I do, or am any good at." I put it aside for months, I suppose—I simply don't know the chronology—until it came to me that there could be a story made from this, and as soon as I had the sort of person who, in my stead, would be able to write passionately about these two parrots—so, someone rather pedantic, rather obsessed, ready to draw the fullest meanings out of the smallest coincidence or ambiguity—I began to have Geoffrey Braithwaite with me, and then I wrote a version—quite a close version, I think, of the first chapter—as a story, as a separate story. But it was clearly a fiction, a piece of fiction. It had Braithwaite, it bounced his life off Flaubert's life and work, and it ended with the second parrot, and had one wondering which was which, or whether one was the true one. And, I guess, shortly after I had finished that, I realised this was not just a short story: this was the start of a project, in which I could play off the real against the fictional and the contemporary against the nineteenth century in a productive way—and I went on to write it.

When I reread that passage, I thought it was quite a good example of what you can and can't do and use as a writer, what is true in life but does not work as fiction—because it really happened that I was there in the second museum, took the cover off the parrot, put it down somewhere, and all of a sudden on a typical grey Normandy day a great shaft of sunlight comes into the *pavillon* and it lights up this second parrot. Now, you can't do that in fiction, because it's just too obvious, it's just pointing the finger, saying, "Look, this is an answer, this is a symbol." But I also remember that I had a debate with myself about whether I could use this at all, and in fact I reduced it finally to a single line. I misremembered my own novel at this point: I thought that I had completely eliminated this obviously banal and sentimental piece of sunlight that suddenly arrived, but in fact I had left in "a shaft of sunlight came in." But I was deliberately keeping it as little more than weather, rather than as an authorial thumb on the scales.

Guignery: Thank you very much, Julian. I find that there are many similarities between Braithwaite's method in *Flaubert's Parrot* and Bouvard and Pécuchet's method in Flaubert's book. In particular I am thinking about when Bouvard and Pécuchet try to write the life of the duc d'Angoulême: there are many common points with Flaubert's approach—that is, in both cases the structure is rather fragmented, it's a juxtaposition of disconnected fragments, and none of the biographers manages to reach an all-encompassing vision. Did you intend this parallel between Braithwaite's method and Bouvard and Pécuchet's method?

Barnes: No. That I can say for certain: I didn't. I mean I may possibly have, at some very, very unconscious level remembered this, but I certainly wouldn't admit it to any conscious or pre-conscious level. I thought of *Flaubert's Parrot* when I started writing it as obviously an unofficial and informal, non-conventional sort of novel—an upside down novel, a novel in which there was an infrastructure of fiction and very strong elements of nonfiction, sometimes whole chapters which were nothing but arranged facts. It was a challenge as to how strong and authentic you can make a narrative when you aren't having anything invented in it; it was partly a challenge to myself to see what I could do as narrative with various stuff. I guess that if I was looking for a comparison within Flaubert, the one that I would choose would be perhaps Félicité's room in *Un Cœur simple* which, you recall, Flaubert describes as a cross between a chapel and a bazaar. And so you could say my novel is half homage and half junk shop. If *A History of the World* is a similar sort of upside down, informal piece of novel-history, this is an upside down, informal piece of novel-biography.

I had one image when I was writing it, which I did not use at all in the book, but it was the idea that a great novelist lies in a sort of unofficial burial mound—something Anglo-Saxon or Egyptian—and there is always an entrance to it, through which he was taken in, and then he was buried and the entrance was sealed up. What biography tends to do, understandably, is to unseal the entrance: it goes in, it finds the body, it finds all the artefacts that the great writer has been buried with, and it is re-creating him backwards from that moment of burial. And *I* thought—my semi-image in my head for what I was doing was, "What happens if you sink in tunnels at lots of different unexpected angles into the burial chamber?" Perhaps this will result in some insights that you don't get by using the official entrance—hence a chapter which has just been so ably commented on about railways. What if you just assemble everything that you can find that Flaubert wrote about railways? Perhaps this will tell us something about him and his work that something sequential and conventional won't?

It's like my second chapter—the three biographies of Flaubert. I thought, it is your duty as a writer (any sort of writer) to establish facts for your readers, so it was my duty to give some sort of account of Flaubert's life early on so that people knew exactly who he was, what he'd done, and so forth. But it seemed to me that the conventional account of his life should be undermined in two ways: you can read almost anyone's life as a triumph—I am talking about the sort of people who get biographies written about them (*ipso facto*, their biographers usually see their lives as triumphs), or you can equally read most of these lives as failures, which is what they often appear to the subject of the biography him- or herself (and that's "Chronology II"). And then "Chronology III" says, "But maybe seeing someone's life either as triumph or as disaster does not actually tell us half as much as just seeing their lives in terms of metaphors." There are many, many, many metaphors and similes that Flaubert used that I did not put into "Chronology III"; as he said at some point—I can't remember the French quote, but the English quote is roughly that similes and comparisons were crawling over him like bugs and that he was always having to squash them. In fact, I think that maybe, of the three chronologies, the one that evokes Flaubert the best is the third, the one which consists of him saying things like, "I feel like an old camembert slowly liquefying."

While on the subject of railways, I meant to add a satirical P.S. to Tony Williams's remarks on trains in my work. I hadn't realised that I had written so admiringly about the Eurostar in the short story "Tunnel." But that explains why shortly after the story appeared I got a letter from Eurostar, asking me if, in exchange for free travel for the rest of my life, I would allow my name and my picture to be used to advertise their services. I left that to M. Éric Cantona, I think—though had I had the wit, I would have written back and said, "No, but I know a famous Frenchman called M. Flaubert who might be willing to do it."

Guignery: In an interview for *Book Club* on Radio Four in 1999, you said that mystification is too easy for a novelist, and you also said confusing the reader is too easy. You said that you devised a strict line dividing factual and reliable information about Flaubert in *Flaubert's Parrot* on the one hand and more doubtful and fictional components on the other hand. And yet I feel that sometimes you do confuse the reader in *Flaubert's Parrot*, for example when you propose contradictory versions: you have just alluded to the three chronologies, and we can refer to the different versions of Flaubert and Louise Colet's affair. You also confuse the reader when you give references without giving the sources: I am thinking about the series of maxims, when at the end you say, "All these maxims are by Flaubert, except for the one by Bouilhet," but without saying which one it is.

Barnes: I think I only confuse the *academic* reader.

Guignery: O.K, let's talk about the academic reader, then.

Barnes: My brother, who unlike me lives in France, is a philosopher and has a very logical mind. When he read *Flaubert's Parrot*, he wrote me a letter saying, "I enjoyed your novel very much, except of course I did not know what was true and was not . . . etc., etc." As I said, mystification is easy, confusing the reader is easy: I intended the rules of the game to be as clear as I could make them. It seemed to me that all the information that Geoffrey Braithwaite gives you about Flaubert is true, or as true as he and I together could make it—I mean I'm sure there are one or two mistakes in it, which perhaps today someone will point out. So everything that he tells you is true, is the rule. He is an imaginary character, therefore all the people he meets are also fictional—except I thought that at the end of the book I was allowed to make the factual and fictional shake hands, when I bring on M. Lucien Andrieu, who indeed really existed and was secretary of the Société des amis de Flaubert, and who solved the problem of the parrots as far as it is soluble, for me and for Braithwaite.

I would not agree with you that giving three chronologies is confusing. I would say that it is actually illuminating. I don't think that, if you read the three chronologies, all the facts, all the statements there are incompatible with one another in terms of human life and human psychology. I think it's like giving an extra dimension or extra depth of focus. I can see that there would be points where the reader might want footnotes, or a question would be raised in the reader's mind to which he or she would only obtain the answer by going off and looking up in a book about Flaubert. For example, in Chapter 3 about Juliet Herbert's letters the reader might want to know more exactly the nature of Flaubert's relationship or to what extent these letters were likely to have existed. Incidentally, when I talked to Jean Bruneau, the extremely distinguished editor of the Pléiade *Correspondance*, he said that he still thought that the letters would turn up, which was very interesting, because that was some years after I had written this chapter.

To revert to the beginning: I thought I was making the rules of the game fair, and if my novel sends people off to either read Flaubert or read a biography of him, or check up some facts for themselves, then I don't think that's a failure.

Guignery: In an interview in 1999, you insisted on the importance of the fictional infrastructure in *Flaubert's Parrot*, and you said that the whole impetus of the novel was aiming towards the chapter called "Pure Story." So can we perhaps say that "Pure Story" is, in a way, the real conclusion of the novel, and that everything that comes afterwards is an anticlimax? It's true that the last chapter has to come last, because it solves—or does not solve—the enigma of the parrots. But, for example, why did you decide to put the examination paper as the last chapter but one?—If you remember!

Barnes: I do remember! No, no, it has more than one ending, perhaps! "Pure Story" tells you the story that has been delayed all the way through the novel—the story that Braithwaite is unable to tell you—which is his inability to tell you the tragic story of his own domestic life. Here is why he is telling you all this stuff about Flaubert, and why I insist upon the fictional element, the fictional infrastructure: without it, it wouldn't be a coherent book. I think it's a book . . . (I hate these sentences which start with "It's a book about . . . ," but I occasionally find myself drawn into them) . . . obviously, it's a book about the shiftingness of the past, and the uncertainty and unverifiability of fact, and so on and so forth, and it's a book, and it's a novel about Flaubert, and so on, and it's a novel about love—how the love of art compares with love of a human being—and I think perhaps beyond all that it's a novel about grief, it's a novel about a man whose inability to express his grief and his love is shifted (I'm sure there's a psychiatric term for it—displacement activity might be the one), is transposed into an obsessive desire to recount to you the reader everything he knows and has found out about Gustave Flaubert, love for whom is a more reliable constant in his life than has been love for Ellen.

Guignery: You were talking just a few minutes ago about Chapter 3, "Finders Keepers," which focuses on Juliet Herbert, a fictional chapter involving two fictional characters, Geoffrey Braithwaite and Ed Winterton. Did you choose to deal with Juliet Herbert in a fictional chapter precisely because there is no evidence for her affair with Gustave Flaubert? In other words, do you agree with Virginia Woolf when she writes, "The biographer is inventing when the evidence runs out"?

Barnes: Yes, I guess I do agree with that.

Guignery: I know that you are not a biographer.

Barnes: No, I'm not a biographer in *Flaubert's Parrot*. Juliet Herbert is a case which reminds me of the time when I worked as a lexicographer for the *Oxford English Dictionary*—I worked on the *Supplement* to the *Dictionary* for three years.

It was at times fascinating, at times tedious, work, and part of the tedium was relieved by things like finding that other lexicographers in the past had found the
work tedious and had therefore inserted jokes into their dictionaries. I can no
longer remember which dictionaries they are, but there's one dictionary whose
definition of a *currant bun* is "bun with very few currants in it." And there's another dictionary whose definition of a *net* is "a collection of holes tied together
with string," which actually is a very—I think—elegant and intellectual definition
of a net. And I use this to say, "You know, this is what a biography is: it's a net.
Things below a certain width or diameter go through it automatically, and are
lost—all the plankton, and the anchovies perhaps (unless you have an anchovy
net)." Some biographers have anchovy nets and boy! their biographies are long!

So, getting vaguely back to your topic, Juliet Herbert is an anchovy who has
slipped through the herring net cast by biographers. Flaubert's letters to her have
disappeared, none of hers to him, if there were any, exist (or have been found),
there is no photograph of her. There is a wonderful book by an Englishwoman
called Hermia Oliver, entitled *Flaubert and an English Governess: The Quest for
Juliet Herbert* [Oxford: Clarendon Press, 1980] which assembles all the known information, and even so she remains someone of whom one can only speculate. So
there did not seem to be any other way to go than by Braithwaite meeting some
imaginary person who had perhaps found the letters and then done something
beastly with them. I think this was one of the earliest chapters I wrote, maybe
the second or the third, and I think I was still searching, finding my way with the
book when I did; and perhaps, I thought, it had better have a chapter in which
there was a bit of narrative excitement—how about one with some lost letters? I
remember Kingsley Amis telling someone he gave up *Flaubert's Parrot* at about
Chapter 3 because no one had come through a door with a gun in his hand by
that point. His taste in literature somewhat declined as he grew older, alas! Have I
answered your question, or not?

Guignery: Yes, you have. In 1999, you published an article in the *Times Literary
Supplement,* "Letter from Genoa," in which you explained how you tried to trace
The Temptation of St. Anthony, the painting by Bruegel, by going back to Genoa.
First, could you explain why you wanted to find that painting in the first place,
and is this related to the quest for the parrots?
Barnes: When Flaubert was travelling with his sister and his parents on his sis-
ter's honeymoon, they went to Genoa, and it is there that he saw the Bruegel,
which has subsequently been reclassified, I think, as painted by Jan Mandyn, *The*

Temptation of St. Anthony. He makes two entries in his travel journal about this: a short entry at first, and then a few days later a considerably longer entry, in the course of which he says this might be the subject for a play. This is rare evidence of the exact beginning of a literary work and a literary obsession. We actually see it on this day he saw this painting in this place, in the *Palazzo Balbi* in Genoa—and after all, it was a theme which obsessed him all his life, for some thirty years, until he finally published *The Temptation of St. Anthony.* So, not surprisingly, I wanted to be there to witness this painting *in situ* if it was still there, and I found myself going to Genoa with some friends, one of whom was a painter. We were looking for it and had various contacts with the art world, but it just wasn't there. It was not clear what the *Palazzo Balbi* had turned into, what had happened to their collection, and so on and so forth. There is a reference to it in I think the Pléiade *Letters*—a footnote which says it's still in Genoa, belonging to someone, and this footnote is repeated, I note, in the *Œuvres de jeunesse,* first volume, in the Pléiade edition, which I bought here this morning, appropriately enough. I looked up the editor's note, which said that it had been proved in 1946 that this was still in Genoa. But *I* know that it is *not* there! Because I know an English picture dealer who has established that it's actually in a private collection in Rome. But I haven't yet been to Rome to write a "Letter from Rome" about it. I'm going to Rome in May, so I shall try and find it then.

Guignery: You visited the two Flaubert museums in Rouen and in Croisset, as you just said, twenty years ago. You also said that you visited French writers' houses for this book which you were supposed to write: are you interested in museums devoted to writers, or are you sometimes disappointed by what you find there?

Barnes: I visit whenever I can, wherever I am, any house belonging to any artist of any sort. I like them the more messy they are, the more dusty they are, the more incoherent they are, and I think this is one of the reasons why I found the *Pavillon* at Croisset so engaging when I first visited it twenty years ago; it was, as Braithwaite says, like Félicité's room, half-chapel, half-bazaar. In that sort of museum, you often find more objects which speak to you directly, which draw you into contact with the writer, artist, composer—whoever it is—than you do in the ones where lots of State money has been poured in and which have been perfectly decorated, with a Study Centre downstairs, and you feel it's sort of antiseptic and everything is kept behind glass and in a perfect state of preservation—which in many ways is admirable. But at the same time, the moment when you have to get down on your knees to look into a little display cabinet, and there you see in handwriting from about 1905, when I think the *Pavillon* museum was set up, "*mouchoir* with which Flaubert mopped his brow just before he died," and when next to it there is this very ordinary glass which says "glass from which he took his last sip of water," that has an immediacy which no amount of video presentation and trying to make older art "relevant" to twenty-first-century visitors will achieve, it seems to me. So, I am all on the side of mess, because if you go into any writer's study, that's how they should look like.

If you go to *my* study, the last thing I did before leaving my house on Thursday morning, because I knew that the cleaner was coming, was to leave her a note (I do not normally allow the cleaner into my study at all, but made an exception since I was going abroad) saying, "Please clean the floor (and only the floor) of my study," because you can't see anything but the floor, anyway. And this is what writers' studies look like.

Actually, one artist's studio that I would love to see is that of the great British artist Francis Bacon, who died a couple of years ago. I have only seen photographs of it, but it looked like something between an extremely grubby automobile repair workshop and a place where many deranged children had been let loose with tubes of coloured paint. It has been faithfully bought and transported, in all its amazing squalor and disarray, to, I think, Dublin—certainly to Ireland, where he came from originally—and is being re-erected. I just hope that they let people go in and feel it, rather than put it in a sort of glass wall, as you get in a squash court, so you can just see through to it. That seems to me the authentic chaos from which any work of art tends to be created.

Guignery: It is now time for the audience to ask questions.
Barnes: I am quite happy to answer questions on football, politics . . . anything, really!

Terrien: You've just said that you obviously did not write your chapters in chronological order, and we were wondering earlier on about the organisation of chapters in *Flaubert's Parrot*: as the narrative is not linear, it is hard for us to pinpoint the logic. What dictated the order?
Barnes: Well, it's the same with *A History of the World in 10½ Chapters*, which also follows no obvious chronology, and actually seems on the surface even more inchoate than *Flaubert's Parrot*. But, if you think about it, *Flaubert's Parrot* begins with Chapter 1—the problem, the quest; Chapter 2—the facts in the case; working backwards: the answer to the problem—the last chapter. To answer an earlier

question on the last chapter but one, I thought it would be a nice joke to give the reader an examination paper at the end of the book, you know, "You've done your work—I hope it was pleasant work. Here's some questions for you to consider" (whose answers are not contained in the book). Again, it's a sort of upside down examination: it's not an examination paper on the book you've just read—it's telling you a lot of stuff you didn't know from the book at all. So it is a subversive examination paper. Just before that, you get "Pure Story," which is the answer to the *second* quest, problem or query. At the beginning Braithwaite drops a remark about his wife, which you have to then follow through the book. Then there is in the middle a kind of hinge of reality, with the chapter "Cross Channel," which both does the formal Anglo-French link by being a cross-Channel journey in one direction and a cross-Channel journey in the other, and also brings Braithwaite in focus: that's the first time when he speaks to you—apart from the first chapter— fairly directly and tries to explain himself and breaks down at some point and fails, and gets rather cross with you.

So, it's like the way dentists build up bridges in your mouth: they have certain pins which they put in certain teeth in certain places, and then, on that, once they've got those in place, they know that they can build a solid structure. Those are five or six of the posts on which the rest of the structure can rest. Obviously, what you're balancing is narrative drive, narrative continuation, against the pleasures of going off the tangent, and writing separate discrete chapters which don't follow the straightforward narrative through, but exist there, in some sort of parallel relationship to it, or explain it indirectly.

Trying to re-imagine myself back into the time when I was writing it: you get the key chapters in place—that does not necessarily mean you write those ones first—but you know there are going to be those ones holding it together, and then you think about what the other chapters might be, and some ideas come to nothing, some ideas you turn into a chapter. And at that point, it's more a question of setting them against one another in terms of "tonality," than moving the story forward. There comes a point, though, when most novelists run out of the ability to explain, and you say at this point, i.e. now: "I did it because it feels right, I did it because I thought that chapter would work better—I can't explain more than the words 'work better' say—by putting it there rather than here."

Tony Williams: There's one broad issue, I think, that is relevant to what you were saying about the quest to find Flaubert. At one stage, Flaubert jokingly said he'd like to be buried with all his manuscripts in this tomb you were talking about, penetratingly. Did you ever consider making Geoffrey Braithwaite go off to the *Bibliothèque nationale* in Paris, and look at the manuscripts of *Un Cœur simple*, in an attempt to solve the riddle of which was the right parrot? I mean, would the *avant-texte* of *Un Cœur simple* have provided a different set of indicators—or was that something you deliberately closed down as an avenue of enquiry?

Barnes: There are three answers. I think that Braithwaite is the sort of cranky amateur scholar who would have a slight fear of manuscripts, of libraries: it's an obsession which is in some way private, and to do with his own life—as I was trying to explain when I referred to displacement activity. On the grounds of character, he probably would go to *Bibliothèque nationale*: his solution is of course the more practical one, which is to go to the Museum of Natural History in Rouen, from which Flaubert borrowed the parrot, and to try and work out from that which is the true parrot. You see, as M. Andrieu explains at the end of the book, very lucidly, and correctly—which seemed obvious when he told me since it had not been something that I had thought—just because Flaubert borrows a parrot from a museum, it does not mean that the parrot that he then describes in *Un Cœur simple* will resemble this parrot: because after all, the one thing that we do, as novelists, is we make it up! And so the colours that it might have might change because of the sonority of the sentence.

Funnily enough, further on in this notebook, there is an entry on that problem. I came back to Rouen about a year or so later, and I went to the Museum of Natural History, and I tried to solve it. There's a booking-out system, from which it's clear that Flaubert has booked out a parrot and has returned one. There's a system of numbers, which are attached to the base, I think, of the parrots: it's clear that both parrots came from the museum—but whether or not one of them was actually borrowed by Flaubert is uncertain. And there is a problem because one of the parrots has a big screw through the place where the number is. It's quite clear from my notebook, from these notes which I made nineteen years ago, that I thought that I had solved it: but re-reading my notes, I can't understand what they're saying!—which seems to me completely appropriate, since just as there is no solution in the book, there is not even a solution in my notebook that is lucid any more.

I think in any case this is appropriate to the book, and also to the sort of novels I write: there isn't a solution. I like the kind of novel or work of art or film which implies that it's going on after it ends, which leaves some things unresolved. If you set up a novel in which there is a sort of symbolic chase for the writer's voice, which is emblematised in one of two parrots, I think it's only fair that the writer's voice, that the feeling of getting finally in touch with the great writer, fails in the end. Let him have a little bit of privacy, and let him keep his secrets, I say.

Matthew Pateman: You seemed to encourage this one by asking us to ask you about football. One of the things you did manage to avoid yourself doing, which I am sure must have been a strong desire, is to make the obvious football joke about being "sick as a parrot"—and Braithwaite, I think, doesn't make that joke, does he, during the course of the book. But given that you wrote *Putting the Boot In* and the usually improbable idea of Leicester City winning the F.A. Cup at the end of *A History of the World*—and there's obviously a footballing delight there—how is it, do you think, that you managed to avoid being part of that whole crew of "New Lads" when football became suddenly rather popular in the mid-1990s with intellectuals and academics? You seem to always be, to my mind, rather pleased to be excluded from the whole "New Lad" catalogue, despite the fact that you are one of the first major novelists to have included it seriously in a novel.
Barnes: I'm too old to be a "New Lad"! Yes I did put football in *A History of the World in 10 ½ Chapters.* I am very interested in football, and indeed many, many, many other sports—but I tend to speak only to the Leicester City fanzine, which is full of other nutters writing. Did I say nutters? Let's say we have lots of distinguished supporters of the great game writing there.

"Sick as a parrot" was naturally used in the cartoon when the book was shortlisted for the Booker Prize; there was a picture of two footballers, with a ball between them, and one was saying to the other, "I suppose he will be over the moon if he wins, and sick as a parrot if he loses." I actually wasn't tempted to use the phrase—"sick as a parrot" was a sort of young football lad's joke twenty years ago, wasn't it? It was not the Geoffrey Braithwaite type of joke: so I think that would be my answer—it would be out of character for him.

Guignery: He's too old.
Barnes: He's too old, yes. And he doesn't actually say he likes football. I don't think he mentions sport at all, as far as I can remember.

Cool, Clean Man of Letters

Nadine O'Regan/2003

From *Sunday Business Post*, 29 June 2003. Reprinted by permission of the publisher.

Julian Barnes has a voice that could cut through ice. Sharp, crisp, and quintessentially English, his are the kind of tones that remind you why Hollywood regularly casts Englishmen as villains in its films.

Happily, Barnes is no natural born baddie. This is a man who exclaims with delight when he sees his shortbread biscuits arriving at our table in Dublin's Fitzwilliam Hotel, and kindly refrains from commenting on your correspondent's appalling efforts to pronounce the names of his favourite French authors.

Barnes is both terribly nice and terribly clever. Though willing to converse about his own work, he is just as interested in the creations of others. He is in Ireland to give a reading at the Dublin Writers' Festival, and has spent the morning visiting the Francis Bacon studio and the Writers' Museum, where he chanced upon the exciting new word "stuccodore."

"Wonder if I could use that?" he muses.

Barnes has managed to pack more culture into his weekend trip than most Dubliners manage in a lifetime. It makes a certain kind of sense, then, that the fifty-seven-year-old's most famous book is actually a tangled-up meditation on another writer's work. *Flaubert's Parrot* tells the story of a man obsessed with the French author Gustave Flaubert.

As the narrator attempts to track down the stuffed parrot that once sat on Flaubert's desk, he relays snippets of information about the author and analyses his prose. In this way, the book combines fiction with literary criticism.

In France, *Flaubert's Parrot* won the prestigious Prix Medicis and brought Barnes to the attention of a new audience. But the novel was his third full-length work of fiction, and Barnes has published six more since it came out in 1984. Does he mind that he is still best known for *Flaubert's Parrot*? "No," he says. "I remember once seeing a band wrapped around a new book by one of those very respectable, middle-ranking British novelists. It said, 'His 21st novel.' and I thought,

'That's all they can say because he has never written a book that anyone has ever heard of.' It was a case of, 'Here's another novel by someone whose other novels you haven't read.'

"Kingsley Amis was once asked if *Lucky Jim* was an albatross around his neck, and he said it was better than not having a bloody albatross at all. That's my perspective." In a few months, Barnes's new collection of short stories will be published. It has the rather enigmatic title, *The Lemon Table*.

"In Helsinki," he explains, "at the turn of the previous century, there was a table at a particular restaurant to which the composer Sibelius used to go. It was known as 'the lemon table' because the lemon was the Chinese symbol of death, and when you went to the lemon table, you were obliged to talk about death. The late nineteenth-century generation thought and talked about death a lot more than we do." When asked if he contemplates death frequently, Barnes nods. "I've been thinking about it for a very long time. I think about it most days of my life. I have since I was sixteen." He smiles. "I don't get anywhere with it. I don't come up with any answers. But I suppose it must inform the way I live and write." Is he religious? "I'm not. My position is: I don't believe in God, but I miss Him. Sometimes, when you see great religious art, or you listen to a great choral work, which is a religious work, you think how wonderful it would have been to have been alive when these things were being painted or composed, and to believe it all." Barnes is aware that people often become more religious as they grow older, but he is certain this will not happen to him.

"It's feeble to become religious because you're afraid of death approaching," he says. "The idea that God created the world in which we live, given its inequalities and injustices, is incredible. If He were an unjust God and He created the world, on the other hand, that might make more sense." This is typical Barnes: logical almost to a fault. Brought up in a family of schoolteachers, the Leicester-born author is a meticulous user of careful language, who always pushes arguments through to their rational conclusions. This has frequently resulted in him being characterised as cold or snooty.

His friends feel this impression is essentially inaccurate. "He has very high standards," the writer Jancis Robinson has said, "by which I don't mean he worries whether or not the napkins are folded correctly. He wants everything to be good quality, whether that is a decision, a moral stance, or a hunk of beef." Barnes also possesses a wry, highly refined sense of humour. During the war in Iraq, he wrote a powerful article for the *Guardian*, attacking the actions of the Bush administration.

He was taken aback to discover that the angry letters he soon began receiving were not in response to this piece, but instead to a cooking column he had penned for the same newspaper.

"I didn't get hate mail about Iraq, but I got hate mail about Nigel Slater," he laughs. "I wrote a column saying that a recipe of his didn't work. Not since I attacked Torvill and Dean in my *Observer* television column have I had such a vituperative response. Nigel Slater is obviously a domestic god, and if this recipe didn't work, it was because I was incompetent." Barnes may be many things, but incompetent is not one of them. The author maintains an almost prodigious work rate, writing newspaper articles, essays, short stories, and novels. He is diligent and extremely clear-headed, never taking an advance prior to the publication of one of his novels, for fear it would have a debilitating effect on his writing.

"It could be psychologically dangerous," he says. "Whenever I read about three-book advances, I always think, 'Well, they know they've got X pounds guaranteed, so isn't this going to make them lazier?'" Is he ever envious of the large advances earned by some debut novelists? "No," he says. "You raise an eyebrow. You think, 'They wouldn't pay this to a middle-aged man with a beard.' It puts an awful lot of pressure on the novelist, which I'm not sure is right. I don't feel envious." It might not be the best strategy for Barnes to complain to his agent, however. Pat Kavanagh is not just his literary representative, but also his wife. Does this unusual situation ever cause problems between them? "Not from my point of view, because I think she's the best agent in the world. But she knows that people know that she's asking for money for her husband, so I think she would be happier if someone else represented me. But it really has given us very few problems." Presumably, this is due to the high quality of Barnes's output. As a novelist, he ranks alongside Martin Amis, Ian McEwan, and Salman Rushdie as one of the great innovators of English literary fiction. He may have matured into something of an elder statesman, but his passion for his work continues unabated. Retirement, for Barnes, is not an option.

"I don't think I'd be happy if I just stopped writing," he says. "Writing has become necessary to me. It is a necessity as well as a pleasure." How would the author like to be remembered? Barnes mulls over this for a moment, then grins. "I hope when my obituary is written, it doesn't say, 'He wrote twenty-one novels whose names we can't remember.'"

Big Ideas—Program 5—"Julian Barnes"
Ramona Koval/2004

Transcript from *Big Ideas*—Program 5—"Julian Barnes," first broadcast on ABC Radio National, 31 October 2004, by permission of the Australian Broadcasting Corporation and ABC Online. © 2004 ABC. All rights reserved. A copy of the program transcript can be found at http://www.abc.net.au/rn/bigideas/stories/2004/1228319.htm.

Ramona Koval: Hello, Ramona Koval here again on *Big Ideas*, and this week, the biggest idea of all—a conversation about death with English novelist and essayist Julian Barnes, whose new book of short stories, *The Lemon Table*, is full of ways to die with dignity and ways to live as if it really mattered. Julian Barnes's first novel, *Metroland*, was published in 1981 to critical acclaim. It went on to win the Somerset Maugham award for a debut novel. He's since written many novels and essays and short stories. Under the pseudonym Dan Kavanagh, he's written four crime novels. A committed Francophile, he was the first Englishman to win both the Prix Medicis and the Prix Femina. He has been nominated for the Booker Prize twice, once for *Flaubert's Parrot* and the other time for *England, England*. Julian Barnes once wrote, "I am a writer for an accumulation of lesser reasons: love of words, fear of death, hope of fame, delight in creation, distaste for office hours—and for one presiding, major reason: because I believe that the best art tells the most truth about life."

The title of this new collection is taken from the last story, "The Silence," where a dying composer goes out by himself to dine alone and reflect upon mortality—or sometimes to a restaurant to join "the lemon table." "Here it is permissible," he says, "and indeed obligatory to talk about death. It is most companionable." Therefore, in this conversation I had at the Edinburgh International Book Festival, it was permissible—indeed obligatory—to talk about old age and death; because, of course, talking about death is talking about life.

Let's start with the story called "The Story of Mats Israelson"; it's full of yearning, isn't it? Full of yearning and missed opportunities, that story.
Barnes: Yes, absolutely. I quite like putting facts and real things and real stories into my fiction. But when you do, they always have to do double work. They have

to be true but they also have to be sort of radioactively relevant. They have to give off something which then infects and inhabits the rest of the story. And the story actually began when I was in that sort of state of reverie which either leads to creativeness or to complete noncreativeness, depending on your luck. And I was thinking about the fact that nowadays, in the emotional life, on the whole, emotions tend to be indulged. Once they arrive, they tend to be gratified in some way, on the whole, speaking very generally. And I was thinking about what it was like when emotions arose which couldn't be gratified and which also became intenser with time and which became more frustrated with time because the two individuals involved were still living close. So I felt, well, this is probably, unless I find some small closed community now, this is probably looking back a hundred years or more. And I thought, where shall I set it? And I was thinking somewhere where the landscape or something about the countryside or the buildings or the towns or the overall moral landscape would mean that two people can meet, fall in love; something could stop them—I won't tell you what—and yet they live in the same community for twenty or thirty years and then something happens at the end.

And I was thinking northern Germany for some reason, I don't know why. Probably I was reading Fontana at the time. Then I found myself browsing in an old Baedeker to Norway, Sweden, and Denmark. And I came across the story of Mats Israelson. And instantly I knew, right, that's it. Now I know exactly where this story happens and exactly when, because the story of a body preserved for forty-nine years perfectly and then recognised at the end by the former fiancee of the man who perished in the mine—is exactly the sort of correlative that you put in the middle of a story for a story which is about someone who puts his heart into deepfreeze at a certain point in their life. I don't know what your question was at the beginning, but that, none the less, is the answer.

Koval: And a fine answer it is. And it makes me ask, though—you say it was a time when people were a little bit more reticent about their emotions, but aren't there some people who just grab life by the throat no matter what time it is, and others who don't? And in fact a lot of these stories really explore the different ways of living, really.

Barnes: Yes, I think that's true. I think there always have been people who have grabbed life by the throat. And when I was growing up I somehow assumed, as each generation does, that there was absolutely no sex at all except in very, very limited circumstances called marriage, until the 1960s, when I was eighteen or so. And then you discover, this is obviously completely untrue. But I think it's slightly dangerous to assume that when we look at the past, what we find there is what reminds us of ourselves. And I think that's how I used to look at the past. You used to think, oh yes, of course, romanticism, Byron and so on—it's just like me, it's just like us. But the more years I have on the clock and the more reading I do, the more I think it's important to emphasise how very different it was, rather than flatter ourselves by saying, "Well they were just like us really but a bit more primitive". I think often they were a lot less primitive.

Koval: That reminds me of another story—I think it's called "The Revival"—in this book, with the aged Turgenev looking back on his life at a moment of happiness or a half-hour of happiness when he puts on a revival of a play and falls in love with the young actress who was one of the leading characters there. But there's a narrator of that story who is looking back on history in a similar way to what you've described.

Barnes: This also has a true incident at its heart. Turgenev's plays, which I'm sure you know, were absolutely wonderful but were completely unsuccessful and he was a playwright before he was a novelist and short story writer. And then when he became famous throughout Europe as a prose writer, his plays were put on again in St. Petersburg. And *A Month in the Country* was put on there something like thirty years after it was first written. It was written I think in Paris and then banned by the censor, and then put on in the 1870s, '80s, I can't remember exactly, in St. Petersburg. And he met the actress, who was one of the most famous actresses of her day, and fell in love with her. But he fell in love with her in a very Turgenevian way, which is, he was a great expert at renunciation, so he fell in love with her and yet was already trying to move on to the next stage, which is—wasn't it wonderful when we fell in love and didn't do anything about it? Which again, I fancy, is something that doesn't happen too much in the twenty-first century in our modern cities.

And there's a bit where a letter of his is quoted, how his heart is like a bonfire and how he wishes to kiss her hand. And the narrator of this story, he was the narrator from a contemporary point of view, recognises that when a modern reader reads about hand-kissing they think that a slightly snooty reaction might take place. So he just briefly says, "When did you last have your hands kissed? And if you did, how do you know he was any good at it? Further, when did anyone last write to you about kissing your hands?" Here is the argument for the world of renunciation [that's to say, Turgenev's world]. "If we know more about consummation, they knew more about desire. If we know more about numbers, they knew more about despair. If we know more about boasting, they knew more about memory. They had foot-kissing, we have toe-sucking. You still prefer our side of the equation? You may well be right. Then try a simpler formulation; if we know more about sex, they knew more about love."

So part of any writer's job is corrective in as nondidactical sense as possible. But to say, it wasn't like that; it was like this—that holds in lots of areas and I think especially when you're looking at the past. Maybe I'm a frustrated historian, I don't know.

Koval: You often write about historical figures; Turgenev, or Sibelius later on in the book, or indeed, Flaubert. So when you think about these historical figures, do you speculate on the unknowable parts—things that you read between the lines—or do you like to use only what you know and then play with it or recast it?

Barnes: I don't think there's a general answer to that. I think it depends, brutally, on what use I want to put them to. It sounds rather as if they're glove puppets. They aren't, of course. But in the Turgenev case I just wanted to take this incident of love and renunciation and spin something broader out of it. Sibelius, I've always been a great admirer of his music, and it's one of those careers which is full of music and ends in silence. He's famous for the thirty-year silence when he wasn't writing, when he was trying to write his eighth symphony and never did, and was going into his workroom at midnight with a bottle of whisky and some music paper and at three in the morning his wife would come and take the whisky bottle out of his hand, with his head slumped on the music paper, and he hadn't written a note . . . and so on. And it was about how everything leads to silence; that's the metaphor there. I don't think I have a generalised approach to these people when I use them. It's just that they suit the story. They could be someone else, but they happen to be them.

Koval: It's also about art. Why choose these artists?

Barnes: Yes. When I do choose such people, it's because I'm interested in them as writers, musicians, composers, whatever. I think it would be hard to write—though your job is always to be on the side of character, your writing, even if it's Martin Borman or someone like that, you have to see the good side—or you have to see the inside—of the character. And therefore, to a certain extent, to have to inhabit them and sympathise with them and see what there is to be said for them. I don't think I could write anything substantial about a third-rate painter, or a fourth-rate composer. I think I wouldn't want to spend that amount of time with them. I haven't tried it. Maybe I should.

Koval: I tell you who I wanted to spend a lot more time with; my favourite character in this book is one of your old ladies. You've got quite a few old ladies, obviously, because old ladies know a little bit more about approaching death than . . .
Barnes: Old ladies are great, yes . . . especially when they buy my books.

Koval: Now Sylvia Winstanley in this marvelous story called "Knowing French." It's a group of letters. In fact it's her letters to a novelist called Julian Barnes. We don't have any of his—this novelist Julian Barnes'—letters, because that correspondence was destroyed. Unfortunately she . . . something happened.
Barnes: She kept it in the fridge and the fridge was defrosted one day. And the letters were rendered illegible.

Koval: And because you put yourself in this story—or a Julian Barnes very similar to you who has written some of your books and has used some of your characters—and because you don't show us the Julian Barnes side of the correspondence, even though you could have so easily added them, since they purport to come from you . . .
Barnes: My letters were destroyed in the refrigerator . . .

Koval: Of course I have an overwhelming urge to ask if anyone like Sylvia existed and wrote to you, and yet I know I shouldn't ask that.
Barnes: No, you shouldn't, but I shall reply anyway. It's an epistolary story, except that only, as you say, only one half of the correspondence is there, and the letters from Julian Barnes—or Dr. Barnes as she mistakenly calls him to begin with . . . well, stories often have multiple beginnings, and it's partly what the technical challenge is and what the thematic challenge is, when they come together, then they often start the story. Something got me thinking about telling a story from— I mean, you often tell stories just from one side—but what about telling a story in which traditionally there are always two sides but you just give the letters from one person and not the replies?

Then I thought, this is actually a very good notion, because my replies probably wouldn't have been very interesting anyway, even if they hadn't been destroyed in the refrigerator. And I thought back to a correspondence I had had in the '80s with a lady who wrote to me from an old peoples' home—not called that, obviously, and not in that town. And she wrote to me because—part of the story is about coincidence. It's about approaching death and it's about reflecting on life. The story begins with a coincidence which I shall explain in a moment, and it ends with her question to the me character, which is, well if you don't believe in

God or anything like that, I suppose you just believe that life is a coincidence. But the question remains, what sort of a coincidence? And the question is left hanging in the air.

It began when this lady wrote to me and said, "I've just gone into an 'old folk-ery,'" as she described it. She was one of these very strong, opinionated, privately-educated-and-then-got-into-Oxford women who knew their own minds, never married, interested in lots of stuff; and she decided when she got to the old folk-ery that she would go into the local library and start reading fiction, from A to Z. And so I remember she said at one point, "I have read these two characters called Anus—a lot of descriptions of pubs and women's breasts. So I pass on to B." And then she described how she saw this one—*Flaubert's Parrot*, she said, "Yes, and I remember that from reading *Un Cœur simple* when I was young. And then as I was reading it, I was walking down the street and there was a parrot in the window . . ." and so on. And so because of this, she wrote to me and I replied, and we had a correspondence for two, three, four years, and then it sort of ended. So I took that as a starting point so, as always, that's the starting point. But the story is going somewhere else, and so the story moves on to her reflections on life and death and the possibility of some divine coincidence existing—because it seemed to her (this is me taking over the story at this point; our correspondence was more formal and less intimate and less about grand matters, but I took the tone of it as I remembered it, and the way that she would just—as some people do—just say things to strangers they've never met because they've read one of their books, that they wouldn't necessarily say to other people living around them). And I took that and ran with it, and so it leads on to her reflections about the four last things.

Koval: She's got a nice, shorthand way of describing and summarising things. It's as if she knows she hasn't got a lot of time ahead for waffling. She gets to the point, doesn't she?

Barnes: Yes. But I think that is characteristic of English women of that genera-tion and also class, that they will come up to you and say, "That's not a very [nice] suit you're wearing," or something like that. In a perfectly friendly way. And if you're me, you find yourself saying, "Yes, I'm terribly sorry about the suit. It was a mistake."

Koval: And what's that code for? Pardon me for not knowing.

Barnes: Well, that's code for straight speaking. And it's a way of being friendly and yet also putting you down. I quite like it. But we won't go into my psychology too much this morning. Bit early.

Koval: She makes a big point of saying that there's a difference between knowing French and being very good at grammar. And this is a very fine and subtle difference about the way to live. Can you talk about it?

Barnes: Yes, the story's called "Knowing French" and at a certain point she talks about how she studied French through, really, through talking it. Through being in France and talking to French people. But she hadn't gone through the normal educational system and so she didn't have proper grammar. Though of course this makes her, in a way, more French, because a lot of French people don't have proper grammar. You just try using the subjunctive in France in a French conversation, and they'll look at you as if you're a completely mad foreigner—which you are. So at a certain point in her life, I think after she left university, she went to be a teacher at a school, or trainee teacher, and she was not allowed to teach children because she didn't have proper grammar. So out of this comes obviously the metaphor that when you start off looking at life and what life means, you're taught the grammar of it. You're taught the rules and the nuts and bolts of what is given and what is supposed and what is assumed to be correct, and how things fit together. But that's just knowing grammar, that's not knowing French. And that knowing French comes from—I mean in the metaphorical sense now— knowing French comes from living life, from feeling life, from understanding life. And again, she's telling me, you're still young, you may know grammar; I know French—because I think at that point in the story she's asking about whether I believe in anything beyond this world and I say, in my grammarian's way, "No," and she says, "When you get to my age . . ."

There's an English writer, I don't know if anyone remembers him, called William Gerhardy, who every so often is revived, and Michael Holroyd was a supporter and friend of his. And I was writing a column for the *New Review*, a magazine which flourished for about ten years in the late '70s. I was doing a little comment, gossip, interview column. And I was the last person to interview William Gerhardy, who was then bedridden and about ninety. And at a certain point he started taking over the interview and asking me questions. And he said, "Do you believe in God, young man?" And I thought, what do you do in this circumstance, where someone wasn't well . . . But then I thought, well, he asked the question, so I'll give him the answer. So I said, "No, I don't, actually." He paused and he said, "Well, by the time you're my age, maybe you will." Which was a very gentle rebuke, I thought.

Koval: And as you're a little bit closer to his age now, do you?

Barnes: Come back in thirty years.

Koval: I just said a "little bit" closer. What about the first story, "A Short History of Hairdressing"—a man goes through three ages of hairdressing and learns how to cope with the guy who's doing his hair in three different ways, and it's over a lifetime. All kinds of things change in the outside world, but he changes too. But the idea of the men's hairdresser as a kind of theatre for all kinds of possibilities, all kinds of sexual possibilities and learning how to be a man. I hadn't thought of it like that before.

Barnes: Yes. It's one of those small areas of life that you suddenly realise that within my lifetime—from first going to what was called the barbers, to the sort of places that you sometimes stumble into by mistake nowadays—there's a complete sea-change in what happens when you're there. The attitude of the people who are cutting bits off you and the social side of it and the décor side of it and so on. So I thought three stories, three different times, taking the boy at, say, ten and then again at twenty and then again at forty or something like that, and using what has happened to "the barbers shop" to the modern hairdressing salon as a sort of way of marking time moving on, and then clearly, what happens to him, and the first intimations of aging, and that whereas the change from being a small boy sat on those big rubber mats so that you're just high enough to have yourself shorn by some brutal Borstal inmate as it seems to you—to having your hair cut by young girls wearing almost nothing and yet regarding you as completely not an object to be flirted with, seemed to me—I'm obviously talking about the character in the book, not myself—this seemed to me to be a way of introducing the general theme of the book, which is not just aging but what happens when things start getting out of kilter.

When I was growing up I went through the normal middle-class English scholarship educational system, where everything was targeted to getting you to university, basically—my parents were school teachers—this is what your life was for. So I found myself arriving at university intellectually, at eighteen, overdeveloped; socially and emotionally drastically underdeveloped. And then gradually things began to shake down a bit and the other bits caught up. And then at some point you have the illusion that as far as you're ever going to be, there is some sort of integrity now to your existence and your personality, and that it's called maturity; and that your brain has now got to the level it's going to level off at, and so your capacity for the emotional life and your capacity for being a person in society have also reached this sort of point. It may not be perfect, but there's a sort of balance and harmony there. I think one of the impulses behind this book was realising that once I'd got to that point, I thought somehow it's going to be like this till closure. That, sure, the brain will drop off a bit, the body will drop off a bit, the emotions won't be quite so fierce, but that's all going to be fine, you know?

There's one story I didn't write about in this, but in a way it's a story that lies behind the book, because it was told me when I was about twenty-five by a friend of mine. And his father, who was then—he was a late child and his father was then in his seventies—and he was a clergyman in the West Country. And once a week his wife would take him into the local county town to do the shopping. There was a large department store there, of the sort that probably still exists but less so now. And she used to park him at the cash desk while she went off and did her shopping. I think I've imagined the story so many times, that I'm not sure anymore about the details that were actually told to me, apart from the heart of the story. But in my imagination I always see it as one of those cash desks which had a series of overhead wires running to it, and those little pneumatic tubes— because shop assistants couldn't be trusted with money, so they had to put the bill and the money in one of these pneumatic tubes and then they'd attach it to something. Maybe it wasn't pneumatic, maybe it was . . . anyway, you'd pull a handle and it would go "chung" round the shop and land at the cashier's desk, like that, and then unscrew it and take the money out or the cheque or whatever, put the change in, stamp the bill, put the bill in, put it back in the machine and "chung" it would go back to the department. I always imagined him standing at this store. Anyway, he got talking to the cashier, who was a young woman, and fell in love with her. He was a married vicar in his seventies with two children. And one day he was discovered in the middle of the road, trying to get run down by a car, because he couldn't bear his life.

I was told this story when I was twenty-five, and I thought, "It's not going to be straightforward, then. You can't really count on anything, then, if that's the case." I mean, he didn't succeed, fortunately. But the notion that there are elephant traps out there should not be underestimated, is what I thought.

Koval: There's elephant traps, but there's also all kinds of possible excitements, aren't there?

Barnes: Oh yes, absolutely. It's a sort of book against serenity, I suppose. When I was in my teens, I would look at my grandparents and I would assume that just as you banked up the fire with coal at the end of the day, that that's what happened with life, and everything was quiet and orderly and regulated. And then I began to think, "Well maybe this is one of the great illusions of life," and that in a way this is one in which people like my grandparents would conspire against the young by putting up this front. I don't know, I never asked them, and they would never have told me whether their life was as serene as it appeared to be—or at any rate, as lacking terrible tearings in it.

I go on like this for a while, you see, and then someone in the audience says—it's a very sweet rebuke I got at another literary festival which probably should remain nameless as you're probably not allowed to name other literary festivals. The lady said, "I'd just like to point out to you, Mr. Barnes, it isn't as bad as you're making out."

Audience Question 1: You've written lots about this link between England and France. Can you account for the reasons why you chose France in the first place, and do you regard the countries as rivals, or friends?

Barnes: I blame my parents. I'm of a generation for which it was quite unusual to go to France. Nowadays I look at children—I went to Brazil to another literary festival (which shall remain nameless) last year and one of the fellow guests from this country was Hanif Kureishi. He has a charming small son, who—I don't know about the ages of children, but he was that height, so you can work it out. At a certain point he turned to me politely and said, "Is this your first visit to Brazil?" I said, "Yes, it is." I said, "Do you like travelling?" And he said, "Yes, I've been to Greece and I've been to San Francisco. This is my first trip to Brazil." And then he listed all kinds of places and ended up, "I think I'm looking forward to going to the west coast of America again." And I think, "Within my lifetime. Because when I was in the sixth form, I would have been about sixteen, I can remember the first boy in our school who went to America. And he went to America in the summer vacation and he came back with a sheepskin jacket and copy of *The Carpetbaggers*. Both items which seemed impossibly exotic to us all. And I was taken by my parents to France. We got a car when I was about thirteen, and my parents were great Francophiles, and so we set off in our car to go on a major tour of France when I was thirteen. And I was probably the first boy in my class to have gone to France, and that's where we went for holidays every year. And that was the only European country—the only other country—I went to, unless you count the Channel Islands, until I was about eighteen.

So I was early indoctrinated, inoculated, whichever you prefer, with France. And I read French and Russian at university, and so it was always my other country. And maybe there would have been a lot more about Italy if they'd taken me to Italy. At a certain point you're unaware of other people looking at your writing, and after I'd written about four or five books, someone said, "Why does someone always go to France in your books?" And I said, "They don't." And they said, "Oh yes they do. Check it out." And then I think I decided to write a book where no one went to France, and then you think, well that's a bit self-conscious as well.

Are they enemies or friends? Well, I suppose it depends who you are. They're both. To me they're not enemies at all. In many more recent political decisions, they're people who have political wisdom on their side.

Audience Question 2: Julian, you said, in "The Story of Mats Israelson," that men mature like trees until they're seventy. As a man of seventy, that's very good news for me. You've told me that just in time, because I'm at the stage in life when I'm doing a sort of Desert Island Discs on what music will be played at my funeral. Now you've been talking a lot about aging and death, and apart from your books, what defenses do you think people of my generation—and others—would have against the thought of death?

Barnes: Well firstly, if you're consoled by the fact that someone in one of my books says that the man comes to full ripeness at seventy—a) I write fiction, and b) this was true in the nineteenth-century Swedish village. So take that with some caution. As to the second part of your question, I hesitate to answer, because I think "see me privately" is almost the answer. I tell stories rather than give advice, however friendly. But, you know, the answer is implicit in your question, I think, which is that unless you are of a religious nature, then some of the consolations of age lie in art, obviously. And also if you're a reader, it's not so much a consolation, but it's a constant interest, not just reading and discovering new work, but also rereading and rediscovering things you thought you knew very well—and suddenly realising . . . I mean, I'm always very grateful to Vikram Seth for writing that incredibly long novel that he did, because I remember when it came out and I thought, but I haven't read *War and Peace* for thirty years. So I thought, I'll read Vikram Seth's novel when I've reread *War and Peace*. And then I thought there's also the—and it is a great book—Ford Madox Ford's *Parade's End*, so I read that. And he's got me reading all these long works. Anyway . . .

Koval: Anyway, look, *The Lemon Table* is not a long work, but it's a fine, lovely work.

"It's for Self-Protection"

Stuart Jeffries/2005

From *The Guardian*, 6 July 2005: 8. Copyright Guardian News & Media Ltd 2005. Reprinted by permission of the publisher.

Julian Barnes does not read his reviews. Which is a shame because he's getting some very good ones for *Arthur & George*. His tenth novel is based on the real-life whodunit that more than a century ago led Arthur Conan Doyle to metaphorically don his most famous creation's deerstalker and investigate. Peter Kemp in the *Sunday Times* wrote of it that "Barnes's suave, elegant prose—alive here with precision, irony and humaneness—has never been used better in this extraordinary true-life tale, which is as terrifically told as any by its hero Conan Doyle himself." Tim Adams in the *Observer*, too, reckoned that Barnes had "taken the bones of a long-dead history and imbued them with vivid and memorable life."

No matter: Barnes will not be tempted. "When I started off, I would read everything obsessively," he says over coffee at a pub near his north London home. "Regardless of the quality or lack of quality of a book, you would get a range of reviews from good to not so good."

"When my first novel *Metroland* [1980] was published, it would be reviewed with Melvyn Bragg's new novel. One would say 'Next to Bragg's symphonic new book, this batsqueak of autobiography bears little scrutiny.' The next would say 'Besides Bragg's monument of windbaggery, this tightly constructed . . .'"

Surely it's not the irritating spread of opinions that hurts—just the hostile ones? "I don't get any better at reading bad reviews. So seven or eight years ago I stopped." That was around the time that *England, England* came out—a book whose reviews were certainly mixed. D. J. Taylor wrote in the *Spectator*: "Despite its weighty themes, this is a rather trivial and laboured performance," while in the *Sunday Times* John Carey claimed the book was "both funny and serious, a double-act that English novels rarely manage." You can see Barnes's point: which is nearer the truth? Better, perhaps, to adopt the Olympian pose of Martin Amis, who said during the papers' mutty mauling of *Yellow Dog*, that he would trust posterity to get it right.

Was it *England, England*'s reception that made reviews unreadable for you? "No, it's a question of self-protection and not having stuff that can fester in your head the wrong way. Some people don't mind—I read an interview with William Boyd in a French magazine recently in which he said: 'J'ai une peau épaisse.'" [I have a thick skin.]

Do you have a thin skin? "I'm not as bad as Philip Roth. He leaves the country when a book comes out." Indeed, for publication, Barnes has returned to this country with his wife, literary agent Pat Kavanagh, from a walking holiday in France, his spiritual if not actual second home. He may not read the reviews, but he has a code ready for interpreting the Barnesian brouhaha in the papers: "They'll tell me: 'X can come for tea. Or Y will not be welcome for tea.' I get the picture that way." What a fuss! Maybe the fifty-nine-year-old, one of Britain's most feted writers, should just read the bloody things and get Pat to hover with smelling salts.

Unwittingly, I put something in Barnes's head that festers during the interview. I suggest that Suzanne Dean's charming retro jacket design for *Arthur & George*, a dark mustard cloth binding embossed with a *Punch*-like illustration of the two protagonists, is Edwardian whimsy, of a piece with the style of a book that echoes the stateliness of certain Edwardian novels, notably Conan Doyle's. Mildly affronted, Barnes repeats "whimsy" several times during the rest of the interview.

The more I think about it, the righter Barnes is to be affronted. *Arthur & George* is better than whimsy: it's a compelling, elegant if middle-brow return to form that is already being talked up as a possible Booker winner, in a year when Barnes is likely to go toe to toe once more with Ian McEwan, whose novel *Amsterdam* beat Barnes's shortlisted *England, England* to the Booker Prize in 1998. Barnes has never won the Booker, though *Flaubert's Parrot* was shortlisted in 1984. This year, he and McEwan may well be shortlisted along with Ishiguro, Rushdie, Coetzee, and Zadie Smith.

Barnes, on being told that the *Sunday Times* is suggesting that these big boys (Smith excepted) of undead EngLit are poised to carve up the Booker between them, says the idea is "ridiculous. It's just the way books get talked about. It just so happens that Ish, Ian, Salman, and I have books out at the same time."

Moving on. Why did you write a book about the least interesting of eminent Edwardian writers? Why not about Ford, Wells, James, Kipling, Conrad, or Shaw? "Because he came with the story." And it was the story of George Edalji, a Birmingham solicitor of Parsee origin, and his wrongful conviction for a series of horse and cattle maimings around Great Wyrley in Staffordshire, that sucked Barnes into its vortex, as inexorably as his treatment of it will, no doubt, seduce his readers across continental beaches this summer.

The book, despite its many meditations on a long-dead literary icon, is no *Flaubert's Parrot*. It could have been called *Conan Doyle's Hobby Horse*, though that was not one of the thirty to forty titles that Barnes considered for the book. "One suggestion was *Conviction*." That's very good. "Yes, but it was too much like *Atonement*. Then there was *News from Distant Lands*, which was too much like a Jonathan Raban travel book. In the end, I went with the working title, which other people seemed to like but I hadn't."

It was the great (and, since April, late) historian of France, Douglas Johnson, who suggested to Barnes that the Great Wyrley Outrage was the British parallel to the Dreyfus Affair, a miscarriage of justice in the heart of England that equally pointed up the nature of an imperial society shuddering into a new century. Racism, fears of miscegenation, imputations of sexual dysfunction, an establishment cover-up, suspicious footprints—the story had everything.

It even had its Emile Zola—Conan Doyle—who, after nosing around Staffordshire, wrote a pamphlet that accused the constabulary of convicting the wrong man. It wasn't Edalji, the son of a Church of England vicar, who was responsible for the fatal slashings of livestock, he claimed, but some ne'er-do-well from Walsall with sociopathic tendencies and a plausible blade hanging in the kitchen.

"I think both cases say something about their different countries," says Barnes. "It shows the way that the French are actively engaged with their own history. In Britain we are not. George remarks at one point that in Britain if there's a problem, we solve it and then forget there was the problem."

You're analysing jolly old England again, aren't you? "I guess, but obliquely this time. In *England, England* I tackled it head on. The idea there was that the notion of England, an artificial notion in the first place, had become endangered, commercialised, Americanised, and Europeanised." I wonder if a nostalgia for a lost England accounts for your excavation of a long-forgotten Edwardian scandal? "I'm certainly regretful. I like the idea that countries are different."

And England used to be different. At one point in the book, for instance, Conan Doyle, seething over the "balderdash" of a Home Office report, refuses to smoke a pipe to soothe his nerves, even though his wife urges him to do so. "Never in front of a lady," he barks. Barnes says he read that Conan Doyle had once been with his son in a railway carriage, when the son started smoking a pipe in front of a lady. "He broke it in two and threw it out of the window."

Throughout, there is something cherishable about Conan Doyle's Blimpishness and his chivalry towards women, even if his sexual chasteness is, frankly, weird. "There is a tradition of English emotional reticence which can easily fall away into emotional inexpressiveness and frigidity," says Barnes. "I prefer that to the Oprahfication of the emotions which is what has happened. People talking about their emotional lives in staggering detail on *Celebrity Love Island* is so banal. It's Princess Diana's fault. When things are wrong in England, it's always her fault, or Mrs. Thatcher's, isn't it?"

The book unfolds with alternating narratives juxtaposing the eponymous characters' developments. George is raised in a C of E vicarage; Arthur by a Catholic mother in shabby-genteel Edinburgh. Arthur becomes a doctor and then an overnight success as a writer; George remains a plodding solicitor, publishing a small guide for rail passengers on their legal rights.

Most intriguingly, Arthur is a one-time eye doctor who hopes to correct a misperception (i.e., the case against George), while George is chronically shortsighted though capable of great insights. In one of the novel's great scenes, George wanders near the Albert Memorial and imagines: "And in that moment, George was struck by the realisation that everybody was going to be dead." George's imaginative insight spreads across the park like a neutron bomb, wiping out everybody. And yet again Barnes has broached one of his favourite literary subjects, death.

Throughout the book, how one moves from what little one actually sees to what one infers from it, how characters construct vast, teetering structures—from the Staffordshire constabulary's flimsy case against Edalji to the equally implausible rival case that Conan Doyle assembles to indict the Walsall ne'er-do-well—is incessantly dramatised.

The book also deals with Conan Doyle's spiritualism, itself a close absence. At one point, during a séance for the dead writer in the Albert Hall, George looks through his binoculars from the balcony to the stage where a chair has been left for Conan Doyle. Will George's feeble eyes ever behold the dead writer's spirit that has reportedly been trying to communicate with the throng? It seems unlikely.

What are the links between these ocular themes and the detective story you are telling? "It's about what you can prove, not just in the criminal sense but the emotional sense," says Barnes. He suggests that the will to believe is often more important than what one actually sees.

Was he ever a Conan Doyle fan? "I read the Sherlock Holmes stories when I was a child. But I am not anything like him. I am not going to put a deerstalker on. Or grow a walrus moustache." Nor is Barnes a man of action, like Conan Doyle who, in *Arthur & George*, is forever doing—skiing Alpine passes, doctoring during the Boer war, clubbing seals in Greenland, clubbing golf balls in Surrey. It's hard to imagine him sitting still long enough to write a book. Barnes, by contrast, has emphasised that writing is "life declined." "Yes, I think I wrote that in a story about Turgenev. It's one of those things that you come up against as a writer. To what extent is writing an avoidance of life? To what extent is writing the most intense involvement with life? Flaubert once said: 'I have always tried to live in an ivory tower, but a tide of shit is beating at its walls.'" Which is no way to talk about nineteenth-century Rouen or indeed twenty-first-century Tufnell Park.

Though Conan Doyle can never replace Flaubert as Barnes's literary hero, there is a parallel between them. Barnes created a sleuth, too. Under the pseudonym Dan Kavanagh, he wrote four novels in the '80s about a bisexual sleuth called Duffy. He did not prove as popular as Sherlock Holmes. When Holmes plunged to his death at the Reichenbach Falls with his nemesis Moriarty, City men wore black ribbons on their boaters. Eventually, Conan Doyle brought the sleuth back from beyond the grave. Duffy's return has never been so hotly demanded. Perhaps, then, Barnes sought to satisfy his long-neglected urge to write detective fiction in *Arthur & George*. Maybe he is using Conan Doyle as a springboard to dive into different waters.

Barnes denies this. "I deliberately didn't want to write a book that bounces off his work." A cunningly forensic mind is none the less behind *Arthur & George*. No wonder that after Oxford graduation, Barnes read for the bar; no wonder, either, that a former detective writer can give Conan Doyle a run for his money in terms of well-laid twists and turns.

That said, Barnes cannot imagine being a campaigning writer as Conan Doyle became, bothering the establishment with his passionately held views. "I'm not a public platform person, either by my own personal temperament or my literary temperament. I don't write novels in order to persuade people of things." Why then do you write novels? "Oh what a G2 question. I can't answer that in a soundbite. I'll give you a reply in 3,000 words in a few weeks."

I'm not sure if he's joking. If, Mr. Barnes, you are reading this, and you were serious, please send me your reply soonest so we can run it in the paper. That, though, will probably not happen—if you don't read reviews, what chance is there you'll read this?

Interview with Julian Barnes

Xesús Fraga/2006

Originally published in Galician on the Rinoceronte Editora website as "A entrevista a Julian Barnes: o documento completo," 10 July 2006. This interview is published here for the first time in English with permission of the author. Xesús Fraga is Barnes's Galician translator.

Xesús Fraga: We can start talking about *Arthur & George*, and I suppose then the conversation will deal with other parts of your work and writing in general. When people read the book, they see Arthur as a well-known character, a famous person, but I think you started the book because of George, not because of Arthur. Can you explain how you got to George's story, because by now it must have been quite obscure and forgotten?

Julian Barnes: Yes, I was never interested in Arthur Conan Doyle, to be honest. I hadn't read a word of him since I was twenty, when I read some Sherlock Holmes. But I was reading a book about the Dreyfus case in France, and the English historian who was writing it said there was a parallel case in England with many features in common: a horrible crime, a miscarriage of Justice, handwritten evidence was very important, a sentence of hard labour in both cases, and a famous writer coming to the rescue. I thought, "I've never heard of this case and I don't even know how to pronounce the name of the man involved."

Fraga: Like many of the characters in the book.

Barnes: Like many of the characters, exactly. So I thought that I wanted to read about it and try to find something about it and, to my amazement, I went on the Internet and Googled it and went to Abebooks and all that, and no one had written about it, no one had touched it since the day nearly a hundred years previously when Conan Doyle wrote his article. So it was part out of frustration that there was nothing written about it that I thought I might write something. And you're right: I came to it through George, and Arthur just happened to be attached. At the beginning I was rather irritated that I was obliged to write about Arthur Conan Doyle, and then as I read about him I found him a much more interesting man than I had imagined, and his career ending as a sort of spiritualist evange-

list I found fascinating. I also realised that I didn't have to write an homage to
Sherlock Holmes; I didn't have to write a book in which people who love Sherlock
Holmes would find lots of references towards the story. I could write my own
book. It was very much what happens when a writer leaves his desk rather than
when he works at it—I find a way to make it my own book.

Fraga: Did you find yourself in a similar situation as Conan Doyle? I mean, famous writer comes to the rescue of a character, now that he's long forgotten;
Conan Doyle investigates Edalji's case, and now you investigate again his case
and his relations with the society he lived in . . .

Barnes: Yes. I mean, at the very, very beginning of it I didn't know what sort of
book it was going to be and I didn't know whether it might have been a short
nonfictional account of the case. At one point I thought of writing it differently.
I thought, "I don't want to write a novel that only happens in the past; I'll write
a novel with that story and then a contemporary story of racial prejudice." But I
thought that would be too convoluted, and, partly, the strength of the original
story was such that you don't have to put a parallel story today into the book
in order for people to realise that it's about today as well as it is about a hundred years ago. So at one point I thought, "No, the story will do for itself." If
people don't notice any contemporary parallel, then they're not very good readers anyway.

Fraga: The first part of the book is very important because it gives you the impression that you are reading a book that deals with how the mind works. Both
Arthur and George start with their first memories and then you go on to describe
how they grew up, how they were educated. It's not just an account of how they
met and what happened; there's a lot of background.

Barnes: Yes, I wanted them to be real people so I had to get inside their heads to
start off with. I suppose my way of getting into that period and evoking that period for readers today is to do it through the way the characters think and the way
that they talk and through the language of the prose rather than amassing a great
amount of historical detail. There are occasional references to clothes or furni-
ture, but not really very many. That seems to me a very ponderous way to write a
historical novel. You can do a lot more using just a few words that give you the period. I realise this means trouble for my translators; they have to find a language
which evokes the period of a hundred years ago and which doesn't have any
modern anachronisms in it. It will obviously vary from language to language according to how each individual language has developed in the last hundred years,

and there are some languages which have stayed fairly constant and so it won't work. I've discovered this before when writing a book about which my German translator said, "Look, I can't do this because German in this period has stayed exactly the same, so there's no way I can indicate with the flavour that this is the eighteenth century, which of course you can do in your own language and you're very conscious of it."

Fraga: George has a way of expressing himself that I suppose would even sound strange in his own time. Take his conversations with Sergeant Upton, for example.
Barnes: Yes, yes, yes. I can imagine boys like that today, but he's very pedantic and very literal. That's his strength and his weakness, I think.

Fraga: There are a few similarities between Arthur and George. They are both persons who have been educated with a strict code of honour; they appreciate honesty and their own values. They live as if they expected the world to act and react according to the code they set, but then the world goes in a different way, and that's they suffer. They suffer a lot because of that.
Barnes: Well, George does especially. But I think that's one of the things that happens to most people. Most people are brought up by their parents or by their school or by the Church with certain values, and it always comes as a surprise to realise that the rest of the world doesn't work according to these values, or that enough of the rest of the world doesn't work with them. I suppose the opposite applies too—if you're brought up in a criminal milieu where your only values are those of self-interest and dishonesty, it probably comes as a shock to discover that in the world there are people who like virtue and truth. Though I suppose that shock is less of a blow to the system than the other way round.

Fraga: Arthur is also quite shocked because he thinks he can be Sherlock Holmes: if he has created the character and the character obeys him, then this case proves him wrong all the time.
Barnes: Yes, well, that's another parallel of what we've been talking about, that Arthur discovers that real life detection is very different from detective stories. When writing, I deliberately played that up, that aspect of things, that Arthur keeps getting things wrong as a detective and he jumps to conclusions. And indeed he did, you know. He read the anonymous letters and he decided there were three writers. And then he found the people he thought were responsible, but there were only two brothers, and not this young boy that he had extrapolated from the letters. That's why there's such a confrontation with Anson, when he goes to stay with the Chief Constable. And that's part of the collision with the re-

ality of other people's assumptions and the reality of how police investigations are often carried out.

Fraga: Yes, he gets very irritated when everyone keeps telling him, "This is not a novel, it's real life." At first he's quite shocked that people react that way, but in the end I think he has to give in and admit that real life is different from fiction. It's interesting to see how fiction contaminates our lives.
Barnes: Yes, yes . . . I don't know if that's a question [laughs].

Fraga: I mean, it's quite a Quixotic issue. Arthur is like Don Quixote, who wants to help people in distress, but mainly because of what he's read. Don Quixote has read knights' stories; Arthur has, as well, and he even has his own Sancho Panza—Woodie.

Barnes: Yes, or his own Doctor Watson, depending which comparison you need. You would say that Don Quixote's imagination had been deformed by the books of chivalry he read, as you would say Emma Bovary's mind had been perverted by the sentimental romantic fiction that she read. In Doyle's case it's more that these are the values that his mother gave to him, I think. But there is certainly that element of the public righting of wrongs. I think that this is more true of how writers were a hundred years ago than now. Writers like Bernard Shaw or H. G. Wells and so on, and Kipling and Conan Doyle, were such public figures that their remarks on issues of their day were taken seriously by No. 10 Downing Street. And now I'm afraid that doesn't apply today so much. I mean, obviously writers still campaign against injustice and sign petitions and tell stories and so on and so forth, but their public influence is less than it used to be. You could say, "That's because all the writers now are small and they used to be big." That's possibly the case, but I think it's more the case that politicians always know who is useful to them, and nowadays if Tony Blair could be sitting on the platform with some member of U2 or Ian McEwan, he would choose the rock star any time—that's where the votes are. So to that extent it's the way that culture has changed, whereas a hundred years ago Kipling or Conan Doyle would say, "No, I think young men ought to be put into the Army for a period of conscription for three years," and they would write to the Minister of Defense who would take it seriously. If I wrote to the Minister of Defense and said that the Iraq war is a disaster, that we should leave, I wouldn't even get a reply.

Fraga: We'll talk of writers' attitudes later on, but I wouldn't forgive myself if we didn't talk about the other characters in the book, like George's sister, for example, who comes in as a real surprise at the end, or Arthur's mother or even

Woodie. Arthur and George are the main characters, but without the others the novel wouldn't be the same. They act as a balance; they give humour, seriousness; they put the characters into their places when they fantasize too much . . .

Barnes: Yes, that's right. It's the longest novel I've written by some distance, but it's also the novel with the most number of characters in, and part of me was always thinking, "My novels don't have many characters in them." They only have as many characters as they need, which isn't very many. I used to think that this was because I come from a family which isn't very large, and so I used to envy writers who (well, as a writer you always envy what other writers have) came from large, sprawling families, lots of cousins and uncles and brothers and sisters. I come from a very small family and also not a very close family either, so I used to think that perhaps there was a connection between the fact that I come from a small family and that all my novels tend not to have very many characters. Part of me was determined to write a novel which had a lot of characters in it, as many characters as it needed. But sure, at times I was worried that, as it was, Arthur and George would dominate it too much. Maud I think is a very interesting character. Then again, I don't know if she was like that in her life; it's a complete guess. That was one of the difficulties of the book. You're going from characters on the one hand who had many biographies of them and whose every action was recorded, to those who were completely unknown, just a name. Bringing them up to the same sort of weight was difficult.

Fraga: I haven't written many books, but it's funny because I'm an only child and my main characters are also only children. I've been quite obsessed with writing a story where the character has brothers and sisters.
Barnes: Yes, yes.

Fraga: Just to prove myself it's not a weight on me.
Barnes: Yes, I know that case. You do have those anxieties. I'm not an auto-biographical writer—very, very rarely—but you have those anxieties that your imagination is bounded, limited by your experience.

Fraga: But I think most readers don't pay attention to these things. I mean, a novel is like a clock, you just see the time going by, but not the mechanism, the book's structure.
Barnes: No, that's true for most readers, but there are also readers and some critics who think that any story that's told in the first person must be autobiographical. And that anything bad that happens, especially to do with the emotional or

sexual life, must be autobiographical. I have a friend who is a very good short story writer called Helen Simpson, and she wrote a story which was published in *Granta* magazine about a woman who lived in circumstances rather similar to hers and whose grandfather was dying with Alzheimer's disease. And the editor of the magazine after it was published said in a very sympathetic voice, "Were you very close to your grandparents?" And she said, "I've never met any of my grandparents. They were dead before I was a child. And I've never known anyone with Alzheimer ever." Which is both an encouraging story in terms of what imagination is and a depressing story in terms of how reductive and autobiographical some readers can be.

Fraga: A Spanish author, Javier Marías, wrote a novel called *All Souls* . . .
Barnes: Yes, I remember when that came out.

Fraga: . . . and he spent two years in Oxford as a teacher and the main character in the novel is also a Spaniard who spends two years in Oxford teaching. At the end of the novel his character has a child, so when Marías went back to Spain and started giving classes at University pupils used to wait for him at the end of class to ask him questions, and one of his students asked him about his son. He replied he wasn't a father, but the girl had read the novel and thought he and the character were the same person. And also one of the most respected critics in Spain, Francisco Rico, asked Marías deliberately to place him in a novel as a fictional character. So fiction still has a great power, and to be in a book. It's also George's dream to be a footnote in legal history because of his book. If he could see what you've done, he would be very pleased!
Barnes: [Laughs]. I don't know! You can't tell. He might be cross. It's very difficult putting people into books. I once borrowed someone's name. When I was working as a journalist, there was this woman in another department whose name was Jean Serjeant. And when I told my wife I had been talking to a woman called Jean Serjeant she said, "What a beautiful name, what an interesting name." So I thought, "I'll put that into a book." I asked her, "Can I use your name? It's got nothing to do with you at all. This is a story of a woman who grew up before the last war and so on." And she said, "Yes, that'll be fine." I used her name, and after the book came out she wrote an article saying how she had read this book and how she was very irritated that this woman wasn't very intelligent [laughs].

Fraga: Religion is also an important issue in *Arthur & George*. Funnily enough, it doesn't work. George is part of the Church of England, but that doesn't help him.

He's very deep into this religion which is the establishment, but it comes against him. And on the other hand you've got Arthur, who starts in an established religion but he grows apart from it.

Barnes: Well, they follow different courses. They both start in the Church, that's true. George's development is that he finds that religion as presented by his father is of no help in his suffering, in the ordeal he has to endure. And that his father has this preposterous notion that he's being tested, a martyr, and George doesn't see any point in this, in the God that's inflicting such suffering on him. That's because he has no imagination, as he says, and he takes things on a very literal level. Arthur's impatience is obviously of a very different source. It's the impatience of one who doesn't think that faith in itself is good enough, that a religion is only sustainable if it can be proved to be true. And that's why he gets involved in spiritualism. Rather curiously, lots of interviewers have asked me things like, "How is it that someone who could invent Sherlock Holmes, the most rational and scientific of detectives, gets involved with spiritualism, which is the most deeply irrational form of religion there is." But the answer is in the book, and it seems to me to be quite straightforward—that at the beginnings of its life spiritualism, at least as far as the Society for Psychical Research and those sort of bodies were concerned, was actually a rigorous scientific organization designed to detect and root out fraud and make spiritualism and psychical research into a proper discipline. As Arthur says, "Of course there's a lot of fraud. It's the sort of activity that attracts fraud. When Jesus Christ was in the world there were also a lot of rival prophets claiming to be the true prophet. But all you need is one proven case of the spirit surviving death, one scientifically solid case. And that's proof for everyone." So that's what they were after.

Fraga: It was a very important thought for the Victorian age.

Barnes: Yes, and it was the time, the turn of the century, when all sorts of scientific breaches were happening, which were discovering things that just lay beneath the surface of things. One of the early titles of the book was *The Skin of Things*, because it was about the surface of the world and what was immediately underneath it and the skin of George and the skin of Arthur. But I dropped that [laughs].

Fraga: Yesterday I remembered that aspect of the book when I visited with my family the Science Museum—there was this big X-ray machine, the kind of advance they would have admired.

Barnes: Yes, suddenly X-rays exist, suddenly the wireless exists. You know, why is telepathy any more strange than those? We must be out to prove that telepathy is also something that really exists. And, from that, spiritual messages from those who are dead. After all, the Christian religion they were brought up in maintained that we lived after death, and why shouldn't there be a means of getting in touch? It seemed logical.

Fraga: The skin theme is also important from a racial point of view. George thinks of himself as a 100 percent British citizen, but the establishment keeps reminding him that they don't consider him as such, or not at least 100 percent. It's moving and pathetic at the same time to find someone who thinks himself part of something and that something keeps expelling him.

Barnes: Yes, that's right. And I think the idea of a victim who doesn't understand why he is a victim is also very poignant and also very useful for a fiction writer. George did write some newspaper articles, and in one of them he said one of the most astonishing things for me when I was starting my research, he said, "People tell me that my case has to do with race prejudice. I don't believe that's the case. I think there might have been a couple of people in the neighbourhood of Great Wyrley who have suffered from race prejudice, but I never really encountered it, so I don't think it's relevant to the case." It's quite understandable he would want to think that, because race prejudice isn't logical, it isn't rational, and he was a rational person.

Fraga: It also connects with your book *England, England.* When George thinks of himself as an Englishman, it brings up the subject of what made you English in the nineteenth century, when people from the colonies were starting to live in England, and also what it means now, in the twenty-first century, with this very complicated society where it's difficult to assemble all the pieces from other cultures. And with the cases of Scotland and Wales, the English are starting to see themselves more English than British. There's this big issue about the flag of St. George and what it means to be English now.

Barnes: Well, I don't know if we'll ever get to the answer, because one of the things about the British, the English particularly, is that they're not very good about what it means to be English. No, I think it's partly a lack of imagination; it's partly the fact that they spent two hundred years, or how long it was, being about the most powerful nation in the world. And if you were the most powerful nation in the world, as you can see with America at the moment, you don't think very clearly about what you are. You think that you are the norm and that everyone else is a variant form of what is the norm. The Welsh and the Irish and the Scots have always had the English to define themselves against, whereas the English don't really know who to define themselves against. They don't know whether it is the French—it's usually the French [short laugh]—sometimes it's the Germans, though at different times we have been both very close to the French and very close to the Germans.

Two things are going on simultaneously: one thing is that there's a sort of a move to the English being more nationalistic-English, which seems to me as very retrograde. One of the nice things about the English is that they aren't very good at thinking about being English. And the other is the attempt by Tony Blair's number two, Gordon Brown, to have some sort of defining terms of Britishness and lay down the elements of what it is to be British, which I think is also disastrous. And, indeed, in *England, England* I did a version of what happens when you try to reduce the nation to certain key elements.

But at the time of *Arthur & George*, Englishness seemed much more about being inclusive or seeming to be inclusive, and so you would aim to be English, you would aim to conform, whereas now Englishness, and Britishness especially, have many forms and a lot of people don't care about it. A lot of the young think it's ridiculous to even answer that question. The young are more international with each generation. I'm very divided about the whole question. I don't know the answer. On the one hand, I like the idea of individual national cultures and what they have built up over the years, but they're so often used as an excuse for narrow-mindedness and chauvinism and aggression. It's like the European Union—given the history of wars in Europe for a thousand years, the European Union, or its various forms, has actually been rather amazing. There hasn't been a war since 1945, apart from Yugoslavia, which is an amazing achievement—at the price of much greater homogenization, internationalisation, thinning down of the national culture of each country. It's the price we're paying, how you do the trade. You want the young as they come up to get out into the world, to understand difference and diversity, to be peaceful, and to make friends all over the place. At the same time, when they say, "I'm not English" or "I'm not British," "It doesn't matter. Let's forget about nationality," I have a sense of regret that languages disappear, cultures disappear, and whether at some point there'll be some sort of strange little vestige of people pretending to be English, just like the Welsh get together and they dress as druids. And everyone will use a shared international English and then there'll be a small group of people who will meet in order to preserve in its rather antique form all the distinctions that existed in

English-English before American-English took over the world. I imagine this in a hundred years' time.

Fraga: I think people tend to mix up things from different cultures and sometimes they incur contradictions or they exclude themselves. In London you can see Asian boys with Palestine flags sewed on their jackets but eating a burger from McDonalds. There's this left wing or nationalist approach to things, but at the same time consumer society engulfs it all. It's not about countries, it's about corporations—they are the ones that rule.

Barnes: Yes, and it's not just a question of left and right, because often it plays the other way, that the left is more international and the right is more nationalistic and more concerned with keeping the idea of whatever the nation is. But yes, I think governments increasingly are less powerful and more willing to do what transnational companies want them to do. They are setting the agenda, and the ideal agenda for them is a vast community of consumers, all of whom want the same thing. So that is clearly, it seems to me, the enemy of individuality amongst nations. We can't get too serious about it, but, even so, I remember being in Italy a few years ago and walking with some friend we had met in a little town in the middle of Italy, and I said, "Oh God, there's a McDonalds there!" And she said, "Why shouldn't we have McDonalds? Why should we eat all these old-fashioned foods that you want us to eat all the time?" [laughs]. It's like when the Wall came down in Berlin, all these East Berliners flooded through and the first thing they wanted was to go to sex shops and to eat burgers. OK, that's their right, and we shouldn't have too many illusions about it.

Fraga: Yes, but I think the problem is bigger. For example, a hundred years ago humans cultivated a thousand different species to feed themselves, and now it's come down to 150.

Barnes: Has it? That's very interesting.

Fraga: Yes, there's a United Nations report about it. So it's not prejudice or being fussy about burgers, it's a much deeper thing about the world losing its variety and richness.

Barnes: Yes, that's true.

Fraga: In Spain, for example, fifty years ago you could find fifteen or twenty varieties of melons in the market and now it's only two or three.

Barnes: Yes, that's true. There are organizations in Britain that protect what are called heritage seeds and they send out these seeds to gardeners to try and protect the old species. I have a little garden and sometimes grow these old vegetables. Though, in terms of the market, how they will ever survive against the mutant genetically modified stuff I don't know.

Fraga: I think it's important authors deal with such issues, maybe not in a direct way. You talked about Kipling and Conan Doyle writing to the Minister of Defence; maybe things now should be done in a different way. For example, books like *Saturday,* by Ian McEwan, don't deal directly with the 9/11 attacks, but they reflect a mood and make you think about what has been happening.

Barnes: I remember when 9/11 happened and people said, "We need writers to explain it to us." And my first thought was writers don't know what's happened yet—we need journalists to explain to us what happened and who these people are and stuff like that. I think it's complicated. My friend Jay McInerney, the American writer, wrote a novel which is in the shadow of 9/11, though it doesn't deal with the events directly. And when Norman Mailer heard that he was writing it he said, "Don't do that. Give it ten years."

Part of me thinks that literature should absorb things like that and wait until they can be useful to literature. The high-minded approach in literature is actually what matters. Flaubert once said of the Franco-Prussian War, "Yes, perhaps in the long run the only point of this war is to give a few fine pages to a few writers." Part of me thinks that, and then there's the other part which is urged on by, "This is the hot story in town, you ought to do something about it." I think there's also amongst readers a sort of understandable eagerness to have things explained. John Updike wrote a book called *Terrorist,* which is actually absolutely brilliant, about how a young Arab American living in New Jersey gets turned by a mullah into a terrorist. When I read it in proof I thought, "Yes, I believe every word of this and I understand it better now."

But writers should only do what they are good at doing. And on the other side there are readers who over-interpret things; I've had *Arthur & George* put to me as being in part post-9/11 because it deals with how people with the wrong skin colour are always suspected. And I said, "Well, I'm sorry, but I never thought of it. I didn't think about it for a moment." Ian McEwan is a great friend of mine and I admire *Saturday* enormously. I don't think that book is really about 9/11; I think 9/11 is in the background and that what it's really about is the terror of someone's life going wrong. It's about domestic terror. And then, on the horizon, there is the plane blazing through the sky. I don't resent it, but I think it's been over-interpreted in that way, just as, for example, Philip Roth's *The Plot Against*

America was taken up as a metaphor for the Bush Administration, which he didn't mean at all. But you don't refuse those things.

Fraga: Even *The Lord of the Rings*, when the films came out, was seen that way.
Barnes: Really? Well, I've never read *The Lord of the Rings* and I've never seen any of the films. *Harry Potter*'s all about 9/11 [smiles].

Fraga: Do you think people miss periods like the '30s when they could identify writers with a political option and they went to war, like Hemingway or Dos Passos, when they went to Spain to the Civil War?
Barnes: I don't really know. I don't know whether it helps to give writers labels. I think it's a quite good idea that writers don't have labels, that the only label they have is their own name. I think there's a danger in writers taking up political causes because they think they ought to. There's a danger of writers becoming public spokesmen, but then, on the spectrum that all artists are on the service of some other cause, to the spectrum of art for art's sake, something pure, I'm not in the middle. I'm more weary of art in the service of an idea than I am of art that tends to go off to the ultra-bouts spectrum of things. You can see things going wrong with Tolstoy, you can see how the need to propagandize seeps into him as the years go by, and I think that is a warning.

Writers are also citizens, so you could go to a war as a citizen. I don't know. I don't know the answer. Hemingway didn't necessarily go as a novelist, he went as a war correspondent. I suppose in the '30s there was a very clear divide between left and right, and each had their terrible extremes and it was quite hard to hold the middle-of-the-road liberal position then. And most writers in Britain, I suppose, who we remember now tended to lean to the left, like Orwell and Auden and Spender and the poets of the '30s. I think there were one or two who leaned to the right, but that dichotomy doesn't really exist any more. In this country both the main political parties are indivisible—they're both post-Thatcher right-wing parties, whether they're called New Labour or Conservative. The Liberal Party, which used to be vaguely to the left, is moving to the same ground. It wouldn't really say much if in this country, say Peter Ackroyd was identified as a Tory and Ian McEwan as Labour or vice-versa. I don't think it matters to people.

Fraga: Even *Arthur and George* thought their case would have a much bigger impact, like the Dreyfus case, and they were appalled with such a small reaction.
Barnes: Well, what they could have learnt from the Dreyfus case was that Dreyfus was brought to trial and on the evidence presented was found guilty. And then

there was a long campaign, and he was brought back and given a second trial, and found guilty again. It was only at the third attempt that his innocence was established. So one of the lessons of the Dreyfus case is that the establishment doesn't give up. The other lesson is that life is not a detective story. In life you don't necessarily find out who did it, you don't necessarily get justice—you get three quarters of justice, half justice. And you really don't know who the bad guy was in the end.

Fraga: Do you think many of *Arthur & George*'s readers expected you to name the culprit?
Barnes: Well, one or two were disappointed that they didn't find out, and I said, "That's the point to it. That's why it's a novel and not a detective story." Arthur thought he had found out and he thought it was these two Sharp brothers who had done it, and it quite possibly was, but then you have George saying: "The evidence you've got against them is not really any stronger than the evidence that was produced against me. So why should I help find guilty someone else on the same level of evidence as myself?"

Fraga: Quite honest of him.
Barnes: Yes, well, I don't know if he said that or not [laughs]. So he might not have been pleased if he could come back and see.

Fraga: One last question. Before coming to interview you I met a Spanish writer, and we talked about your book *The Pedant in the Kitchen.* He was surprised you had written so many articles on the subject, but then he said, "Oh, but Barnes, he's half French, isn't he?"
Barnes: [laughs] Oh, that's nice. Well, the illusion about England is that it is a land of terrible food, and the French certainly seem to think this, still. In one way it's just a short book of newspaper articles about my misadventures in the kitchen, but also I realised as I was writing it that it falls within the . . . Put it this way: one of the functions of writing fiction is a corrective one, not to be didactic, but corrective, to say, "Life is not like that, it's like this. Those things you've been told about life, they're not true. Old age isn't a time of serenity, sex can be boring, and so on." And I was thinking about that as I was putting the book together. At the end I was saying to myself, "This is rather like the reality of sex. It's very different from what you read about it, the way it's photographed, the way it appears in movies." And it's the same with food and cooking: the experience of the ordinary person who goes into the kitchen to put a meal together is quite different

from the recipe or the chef's book or the glossy photograph. So what you're saying is, "It's not like that, it's like this." The best thing anyone says to you as a writer tends to be, "I think that too, but I didn't have the words to express it until I read what you wrote." And it's that joy of recognition of the reader that is your best reward. In the same way, people saying, "Yes, I have exactly the same problem when cutting up an onion" [laughs], that's the answer that you want.

Julian Barnes: Are You an Oldie?

Margaret Crick/2007

An edited version of this interview was published in *The Oldie Review of Books* (Autumn 2007): 7. Reprinted by permission of the author.

Margaret Crick: We'll start with a bit of trivia.

Julian Barnes: I hope it's *all* trivia [laughs].

Crick: Yes, but there's a chance to expand if you want. Do you not only talk to yourself, but see nothing odd in it?

Barnes: I don't see anything odd in it, no. I don't talk to myself all the time; unfortunately, I tend to talk to myself more in the street than in the privacy of my own home, so I probably do seem a bit bonkers.

Crick: Do your lips move?

Barnes: Oh, yes. I speak out loud, as well.

Crick: Actually, that doesn't look so odd anymore, because people assume you have a mobile phone.

Barnes: Yes, that's true. Nowadays you can't tell who's mad and who isn't.

Crick: What do you actually say? Do you comment on things as they happen? Or are you rehearsing a speech or something you might write?

Barnes: No, it's certainly never something I would write. It's usually something I would say in a hypothetical situation. It's not *esprit d'escalier*. It's not what I *would've* said; and it's not even what I *will* say. It's what I *would* say if a certain situation arose.

Crick: Do you know any prayers, apart from the Lord's Prayer?

Barnes: No. Not a single one. I'm not sure I could do that a hundred percent, either.

Crick: Do you think in feet and inches?

Barnes: Yes, I do.

Crick: Have you any views about Fahrenheit or the Euro or changing all our systems?

Barnes: Well, I think we should go into the Euro, because either you're in Europe or you're *not* in Europe. It's foolish to pretend you're part of Europe if you're not even in the currency. Though an American friend of mine said a while ago, "I don't know why there is such a fuss in your country about going to the Euro; you're already using a world currency in your credit card." I think in feet and inches. And more in Fahrenheit than Centigrade, though I can do Centigrade.

Crick: And if someone were to say, "How tall are you?" what would you say?

Barnes: Oh, I would say 6′1″. I certainly wouldn't know what it was in metres at all. I think both systems should be allowed, and that the old freedoms of Britain should allow you to sell things in pounds and stones and hundredweights if you want to, and if people can't work it out they won't go to your shop.

Crick: Have you now forgotten where you were when Kennedy was shot?

Barnes: Oh, yes. I don't remember where I was when Kennedy was shot; I don't remember where I was when Robert Kennedy was shot; and I don't remember where I was when Teddy Kennedy swam heroically away at Chappaquiddick.

Crick: Do you find that OAPs [Old Age Pensioners] are starting to look young to you?

Barnes: If they looked young to me I wouldn't know they were OAPs, would I? I absolutely don't believe in saying absurd things like, "Sixty is the new Forty." I think that's a sign of a person in deep denial.

Crick: [laughs] What's wrong with deep denial?

Barnes: I think you should avoid it as much as possible. I think you should live in the truth as much as possible.

Crick: What of the term "OAP"? I find it rather derogatory.

Barnes: I didn't know it was used very much anymore. Do people still use it?

Crick: Well, yes—"Pensioner," "OAP," "the Elderly"—people use those to describe our kind of age group. Do you think there should be another term now?

Barnes: Well, no one has called me a pensioner to my face yet. And I'm not a pensioner, because I earn my own living. Whereas I think of pensioners as people who live off state funding. So you could be a twenty-year-old pensioner in my book. I think we should just throw the term back at them and say, "I am a self-sufficient writer who pays tax, and you're living off the state. You're the pensioner and not me. You're the one in receipt of something from the state to support your way of life."

Crick: But if you were describing somebody who is at that age and who may or may not get a pension, you wouldn't use the term "OAP"?
Barnes: No, never. I think there's something terribly sort of '50s about it. I suppose you could say "Old Fool" instead.

Crick: One of my interviewees said she thought they should be called "Special Senior People" or something—something a bit different, you know. I think "Senior" is almost worse.
Barnes: "Senior" is awful, yes. I once described my former editor and friend Anthony Howard in an essay for the *New Yorker* as the "veteran political correspondent." And when the *New Yorker* fact checkers checked with him about whether he was "veteran" or not, he said he preferred to be called "seasoned." So when I did the index to the book, I put: "Anthony Howard: seasoned or veteran?" as a way of getting back at him.

Crick: [laughs] That's very nice, actually. Do you think there are any benefits to being an "oldie"?
Barnes: No, I'd prefer to harp on the disadvantages. Are there any benefits? Well, you're less foolish, I suppose. You're wiser; you're less foolish; you see things from a longer perspective. On the other hand, I'm sure that you've lost more than you gained.

Crick: What are the disadvantages? *I* don't feel any less foolish; I feel *more* foolish, actually [laughs]. What do you think are the disadvantages?
Barnes: You're much nearer death than you used to be. That's the main disadvantage [laughs]. It's a simple one in my book. Montaigne did say that we die two deaths: the first is the death of youth and the second is the death of what is only old age. And that it's foolish to lament the second, slipping away from old age into death, because the much greater death is always the first one—the death of youth. Though I don't find that especially consoling.

Crick: Do you think it's easier to be an oldie in America or France?
Barnes: I used to think it was easier to be an oldie in France, but then they had that fantastic heat wave when loads of old people conked out and no one claimed their bodies. There were thousands of them in mortuaries and deep-freeze vans,

unclaimed. So much for both the French and the Catholic traditions of family. On the other hand, I would hate to be an old person in America, because you'd probably be pretending to be a young person in the horrible way that they do. And you'd live in awful golf villages where everyone would be taking Viagra. Sounds a nightmare.

Crick: Have you ever experienced ageism? As a writer, you wouldn't experience it professionally, but . . .

Barnes: Well, funnily enough I did, yes. On one occasion a branch of the British Council—I was on a sort of two-leg tour (if you can have a tour of two legs be called a tour)—and one branch of the British Council refused to pay my airfare to their city on the grounds that they were only interested in *younger* writers. It may be that they didn't like my stuff, but the way it was put by the people who picked up the tab eventually made it sound like it was ageism, yes. And I've heard of other cases like that.

Crick: Did you object?

Barnes: I only found out about it later. And in a way I didn't care too deeply [laughs]. It makes it easier for me to criticize the British Council for their lunatic policy of getting rid of their libraries all across the world. These used to be a matter of pride, and local readers loved them. Then Mrs. Thatcher insisted the British Council earn money, so they went over to teaching English and having "libraries" consisting of videos and CDs and DVDs, and those old-fashioned, non-money-making items called "books" were in some cases just put out on the pavement, and in others given away to local library. Five thousand books in Vienna, I was told. It makes me spit and fume.

Crick: Have you ever been tempted by cosmetic surgery or any kind of lift?

Barnes: Yes, I have. I'm not going to tell you what, though. Someone once interviewed me for the *Evening Standard* many years ago and used the phrase, "He has a face suspiciously unlined for a man of forty." And I could never work out what they meant—that I looked as if I hadn't lived enough, or that I must have had cosmetic surgery [laughs]. I don't have any sort of strong views about it. I'd probably have something taken off if I hated seeing it in the mirror all the time, but I think all such stuff shouldn't obviously be done on the NHS. Oliver Cromwell should have had to go private if he wanted his warts off.

Crick: Do you think women who have face lifts look better?

Barnes: Depends on the quality of the face lift and the face, really. You know, a little lift, a little tuck . . . often, I think it's as much about the psychological effect. And if it makes a woman feel better about herself, she'll look better as well. I think you should try to be as honest as possible about the aging process, while also having cosmetic surgery if you feel like it [laughs]. Yes, that's my position . . . [laughs]. I wouldn't dye my hair, for instance, but if it started falling out and there was a treatment to stop it falling out, I'd probably take that, yes.

Crick: Are you getting increasingly interested in the obituary columns?
Barnes: Oh, I always have been. I used to keep scrapbooks and they were filled with people's obituaries. I read them just as religiously as I always did.

Crick: Do you still keep scrapbooks?
Barnes: No, I did give that up when I was about fifty [laughs].

Crick: Why did you do it?
Barnes: Oh, I just wanted to keep records of certain things. You know, all sorts of stuff that interested me.

Crick: Do you write obituaries?
Barnes: I've written one, I think. Maybe two?

Crick: But you were *always* interested, so you haven't become more interested?
Barnes: No, I was *always* interested in people dying.

Crick: And are there at least ten people in your address book who are dead?
Barnes: Oh, definitely . . . definitely. And if you go back to an earlier address book there would be a lot more people dead, yes. I don't like to cross them out. I know people go through their address books crossing people out when they're dead. I feel that's rather rude. I put them in square brackets when they're dead. So if it's a couple and one has died, then the person who's dead gets square brackets around them.

Crick: That's rather sweet. And do you write letters? As opposed to email . . .
Barnes: And I suppose as opposed to business letters and things like that . . .

Crick: Yes. You know, get a pen and note paper out . . .
Barnes: If I'm writing a short postcard, say, I'd probably use a pen, but the only *long* letters I would write in pen would be letters of condolences, because I think they shouldn't be typed. I think they must be handwritten. Though I have noticed in an oldie way that people don't reply to letters of condolence in the way that they used to, which I think is regrettable.

Crick: What about thank you notes?
Barnes: Oh, yes. I write them.

Crick: By hand?
Barnes: Well, it depends on how well you know the person. There's always a moment when you go from the postcard to the email. I thank people by email if I know them very well. I think that's okay.

Crick: So you don't spend a lot of time browsing in stationery shops or anything like that?
Barnes: Well, yes, in that I love shops like Office World where you can buy stationery and you can take a shopping trolley around and just fill it up with stacks of paper and felt-tip pens and staples and sellotape and envelopes. Like most writers, I'm a bit fetishistic about the means of writing.

Crick: Do you keep your pencils in a little row like Jeffrey Archer does?
Barnes: Or that maniac Georges Simenon. No, I don't. I stuff them into a pot, but I have far more than I need. I always take biros and pencils from hotels and things like that [laughs].

Crick: So do I! [laughs] I either have far too many or none at all.
Barnes: They have to be really bad biros for me not to take them.

Crick: Yes [laughs]. The only ones I don't keep are the ones that get sent with junk mail.
Barnes: Yes, if you can tell from the wrapping there's a biro in it, then straight in the bin with it.

Crick: As you were a lexicographer at one time, are you worried about the state of literacy now?
Barnes: No, not really.

Crick: Because you don't think it's worse, or because you're just not worried that it's got worse.
Barnes: I think it's always been quite low. I don't think there was ever a golden period, either for the language itself or for the state of literacy.

Crick: Right. Doesn't it annoy you in a Lynne Truss way when you see apostrophes either not used or used in the wrong way. "Its" with an apostrophe and that sort of thing?
Barnes: No. The greengrocers apostrophe—"Apple's." No, it doesn't really. It

doesn't bother me. When people get into a Kingsley Amis type rage about the misuse of "disinterested," I always like to remind them that in the *Oxford English Dictionary* the first use of "disinterested" is in the sense of "uninterested"; while the first use of "uninterested" is in the sense of "disinterested,"

Crick: Language changes.
Barnes: Language changes. It's always in a state of flux. It's always growing and decaying. It seems to me very healthy and malleable and vivid at the moment.

Crick: And do you text?
Barnes: No. I did learn once, and my wife and I tried texting each other when I was in America. But we didn't know that the mobile phone had to be switched on to receive it, so none of our texts got through. Also, I think my thumbs are too fat.

Crick: When you say "switched on to receive it" . . .
Barnes: Well, I think if a text is coming through and the mobile phone isn't switched on within an hour or something, the text coming doesn't get through. Isn't that right?

Crick: I don't think so.
Barnes: Well, in any case, I keep mine switched off all the time, except if I have an emergency and need to call someone.

Crick: That's a very oldie thing, to keep yours switched off all the time.
Barnes: I don't know the number of it, either. I never even look it up. I don't ever take it except when I'm going on a work trip and something might go wrong.

Crick: Do you like the language of text? You know, "great" as "GR8" and that sort of thing. Does that interest you?
Barnes: No, not much. But it doesn't irritate me either.

Crick: What about email?
Barnes: Oh, I use email all the time.

Crick: It's so immediate, isn't it? The only problem with it is that you never actually know whether somebody has either received it or opened it—if they don't reply to you. But I guess that could apply to letters as well, I suppose.
Barnes: Yes, you do assume a response within two or three days, don't you, at a maximum. The good side is that, for a writer, *all* business is nowadays done on email, so no one faxes you and no one phones you up. So you get far fewer phone

calls than you used to to disrupt you. But the down side is that you find yourself using it with friends. The number of friends I used to ring up and whom I
now email has gone up enormously. So you think, is this somehow changing the
quality of the friendship?

Crick: Are we pen pals?
Barnes: Quite.

Crick: So you like a chat on the phone still, do you?
Barnes: Yes, I do. I do, but on the other hand I don't want to chat when I'm doing
something else . . . but that's normal.

Crick: Do you know anything about computers? For instance, do you know what
a "trojan" is?
Barnes: I assume that apart from a make of American contraceptive . . . That's
probably a trick *Oldie* question . . .

Crick: No, it wasn't actually [laughs]. I just found out the other day.
Barnes: It's some sort of virus that gets in like a Trojan horse, isn't it? I don't use
my computer for writing on, just for email obviously, and for shopping and for
Googling things.

Crick: You don't use it for writing?
Barnes: No, I use an electric typewriter.

Crick: Why is that?
Barnes: It suits how I think. And the time I did try using a computer, when both
my electric typewriters broke down at the same time, I expected to find myself
getting much more prolix and windy, but in fact I found I was over-correcting on
the first draft. And I always rely on having a rather free first draft. Instead, I was
getting something that was too compact and too tight. It didn't really work. It
didn't represent what I was thinking, what I needed as a writer.

Crick: It is very tempting to correct all the time, because you can do it so easily.
Barnes: Yes, yes.

Crick: I find I can't write without a keyboard of some sort. I couldn't possibly
write longhand.
Barnes: I wrote a novel in first draft in longhand about five years ago and rather
enjoyed it. But it is physically more tiring, of course.

Crick: Do you own an iPod?

Barnes: Yes, I do. On the other hand, and this is an oldie thing, I was taught how to put the CDs through iTunes into my iPod and I diligently loaded it for an American book tour with lots of Bach and lots of operas and things I thought I'd need on six-hour flights. And I learned how to recharge it and so on. Took those international plug adapters. But my CDs were so old that the iPod sorted them all out by track number rather than by the work itself—they didn't have whatever identifying codes each track would have nowadays. And so I got the *start* of *Otello* followed by the *The Magic Flute*, followed by some *Goldberg Variations*. It was absolutely maddening. I felt a real oldie then [laughs].

Crick: But you had *CDs*, so they weren't *that* old . . .

Barnes: Well, CDs have been around for twenty years or so . . .

Crick: And have you ever downloaded a ring tone for your phone?

Barnes: Ha, ha, ha . . . *certainly* not. That would be a very decadent thing to do. No, I have the one that it came with, I think. Oh, no, you have a choice, don't you? No, I certainly wouldn't. And I wouldn't know how to do it anyway.

Crick: And you've no interest in learning?

Barnes: No, none at all.

Crick: When you hear the term "Big Brother," do you still think of George Orwell?

Barnes: No, I think of that dreadful program.

Crick: Do you watch it?

Barnes: I've watched bits of it, yes. It's very strange in that, normally, grotesque people are interesting, but what's odd about *Big Brother* is that it's a cast of grotesques who are actually very boring.

Crick: The sort of people who are on programs like that become celebrities, and people are celebrities these days really for doing virtually nothing. Have you ever heard of somebody called Coleen McLoughlin, for example, or Kerry Katona?

Barnes: The first one is Wayne Rooney's girlfriend. I don't know who the second one is.

Crick: No, I've no idea, but they always seem to be in these magazines you pick up at the hairdressers.

Barnes: I did realize the nature of modern fame most sharply recently when I was up for a *Richard & Judy* book award. I went to the evening event and there was a red carpet which you had to walk across past a bank of about forty photographers. And I walked across it without any of them asking me to stop. I was followed by someone who I thought was a writer I didn't recognize, but who turned out to be Chantelle, who had won *Big Brother*. She was considerably more famous than me in the eyes of the photographers. But that's alright, I thought. If they had started shouting, "Hey, Julian, this way," and "Just one more towards me, darling," I'd have to be very suspicious of myself as a novelist.

Crick: When you're watching television, do you have remote controls you have no idea how to use?

Barnes: There are *lots* of buttons on them I don't understand, yes. And there are lots of remote controls—about six of them, so that's about 300 different buttons of which I understand and use about eighteen I suppose [laughs] . . . or twenty at the most.

Crick: [laughs] I've never thought of it that way. It's not an *oldie* thing. I don't suppose many people can use all the technologies they've got at their disposal.

Barnes: I think there is a handset coming in which actually controls *all* the gadgets you've got. But then, about two years ago, I had a French satellite dish put on my roof so that I could watch the Tour de France live and other things, such as the French elections, and that has an *enormous* control and even *more* buttons and they're in lots of different colors, and I just about know how to go from one channel to another on that.

Crick: It's getting rather terrifying turning on the TV at all, actually, what with digiboxes and all those sorts of things. And then when you do, there's very little to watch anyway. Do you save anything? Do you save string or leftovers or . . . ?

Barnes: You mean *pointless* things?

Crick: Yes, well, these are oldie things to do.

Barnes: I don't consciously save things, no. I suppose the things that I save that are most useless are envelopes from hotels where I've stayed. It's a bit like the biro thing. I always take the envelopes out of the leather folder thinking I will use them. But I almost never find anyone who wants to receive a letter with a Liechtenstein hotel logo and address on the cover and a London postmark. So I haven't found the right use for them, and they are definitely piling up.

Crick: I use them for shopping lists. Not necessarily ones from hotels, but I always recycle envelopes and use them for shopping lists, if they're the right sort of envelopes.

Barnes: Yes, I do that, but they're *used* envelopes. So much stuff comes into the house.

Crick: Does that annoy you, the junk mail, or the amount of rubbish we have, or the amount of wrapping we have?
Barnes: I do have the oldie thing of hating anything that comes wrapped in plastic. But that's partly because the digits aren't as strong as they used to be and trying to rip the plastic open is likely to tear a rotator cuff muscle . . .

Crick: Yes, particularly cassette tape boxes and that sort of thing. They're very, very shrinkwrapped.
Barnes: Yes, I had a little rant about that in a novel—about that little tab on a CD cover that it never works even if you can find it. So usually it's a question of inserting a paper knife or kitchen knife into it along the edge, isn't it?

Crick: Which novel was that?
Barnes: It was in *England, England*. Someone has a rant about the trouble with history being that it keeps referring to itself and assumes that you've read all the other history books on the subject already. So where do you start, he asks. It's as tricky as trying to find the tab on a CD. And the historian who's listening says, "Oh, that's very good. Do you mind if I use it?"

Crick: Are you frightened of going to the Barbican?
Barnes: No, I go there constantly. It is one of the worst sign-posted places arts venues that there is. They've now redesigned it so the staircases aren't quite where they were. Which was not done with oldies in mind. But it keeps you on your toes. Like being in a 3D maze.

Crick: Which makes it even more confusing [laughs].
Barnes: Last time I was there I discovered the roof walk from the Barbican station to the Hall—I'd only been going for about twenty years without knowing about it. At one point you go past the Mendelssohn Tree—it's some big piece of oak—and it says, "For explanation see plaque on wall," but someone had stolen the plaque so I was none the wiser.

Crick: You enjoy cooking. Do you think it is only oldies who cook these days? Rather than getting ready-made?
Barnes: I have a friend whose son went to Warwick University about ten years ago, and she taught him to cook, because she thought boys ought to be taught to cook before they go to university. So he went off fully prepared and found that

not a single person—boy or girl—could cook a thing. I don't know . . . I didn't start cooking until I was forced to by living on my own, and not having any money to go out to eat. I suppose it will happen to them. Except there are more poisoned convenience foods to develop diseases from than there were in my day. What was the question?

Crick: I just wondered whether you thought it was just oldies who cooked?
Barnes: No, I don't think so.

Crick: Do you prefer a nice cup of tea, or something like a mocha latte frappachino . . . ?
Barnes: No, I hate all those terms for coffee. I like things to be simple. I go as far as espresso macchiato. But then, when you say it, sometimes they don't know what it is. So you say, "It's sort of espresso coffee, yes?" "Yes." "And hot milk on the side." And then you turn your back and they've given you a pint glass of foaming milk and a tiny espresso and they're very grumpy when you say that isn't at all what you wanted. No, I don't know what most of those coffee names mean, and I hate the way you go into a Starbucks and the word "Small" doesn't exist.

Crick: Do you think there is too much choice?
Barnes: I'd rather have too much choice than the opposite. But it takes you until you're an oldie to realize that a lot of the choice that you're offered is bogus, like different sorts of washing powder made by the same company with slightly different marketing campaigns, but exactly the same properties.

Crick: When you see a fashion style described as new, do you think to yourself, "Oh, I wore that in the sixties"?
Barnes: That very rarely happens to me.

Crick: Have you any views of the state of civil liberties? I saw this film called *Taking Liberties* . . .
Barnes: Yes, I want to see that.

Crick: Well, it's very partial, but it's quite funny.
Barnes: Yes, I do think that things are never in a state of stasis. I mean, either liberty is being expanded or it's being reduced. And since the days of Roy Jenkins and that government, when civil liberties were clearly being expanded, it seems to me that they've been a bit more chipped away at, by both Labour and Conservatives. And that the combination—or succession—of Blunkett and Reid as Labour Home Secretaries has not exactly brought joy to the libertarian's heart.

Crick: Were you a member of CND or anything like that?

Barnes: No, no. I did join Charter 88 when it started. I went on one demo, and it was rather pathetic. There were about fifty of us gathered at Trafalgar Square, and I think we were going to hand in a petition at the House of Commons, but then we were told that marches could not consist of more than three people or something like that. There are fantastic, arcane regulations designed to stop people from having demonstrations, so I think three or four people walked to the House of Commons and handed it in. The rest of us stayed behind rather aimlessly and waggled our signs at photographers, and then went home. No, I'm not much of a joiner or "belonger." But that doesn't have anything to do with being an oldie, I don't think.

Crick: That's more or less it, unless there is something you'd like to have a little rant about?

Barnes: Oh, I don't think being an oldie necessarily makes you a ranter. I think you can be a *young* ranter just as much as an old ranter. I would like to have a rant about those television programs on which oldies rant.

Crick: Yes, like *Grumpy Old Men* . . .

Barnes: . . . and *Grumpy Old Women*. Half of them are middle aged anyway, not old at all. They're just going on television because they would like going on television. And often they're not really grumpy either—they're just putting it on. I think that's a very bad sign—*faux* grumpiness . . . I'd like to have a rant about *that*.

Julian Barnes: The Final Interview

Vanessa Guignery and Ryan Roberts/2007

Interview conducted on April 4, 2007, specially for this volume. Printed by permission of authors.

Vanessa Guignery: You said in an interview[1] that you've always been obsessed with death. This is indeed obvious in your work: for example, the last part of *Staring at the Sun* is very much focused on this subject, and the theme appears even more frequently in your recent publications such as your translation of Daudet's *La Doulou*, the collection of short stories *The Lemon Table*, and now your new book *Nothing to Be Frightened Of.*[2] Do you know where this obsession comes from and why this has been a constant preoccupation throughout your life? Do you think it has become even more so in the last few years?

Julian Barnes: I know where this obsession comes from: it comes from not wanting to be dead and not liking the idea of being dead, and being frightened by the idea of not existing anymore for eternity. I don't really think of it as an obsession, but I realize it's an obsession compared to how other people don't think about the matter. It's something that I was aware of from the age of thirteen or fourteen, I suppose, and it's with me every day. Whether that amounts to an obsession or not, I don't know. Obsession is a comparative word. I know people whom *I* would call obsessed with death. I have a friend who became aware of his mortality at the age of four and spent his whole childhood shadowed by it and thinking about the idea of suicide: that is definitely an obsession with death, I'd say (he's now a philosopher). Mine in comparison is a sort of low-to-medium level, practical, sensible fearing, but in the context of what seems to me widespread ignorance of and resistance to thinking about it, it probably does strike some people as an obsession. It certainly comes into a lot of my books as you say—even into my first novel, *Metroland*.

1. Wild, Peter. "Interviews: Julian Barnes." *Bookmunch.co.uk*, 3 June 2002, http://www.bookmunch.co.uk/view.php?id=612.
2. London: Jonathan Cape, 2008; The first chapter was published as "The Past Conditional" in the New Yorker (25 December 2006/1 January 2007): 56–58, 60, 63–64.

I remember being very chuffed by a review of that book by Angela Carter who, amongst other things, said something like "this book has a very mature attitude to death." I remember thinking at the time, "Well, actually she's a bit mistaken." In the first part of the novel the main character discovers the fear and hatred of death as an adolescent; by the third part he is married and has a child and says that the fear of death has gone away. I thought this was a good example of the critic's autobiographical fallacy, because, boy was—and is—that was not the case with me. But of course, you take what praise you get. I think I probably am writing more about death in recent years but I don't know if it's particularly growing as an obsession: the tumour is staying the same size. The book I'm writing at the moment has a lot about death in it, but then I was always going to write such a book at some time. I always planned to write a book whose first line was "Let's get this death thing straight." That turned out not to be the actual first line, as you know, because you've seen the beginning of it.

Ryan Roberts: When you say "always," do you mean since you started knowing you were a writer? Was there a certain point at which you thought, "Ah, yes, this is something I want to address at some point"? Was there a particular novel that you were working on, for instance, where you thought, "This is something that I'm starting to develop, but I won't start on it here, I need to deal with it elsewhere"?
Barnes: No, I don't think it quite works like that. I don't think when you write a novel you think, "I've got a few off-cuts and leftovers or undeveloped themes which I'll come back to." In my experience, you can only think about the actual, precise book you're writing. Though there may be some other part of your brain which is squirreling away stuff. At some point—twenty years ago?—I wrote in a notebook the line, "Let's get this death thing straight." But I don't think when I wrote about death in *Metroland* or *Staring at the Sun* or *The Lemon Table* I was consciously thinking, "Well, there's still some unfinished business I shall have to attend to later."

Guignery: But you knew your newest book would deal with death.
Barnes: Oh yes.

Guignery: When did you have the idea for this book then, if you knew that you were going to write about that?
Barnes: I'm not quite sure. I think I might be able to answer this in about two years time! It's partly that when you're writing the book, exactly where it comes

from often disappears. When I was writing *Arthur & George*, I could—and would—say that it had its origin in reading about the Edalji case in a book about the Dreyfus affair.[3] What I had forgotten, and didn't remember until I had nearly finished the novel, was that it actually—or also—came out of an earlier interest. The awareness and possibility of being able to write such a book arose some years before. I planned—hoped—to write something fictional about the forgotten and hidden black population of Britain in the eighteenth and nineteenth centuries. I got some books and I read up a bit, and then nothing happened: nothing was sparked. But I had forgotten that. It goes into a piece of dead ground sometimes and it takes a while afterwards for you to see it and remember. You forget because the memory of that earlier beginning is no actual help in writing the book.

My new book starts with the death of my father and mother: he died fifteen years ago, she died ten years ago. I never thought that I'd write about them. Obviously those two deaths had an effect, a personal effect to begin with, obviously, but then a kind of literary effect. At a certain point, I thought, or I realized, or the idea realized itself, that this might be a way in to writing about death. I didn't want to write an essay addressing death in a head-on fashion—what, whither, why, whence—because I'm not that sort of writer. I sensed that the approach would have to be episodic, discursive, memoir-ish, flowing between essay and memoir. By the time I wrote the opening section, part of which appeared in the *New Yorker*, I certainly thought, "Yes, this is the book." I'm now doing what is probably a penultimate draft. When you're working in a form that you haven't worked in before you inevitably don't get it right the first time, or even the second or third,—draft, that is—so there has been quite a lot of radical reorganization. But that's normal, unless you choose to write in an entirely conventional form.

Guignery: Even in the excerpt that was published in the *New Yorker*?
Barnes: No, that section will remain pretty much the same. It had already been reworked a lot. Though I shall probably have to trim out some bits of *New Yorker* editing.

Roberts: Related to that *New Yorker* piece, you obviously deal with more than just death—you deal with religion.
Barnes: Yes, God is in it, as well. Or *not* God is in it.

---

3. The book was *The Anti-Semitic Moment: A Tour of France in 1898* by Pierre Birnbaum, which Julian Barnes reviewed for the *New York Review of Books* (10 April 2003): 32–34.

Roberts: We were interested in this topic, because in *Staring at the Sun* Gregory itemizes a list of possibilities about the nature and existence of God and eventually falls upon a question related to courage and faith, courage being one of the central themes of that novel. And the question, or the pairing of questions, is: Is it braver to believe in God? Is it braver not to believe in God? (pp. 167–68). Twenty years on, and in light of your new work, which view do you take?

Barnes: I don't think there is an overall answer. I think that it's brave to believe in God and to go around declaring it if you live in Stalinist Russia. And it's brave to be an atheist and to go around proclaiming it in certain Biblically-inclined states in America and other such fundamentalist places. That's a sort of external social courage. There's also the internal courage of maintaining the argument to yourself. Each makes up a certain percentage, the external and the internal. I don't know. It partly depends on your individual make-up. I fear death and I believe there is nothing after it, but does this necessarily make it courageous of me not to believe in God? I just think he doesn't exist and that's it. What do you think?

Roberts: What do *I* think? I agree that a lot of it is based on your particular situation, so, for instance, one of the things that you discuss in your piece is that you didn't necessarily have anything to rebel against.

Barnes: Yes. Yes.

Roberts: So, I think even within certain households—it's not necessarily by state or region of a country or the world, but even within a household dynamic—that questions exists: Is it brave to go against what your parents believe, or is it just a natural reaction to parental leanings of philosophy? Would it be just as brave to be liberal in a conservative household or conservative in a liberal household?

Barnes: Yes, well part of the answer to that is what the punishment or sanction is [laughs]. If you're going to get beaten up for saying you don't want to go to church, then it is perhaps brave. I grew up in a very liberal, with a small 'l', household. My mother was politically conservative. My father was more liberal, or liberal/conservative. In a way, and I think I used some of this in *Metroland*, it was almost irritating that there wasn't anything tougher or more oppressive or grotesque about them . . . They weren't overtly tolerant, but on the other hand they often didn't issue orders—most principles of behaviour had to be inferred by a process of osmosis. There weren't obvious things that we had to look up to, like the church, and at times it was quite hard to know what to rebel against. I'm trying to think of a typical moment of adolescent rebellion for you. Yes—I had a record player and I bought Bartók's string quartets. And I sort of knew that they would hate them, and I wasn't even sure I liked them myself, but I knew I ought to like them, because they were one of the peaks of modernism. And so one afternoon, while we were having tea, I brought the record player into the room and said something like, "I bought this record. How about listening to it?" And my father sat there doing the crossword and my mother knitting—this is a reconstruction in my mind, based on statistical probability—and they sat through it all and then didn't make any comment. And I thought, "This is absolutely hopeless. [laughs] What can I do?!"

Guignery: At the beginning of your new book, you refer to your family, your parents, your brother, yourself of course, and your grandparents—and it made me think about *Flaubert's Parrot* where you refer to Flaubert's belief in the insignificance of the writer's personality. Until now, you seemed to agree with Flaubert on that point and never revealed much about yourself. However, in this book, you disclose a few personal elements. Indeed, you just referred to the new form that you were writing in as a type of memoir. Does this reflect a change of direction or attitude on your part?

Barnes: Well, the spectrum goes from Flaubertian objectivity and suppression of the writer's personality and presence in the text, to the full-on autobiographical novel. My old friend Martin Amis is going around at the moment saying "fiction is the higher autobiography." I profoundly disagree with that. On the scale indicated I'm much closer to the Flaubertian end, for two reasons. The first is aesthetic, the second personal. I don't have a very exhibitionist nature anyway, and in any case my life, turned into fiction, wouldn't make very many pages, in my view anyway. But I admit that while I'm a Flaubertian in the broader sense and in principle, I'm an unsatisfactory or defective Flaubertian. In *A History of the World in 10½ Chapters*, I had a chapter called "Parenthesis" which is autobiographical, openly so. But I think my attitude towards using myself and bits of my life in my books is that I'm willing to, if I can get the right distance from it, so that using a bit of me or what I know or have experienced is in the same focus and perspective as if it came from your life—either of your lives. I don't think I have any desire to be confessional, but I think I'm quite willing to use my own life as an example of something. The reason I am starting in memoir mode in my new book is because I think that's the easiest way to lead the reader in to longer sections about death and God which they might otherwise not want to get into. Approach the general through the particular. Also, I think that my family's vestigial to nonexistent sense of religion over successive generations is typical of what has happened to religion in Britain, at least in terms of the indigenous British Anglicans. It's different for immigrant populations who tend to keep their religion longer and it's different for Catholics. But I live in a country where members of the official religion of the state, Anglicanism, produce fewer people going to church every Sunday than Catholics whom Anglicans have been persecuting—often very successfully—for centuries. And there are fewer practising Anglicans than Muslims now in this country. So I'm obviously talking about the traditional white English—also English rather than Scottish or Irish—remnant or whatever we call ourselves, we're a majority—majority remnant. I think that the way that religion has seeped away in our family can be used as an example.

Guignery: Even though some parts of the beginning of your book are quite ironical, would you say that it was also a way of paying a tribute to your parents?
Barnes: I'm not sure. I don't think that it's a tribute that they would want or like. Especially some of the late pages which you haven't yet read.

Guignery: But I found it very touching at the same time, especially the funerals. And knowing that it is indeed your own story made it all the more touching to me.
Barnes: I did love my father and I had a very exasperated and exasperating relationship with my mother, but there were parts of my mother, especially her dying, which I admired. I'm very glad that it does move you because—well, you only have two parents, and even if you don't get on with one of them, they only die once. Even so, you want to describe what it's actually like when someone dies and how it affects you and stuff like that. What the particularities of death are. Like many other things, dying and death and grief do not work in the way that we assume they do, let alone as we've been told they do.

I remember going to the funeral of a good friend of mine some years ago. And the thing that was on my mind for almost the entire service, was trying to work out exactly when the church was built! It was Classical Revival so I was probably guessing between 1810 and 1820 or something like that. And I told my wife, and when we came back, I checked in Pevsner, and I was so happy I got it within at about two years. And there was my friend who had died! These things don't necessarily work the way we want or expect them to, and we shouldn't pretend that they do.

Roberts: You made reference to the half chapter in *History of the World*, "Parenthesis," which deals both with history and elements of truth, but also with love.

Love seems to be a central theme throughout your work, but it's not really been discussed in any of your interviews. Themes such as death and history and truth all get dealt with, but what is it about love that you find particularly compelling as a subject?

Barnes: I think there are two reasons why there isn't much in previous interviews about love: either people didn't want to ask about it or, if they did, I didn't want to answer. So this is going to be one of my shorter replies. It seems to me blindingly obvious that all novelists ought to write about love because it's what most people are most intensely interested in for at least some part of their lives. And it defines them, at the time and thereafter. So I don't think there is any problem about why I, or any writer, or any reader, should be interested in it. I don't know whether I write about it more or less than other contemporary novelists. I simply don't do the sums. I think the difficulty of talking about love, though, is that you might end up sounding like an advice center. And I don't believe a novelist is an advice center in any shape or form. Every so often, I used to be rung up by German *Vogue* who would say, "We would like you to write a piece about love." And I'd say, "No." And they'd ring me a month later and say, more imploringly, "We would like you to write a piece about looooooove." And I'd say, "Nope, sorry." As soon as you start making any general remarks outside the context of a novel, I think you risk sounding either pompous or smug or like an advice columnist in a magazine. So I think I'll probably *never* answer another question about love [smiles].

Roberts: I'm glad to have been the one to ask. Is that part of the approach in *Talking It Over* and *Love, etc,* to provide different angles, different views on love—Oliver's and Stuart's—in each? You dealt with love more directly in *History of the World* in "Parenthesis," but then perhaps you explored multiple perspectives in these later novels because it's such a complex issue. Instead of coming out as, "this is the one view on love," we sort of get the sense, especially through *Talking It Over* and *Love, etc,* that there is more . . .

Barnes: I think love and how we talk about it and remember it does focus the complete disparity of viewpoints, opinions, and memories that people have about shared situations. The epigraph in *Talking It Over* is "He lies like an eyewitness," and I think one of the reasons that love is such a rich subject is that it is where, more than any other area of life, the participants' memories differ. There is a newspaper color magazine article every week in which they have a couple who have broken up some years ago and they get each to describe their past relationship and how it worked and how it didn't work. And the disparity between the two examples is extraordinary. They mention things that the other partner hasn't been aware of at all—often to a mind-boggling extent. But it absolutely rings true.

I was on a German book tour a few months ago and I was being interviewed by a very tall, handsome German woman. And I was developing this line. "I don't know if it's the same in Germany," I said, "but it seems to me that very often when a couple break up they seem to have very different explanations of what happened." And before I could go on she said, "YES! IT'S JUST LIKE THAT!! [pounds the arm of his chair] IT'S JUST LIKE THAT!!" [laughs]. "Oh, so it is just the same . . ."

Guignery: It was interesting that you said you wouldn't answer a question about love, because I remember from the "Parenthesis" chapter in *A History of the World in 10½ Chapters* that at one point the narrator (or maybe you) writes, ". . . we mustn't become sentimental" (233). This is something I find quite often in your work—that is, sometimes you resort to irony or humor or comedy, perhaps to avoid sentimentalism or to avoid too much pathos. Is sentimentality something you're trying to avoid?

Barnes: No. I don't think I'm entirely against sentimentality, and what I mean by that I'll come to in a moment. But I don't feel that is something I might fall into myself. There's a fairly small chance of my becoming sentimental in my writing or in my person. I don't think I have a sentimental side; I'm suspicious of sentimentality. In my experience, sentimentality often goes with cruelty. People who are cruel are often sentimental. By "sentimental" I mean "falsely emotional," I mean "putting it on," "avoiding things that you ought to be emotional about, or that real people are emotional about, and being emotional about trivial or false things." But there is a form of sentimentality which I applaud. Alain-Fournier, writing to his friend Jacques Rivière about a hundred years ago, said, "Sentimentality is when it doesn't come off—when it does, you get a true expression of life's sorrow." I'm in favor of that kind of sentimentality.

Guignery: I was also thinking of scenes involving death—funerals, for example. In your new book, when you describe your mother's funeral, there is a lot of comedy, and I was smiling or even laughing while I was reading it. Also, for example, in the introduction to *Something to Declare*, you explain that you carried the ashes of your parents . . . and accidentally dropped them. So I realized that when there is a rather serious subject, such as death, you tend to deflate the pathos by introducing something comic. I'm not saying it's systematic of course.

Barnes: No, it's not systematic, but I think that's my sensibility and that's how I see life. It's also a very strong strand of British literature, from Shakespeare on-wards. That's why the French disliked and misunderstood Shakespeare for so long because they found that he didn't stay serious about serious subjects: he had grave diggers digging up old skulls and making jokes in what was supposed to be a tragedy, and that wasn't acceptable. But fortunately French literature eventually caught up with British literature in that respect. Flaubert is of course the arch ex-amplar of the mixture of high and low, and the mixture of genres, and the mix-ture of tones all in the same moment.

Guignery: Talking of Flaubert . . .
Barnes: Yes. Good. Now I'm happy.

Guignery: In *Flaubert's Parrot*, you refer to George Sand's letter to Gustave Flau-bert in which she says, " 'You produce desolation and I produce consolation' " (15, 136). As a novelist, would you situate yourself on the side of desolation or conso-lation?
Barnes: And he replies: "I cannot change my eyes." I would definitely situate my-self on desolation if that's the choice, but I would maintain that writing what George Sand would consider desolating literature is and can be consoling. De-scribing things as they are rather than as we would like them to be can have a consoling effect. Bleak truths can be purging. The other Flaubert quote which I mustn't use too many times in my new book, is: "One must be equal to one's des-tiny, that's to say impassive like it. By dint of saying 'That is so! That is so!' And of gazing down into the black pit at one's feet, one remains calm." We remain calm and we also remain sensible, not mad.

Roberts: You've mentioned that you've made changes to your new work, or that the penultimate draft that you're working on may not be the exact draft or the finished draft. In the past you've mentioned, at least to me, that with *Metroland* you edited almost to the point of penalty on the proofs.
Barnes: I did, yes. I had to pay them some money. Not much, but a small punish-ment for being obsessional.

Roberts: You edit up until it's published, but how much editing do you do post-published for new printings or editions? When you think of someone like John Updike, he's continually reevaluating the status of a finished work and chang-ing lines here and there. How do you feel about that? Once a work is published, do you go back and make changes for other drafts?
Barnes: I think once it's come out in a book I haven't changed anything. I've

just sort of thought, let it be there. Though occasionally when I've had mistakes pointed out I then ask the publisher to change them—between the hardback and the paperback.

Roberts: Technical mistakes?
Barnes: Yes, technical mistakes. Not, if someone said, "I don't like this sentence." Then I would tell them to sod off.

Roberts: Well, for instance, Geoffrey Braithwaite suggests in *Flaubert's Parrot* that the author, you, of *Metroland* should change the error about Flaubert's *Madame Bovary*.[4] But you haven't gone back to make that change.
Barnes: No. I suppose I thought it was rather cute to leave it in. But I remember when I was writing a column for the *New Review* and John Fowles published a new version of *The Magus* in which he had gone through the novel and changed lots of things. So I went through sort of tabulating all the changes and it was stuff like, you know, he took the 2:35 from the Gare de Lyon instead of the 3:35, because perhaps some reader had written to him enclosing a xerox of an old timetable. And the changes seemed to me pretty trivial for the most part. And I didn't—and don't—think the amount of time spent doing that is worth it. On the other hand, well, there are two on-the-other-hands. One is that I did intend to do a new edition of *Flaubert's Parrot*, once all the maestro's correspondence had finally come out—I thought there would be more material I could introduce. But I've gone off that idea completely now, and I think: that's the book I wrote then and that's what my third novel is and will remain.

Guignery: When did you have this idea?
Barnes: At the time of writing it. I thought maybe *Flaubert's Parrot* is a work in progress because only half of the correspondence had been published and there was a lot more stuff to come out, and if I read all the later letters and then I discovered there were lots about other animals I could put it in . . . Then it's partly that I haven't got that sort of time on my hands, and partly it's sort of lost. That was the book then and that's where I was then and that's how I wrote it then, and

4. In *Metroland,* the narrator rehearses to himself the best way to kiss a girl without being rebuffed: "With a slow, sensual, irresistible strength, draw her gradually towards you while gazing into her eyes as if you had just been given a copy of the first, suppressed edition of *Madame Bovary*" (93). In *Flaubert's Parrot,* Geoffrey Braithwaite remarks: "The only trouble is, there's no such thing as a 'first, suppressed edition of *Madame Bovary*'. [. . .] I expect the young novelist (it seems unfair to give his name) was thinking of the 'first, suppressed edition' of *Les Fleurs du mal.* No doubt he'll get it right in time for his second edition; if there is one" (78).

if I was going to do it now, it would be different anyway. The second proviso is things like . . . I think Updike was quite right to edit, reedit *The Rabbit Quartet* as a single volume because he didn't start off writing the books thinking they were going to be a quartet. So it made perfect sense. If I write a third volume in the *Talking It Over* sequence and the three books become a single volume, I would probably edit them down a bit. For a start, if you're reading continuously you don't need the necessary updatings the start of volumes two and three would necessarily contain.

Roberts: And how likely is that?
Barnes: It's moderately likely. I found a very good new word for Oliver the other day while doing the crossword. Have you ever heard of the word "trilemma"? It's a dilemma with three horns. It's wonderful, and it's pure Oliver. Whenever I come across things like that I think, "Oh, yes. Oliver can use that. I'll make a note of it." I think I might well do so, yes. Of course, the question of reediting the text is different when it comes to journalistic work. Then it has to be changed and corrected. I don't think you should republish journalism saying, "This is what I thought then. Isn't it fascinating?" if you have completely changed your mind.

Guignery: So you edited, for example, the pieces in *Something to Declare*.
Barnes: Yes. You've got to edit them, not least because you repeat yourself if you do a lot of journalism as I do. You're bound to repeat yourself, or half-repeat yourself. So it's just courtesy to the reader to take out those repetitions.

Guignery: You recently wrote a new ending to *Madame Bovary* in which Emma is saved, called "The Rebuke."[5] I was very impressed by the voice that you created, which reminded me of the intimate voice of Louise Colet in *Flaubert's Parrot*. Was that deliberate? Did you have that in mind when you wrote that piece—recreating that voice?
Barnes: No. There are bound to be similarities in that I was trying to do a French woman's voice of the mid-nineteenth century and render it in a sort of English which has remnants of the French behind it. So I was undoubtedly using the same technique, and I probably would have done the same thing with Louise Colet: I would have read her mementos and such letters as survive, and I would

5. "The Rebuke" was broadcast on BBC Radio 4 on 22 September 2006, as part of a series called *Madame Bovary Speaks*. Five different writers were asked to propose fifteen-minute monologues to celebrate the 150th anniversary of the first episode of *Madame Bovary*'s serial publication. "The Rebuke" was read by Pat Kavanagh, Julian Barnes's wife and literary agent.

have tried to use correct or plausible intonations or phrasing and so on. With "The Rebuke," I would have reread some of the key Emma parts of the novel and tried to find a voice—the voice of an Emma who didn't kill herself and was looking back some years later. But, of course, since some people think that Emma Bovary was based on Louise Colet, I shouldn't be too offended if you thought the voices sounded similar.

Guignery: How did you feel when you were writing that piece? Did you feel that you were substituting yourself for Flaubert?
Barnes: I don't think I was substituting myself for Flaubert. It's one of those commissions where an editor—in this case, in BBC radio—says: "It's the 150th anniversary of *Madame Bovary* and we're going to ask five writers to write pieces about *Madame Bovary* in one way or another." First you think: "Well, which one shall I do?" Because there are three Madame Bovarys in the book, which we forget. And then you think: "What's my take on it?" In a way it was more of a tribute to Flaubert that I didn't try and modify an existing episode from the book, but that I did something subversive. If I had tried to fill in a little gap in the book or something and try to narrate it Flaubertianly, I expect I would have failed. I also started from the consideration that in almost all the great nineteenth-century novels of adultery, the woman has to die. It's true that in the original case, the little provincial anecdote that Flaubert based it on, she did indeed take poison and die. But there are lots of adulterous women in France in the nineteenth century who *didn't* die! And I was thinking: "Well, what if she didn't?" Then there is the question of: "Is this the male author punishing the transgressing female?" It's a hard one to answer, because half the time, male authors probably thoroughly approved of transgressing females. Were they inadvertently or subconsciously punishing them? Or would they rely on the defense of truth to life: "This is what really happened to the woman I based my tale on." Or they would just say: "I'm sorry, but it's a really good ending. I'm sorry, it's just more exciting this way." In the case of my alternative ending: well, since I like—and often write—novels whose endings are more open, I thought it wouldn't do any harm to let her survive.

Roberts: Just prior to this, we were talking about the process of writing fiction, and you have previously talked about the writing of essays. We are interested, in relation to your essay collections *Letters from London* and *Something to Declare*, that you compiled the index for both volumes. Why did you decide to undertake the indexing, especially in the manner that you did. As an index needs to be functional, how did you approach that as a writer of fiction?

Barnes: I think I decided to do it because I didn't trust a professional indexer to identify the important things in the book. I wanted it to be more thematic, as well. And then once I decided to do it myself, I thought I might as well have some fun as well. So I had entries for food and sex and stuff like that. I wanted the reader to be able to wander around in the index and look up stuff you wouldn't normally find there. Though I did want it also to be a basic, accurate index of every important name. There was also plain curiosity about what it was like to do an index. So I just got a stack of cards, and then it was a question of learning on the job, really. And it was all handwritten.

Roberts: And there have been, I believe, two articles in an indexing journal about your work.[6] So it has been viewed as something unique. How does that feel? I mean, you normally have people writing pieces about your fiction, but you suddenly have these pieces written about an index.

Barnes: Very mild satisfaction, I could say. Nothing stronger than that, Ryan [laughs].

Roberts: Nothing stronger . . . See, the librarian in me is very interested in this.

Barnes: No, I did enter myself for some indexer's medal and they rang me up and they said, "Would you like to come along to the ceremony?" And I said, nervously, "Do you mean I've won?" And they said, "Oh, no. You haven't won!" [laughs] And I said, "No. I'm afraid in that case I happen to be unavailable." Pathetic.

Guignery: Talking about the essays, could you tell us more about the process of writing essays? Do you choose the topics that you want to write about? And how do you choose them? I'm not necessarily talking about *Letters from London*, because we know about that process, but, rather, long pieces that you write on various subjects—for example your latest piece about the relations between France and England.[7]

Barnes: It's probably about fifty-fifty. That last one, the *New York Review of Books* rang me up, and I thought I couldn't not do it because it was such a direct

6. Hazel K. Bell, "An Index for Thalia." *The Indexer* 22.3 (April 2001): 147–48; Hazel K. Bell, "Something to Indicate." *The Indexer* 23.2 (October 2002): 102–3.

7. "The Odd Couple." Rev. of *That Sweet Enemy: The French and the British from the Sun King to the Present*, by Robert and Isabelle Tombs. *New York Review of Books* 54.5 (29 March 2007).

mail shot to me. But often I'll propose things, especially to the *Guardian* which is my natural journalistic home in Britain. So I suggested to them "Kipling and France,"[8] or the piece about Zola that I did recently.[9] Most of the *Guardian* pieces I've proposed, I think. And obviously the start of my new book I proposed to the *New Yorker*—No, that's actually not the case. I read it in public at the *New Yorker* Festival, and afterwards they said: "Can we print it?" and I said yes. That's one of the luxuries of being well enough known for different magazines to want your stuff. But I think it's important to come up with your own ideas, because otherwise you'll end up being typecast. Not that you can't typecast yourself, of course. Some editors are creative and some are . . . more repetitive. I know that whenever a new book about Flaubert comes out, you're going to get about twelve requests for it, and sometimes my heart sinks and I'll pass, though even after all these years I find there's some still to be said. So I've already put in to review the last volume of Flaubert's *Correspondence* which comes out, I think, in the autumn. When I reviewed the penultimate volume for the *Times Literary Supplement*, I got a review slip asking, "Could we have a million words, please?" This time they've formally asked for only a hundred thousand, so I think my career is going into a decline.

Guignery: Is it the same for reviews of books? Do you sometimes choose? Would you say, "I'd like to review that book," or do editors ask you in advance if you would like to review such and such a book?
Barnes: Yes, they do. Sometimes they go through the publishers' catalogues in advance and they say: "There's a book coming out about *The Wreck of the Medusa*, would you like to review it?" And you say: "Oh, God!" Maybe you don't quite say that, but you think, "I had all this in my head in 1988 and I'm not sure I really want to go back there." And then someone will ring up and say: "They've just reissued the original rules of the Football Association," and you think, "Oh, that's much more like it!"

Guignery: How do you feel when you write essays? Are they a relief from the novels? For example, would you write a novel and an essay at the same time?
Barnes: No, it's increasingly difficult to do both at the same time. I could when I was younger. I did that piece about the Franco-British relations at a point when I

8. "Soul Brothers." *Guardian*, 5 November 2005.
9. "Blood and Nerves." *Guardian*, 25 November 2006.

needed a break from the book I'm working on at the moment. I took three weeks off—that's how long the reading and writing and researching of such a piece takes. It is often more than a distraction. When I was writing the "Letters from London" for the *New Yorker*, I found that it did interfere quantifiably with my fiction writing. Over those five years I actually produced far less than I would normally have wanted to do.

Roberts: Speaking of your own work, I should preface this by saying this is certainly by no means a question about Dan Kavanagh, but more about your pseudonym use in general. It's fairly well known that you've written as Edward Pygge and restaurant reviews as Basil Seal, but you've also written in the past under a series of other names. Even to one point where a certain Henry Root had dinner with Julian Barnes, Dan Kavanagh, and Basil Seal.
Barnes: I wasn't Henry Root. He was someone else's pseudonym.

Roberts: No, I know. But that sort of mixture of . . .
Barnes: Yes. Yes.

Roberts: Most of these were published in the mid to late 1970s or early 1980s. What led you to use so many pseudonyms during this particular time period?
Barnes: A mixture of reasons. The Edward Pygge name was a tradition of the *Review* and the *New Review*, so he was actually a pseudonym that I inherited. And it was an honor not granted to many people to be Edward Pygge. And you had to write in a certain style to be Edward Pygge. In this certain acerbic and un-illusioned style about literary matters. Basil Seal I used because I was a restaurant critic and you didn't want them to know who you were. I think it was a condition of taking the job somehow. I think I also made a mistake with Basil Seal, because I chose the wrong character. Basil Seal is, as you know, an Evelyn Waugh character, but I thought that he was the man who was always available for dinner. There's a character in one of the novels, in more than one of the novels, who they always ring up when there's a dinner party and they're short of someone. He has a frightful mother. And they always ring him up, and he's always free and he comes on. So I thought this was the ideal guy to have as a restaurant critic, because he always needs a meal. But I think it's someone else—is he called John Beaver?

The other pseudonyms, which are more trivial, or less often used, were simply because of my output at the time. If I was writing the *New Statesman* television column, I couldn't have another piece in the same issue under the same name. So if I was doing fiction roundup or something like that, I simply used a pseudonym. I quite liked using one, there was something liberating about it. Also, I suppose, you could be nasty about someone without them knowing it was you. That is the morally squalid side of pseudonymity.

Roberts: Was it a function of writing for journalism? An extension of that time? Because at a certain point you stopped using them.
Barnes: I stopped doing so much, I suppose.

Guignery: So you don't have pseudonyms now?
Barnes: Ian McEwan is one of my pseudonyms . . . [laughs].

Roberts: One of the things related to this that I'm curious about is that some of your pseudonyms you made up, like Dan Kavanagh. Some of them are characters—so you've mentioned Basil Seal, but also Marion Lloyd, one of your own characters in *Metroland*.
Barnes: Yes, that's right. She was.

Roberts: But then also, in the case of Lawrence Beesley, you used him as a character in *History of the World* and also wrote under his name for several book reviews in the *Oxford Mail* . . .
Barnes: Yes. He really existed.

Roberts: He really existed, although you later gave him an illegitimate son named Paddy Beesley for two reviews in the *New Statesman*.[10]
Barnes: He was some rogue.

Roberts: So, in the case of Lawrence Beesley, why pick someone real to use as a pseudonym? This was at a time prior to publishing your first novel—the *Oxford Mail* fiction reviews were published in the mid-1970s—so why choose someone who actually existed? What was it about Lawrence that made you want to use him?
Barnes: Oh, I didn't like him for reasons I won't go into and . . . I think he was almost certainly dead by then, and I just wanted to be retrospectively cheeky, perhaps. And I thought it was a rather un-guessable pseudonym. I don't think there was a very complicated reason, though I may have made it sound as if there was.

10. Beesley, Paddy. "Be Bad." *New Statesman* (25 March 1977): 407; "Just Like Us." *New Statesman* (4 February 1977): 163.

Roberts: Whereas Marion Lloyd in that particular instance should have been a guessable pseudonym, because the letters were published at a time that *Metroland* was out.[11]

Barnes: I think you might exaggerate the number of readers my first novel had. It was a pretty safe pseudonym. Or maybe I wanted to be found out? This was my persecution of David Caute. I worked for him as deputy literary editor on the *New Statesman*, and—how can I put it?—we were never going to be best friends. Marion Lloyd was the secretary of the Agnès Varda Women's Cooperative. Yes, I was very pleased with that. I wrote this letter, because he'd written a rather shocking diary paragraph which seemed a bit too over-excited about pseudo-necrophilia in some film or other. So I wrote a stern reproof to the magazine as Marion Lloyd. And he thought it was a completely genuine letter and that a gang of castrating feminists were out to get him. Did I tell you the sequel? Francis Wheen, who was then working on the *Statesman*, told me that Caute was so alarmed that he changed his way of going home from the office. He'd come out, look around furtively, then sort of bolt down the side alley, turn left and right, and take a different way. I thought that was a great success. I'm very proud of that. Who says that writing doesn't have an effect?

Guignery: You are obviously interested in other artistic forms apart from literature. You often write long essays on painters for the magazine *Modern Painters* or reviews of books devoted to painters (Magritte, Manet, Odilon Redon, Claes Oldenburg, Degas, Bonnard, Vuillard). Two of your short stories focus on composers: Leonard Verity in "Interference" (*Cross Channel*) is based on Frederick Delius; the composer in "The Silence" (*The Lemon Table*) is based on Jean Sibelius. To what extent do other artistic forms influence your fictional writing?

Barnes: Painting and music are the two art forms that mean the most to me, although I go to the theatre and the cinema, and things like that. But those are the forms that, I think, move me the most deeply. I can't think of any way in which painting has had a specific influence on my work—I mean, apart from the question of content. I think it's possible that I sometimes think of narrative in a comparable way to musical narrative but if so, it will be at a pretty subconscious level.

---

11. Marion Lloyd, from the Agnès Varda Women's Collective, published two letters in the *New Statesman*, in which she reacted against David Caute's review of the film *Bad Timing*. Lloyd, Marion. "Literary Delicacy." *New Statesman* (9 May 1980): 710; "A Taste of Honey." *New Statesman* (13 June 1980): 901.

Flaubert used to talk about the colors of the books he wrote. I think he said that *Madame Bovary* was going to be the color of mold or something like that. I often have a sense of the undercurrent, the pulse, and the movement of the section that I am writing. Whether that's influenced by what I know and like about music or whether that's just something that does happen and ought to happen in narrative prose anyway, I can't really answer. Music being the most abstract and the furthest from the at times banal particularity and relatedness of fiction, it would be a great mistake to try and write a piece of prose deliberately structured in the way that a piece of classical music was structured. I know that that wouldn't work. Very early on, I tried to write a short story which was the equivalent of a chess game and each move was numbered as a chess game is. It was a series of exchanges between probably a man and a woman and it ended in checkmate. I thought it was quite a cute idea but when I actually wrote it, it just looked so artificial.

Guignery: It could have been a B. S. Johnson idea.

Barnes: It could have been a B. S. Johnson idea, that's true. I've never read Anthony Burgess's *Napoleon Symphony*, but I think he said that it was structured like a symphony. But he told so many grandiloquent lies this it might not have been the case.

Roberts: You've placed your archive with the Harry Ransom Center in Austin, Texas, one of the premier institutions for literary manuscripts. What led to this decision and what do you make of the occasional calls, by Andrew Motion and others, for the British government to support the retention of manuscripts within the country?

Barnes: From the beginning I was a complete squirreler away of everything I wrote, of every draft, and I have a collecting nature to me, I suppose, and also I suppose you're very self-absorbed when you start out as a writer. Anyway, I just had every draft of every book and most articles I had written. I used to keep them in a fairly secure place in the house, and after a while I no longer looked at them, when I went past, with any interest. And I thought, "Oh, it's probably time to get rid of them." You know, I didn't need the money. On the other hand, I thought it would be too depressing to think, "If I'm poor when I'm old, I could sell them," because if you're poor when you're old and you're a writer, that means no one wants your books. And if no one wants your books, no one's going to want your archive either, QED. So I thought that's a pretty stupid way of thinking. And so I wondered who I could sell them to—though it was more a question of where they would have a safe, long-term home. I went into the possibility of selling them to the British Library, but the conditions were such that they were extremely discouraging.

I support Andrew's calls for the government to make it easier for British writers to sell their archives to the British Library. One of the key moments in the whole history of it was the case of the Commissioners of Inland Revenue against John Wain, or rather, the estate of John Wain, who was a novelist famous in the '50s and '60s. At the time John Wain died, traditionally all working papers were regarded as a chattels. They were not regarded as something on which you paid income tax. They were something that you owned and, therefore, if you sold them, you paid, I can't remember what the percentage was—something like 20 or 25 percent. As a result of the case of the Commissioners of Inland Revenue against John Wain, which the Wain estate didn't fight as hard as it ought to—or perhaps, didn't have the funds to do so—all writers' papers are now taxed as income. So whoever you sell the papers to in your lifetime, you pay, if you're paying top-rate tax, which most writers will be if they're going to sell their papers, is 40 percent. So that's the starting point. You're going to lose 40 percent of any sum you make. Secondly, in the case of selling them to Britain, you'd also have to pay VAT, which is 17.5 percent on the top, so you're then losing 57.5 percent. (Oh, and you will probably sell through an expert in manuscripts, so count on losing another 5–10 percent on top of that). Thirdly, the British Library, when consulted, said that they were only interested in a one-time purchase, i.e. they would only buy for a set amount of money not just my current archive but all the papers that I would produce in the future, as well. Fourthly, there was a problem anyway in that the British Library is not meant to buy recent literary papers—papers have to be at least twenty years old for them to buy, so they would have to be bending the rules for most of my archive. And fifthly, they would have to get a grant from the Heritage Lottery Foundation, and, therefore, the amount of money paid would have to be made public, with all the usual journalistic repercussions.

Now, all those conditions were mighty discouraging . . . plus, on top of all those, the British Library said, "Well, actually, anyway, we haven't got any money this year. So would you like to come back to us next year?" So I said to the expert who was acting for me, "Just see if Texas is interested." And within a week they said, "Yeah, we'll come and see them and this is what we'll pay."

It wasn't, as I said, finally about money, though if you're going to lose 60 percent immediately, then only losing 40 percent immediately is rather more attractive. Also, I have no connection with the British Library. I've never worked there. I don't know anyone there. Oddly enough, I had been to Texas. I had had an acquaintance there who had shown us around, Kathy Henderson, and I sort of thought, "Oh, I rather like this." And then there was a final reason which came in very late—actually, after I'd made the sale, so it was a sort of posthumous justification. I thought, "If any horrible little journalist wants to go and look at my diaries or my working notes and find something unpleasant to write a short smirky little para about, they won't just be able to pop down to the British Library. They'll have to go all the way to Texas, so that will discourage the bastards" [smiling]. Yes, I thought that.

Apart from the fact that the law was changed when John Wain died, there is a general lack of interest and enthusiasm in government circles for this sort of thing. I mean, I feel sorry for the British Library. They would be able to get money much more easily for Mrs. Thatcher's papers than Ian McEwan's papers, sadly. But then we do live under a very philistine government, as we usually do in this country.

Roberts: The Harry Ransom Center is very good about providing support for scholarship, as well, as far as scholarships for people interested in their archives. Vanessa and I have both received funds to go and work with your archive. As your papers are now at an institution that encourages that type of scholarship, and as there have been several critical studies of your work published in recent years . . .
Barnes: Yes, you tell me so.

Roberts: Vanessa's among them. And as this interview is intended as the last interview in a collection of interviews . . . All of this leads to this question of scholarship. Now, I know you've stated previously that academics, or at least literary theory, does not influence your approach to writing, but literary scholarship, nonetheless, plays a role in the creation of a reputation, which contributes to the longevity of an author's work through continued study, etc. So how do you view such academic attempts to address your work?
Barnes: With sort of benign indifference, I think would be the answer. I mean, Vanessa quite understands that I'm not going to read what she writes about me. Not that I don't think it wouldn't be interesting and true, but that I don't want to know the stuff that people say about my work. I don't read reviews any more. That's partly self-protection, but I think even more would I not want to read an academic study of my work. Not because I'd expect it to be unsympathetic, but

because I don't want to think of other people thinking in broader terms about my work. Because it doesn't help me write the next book. As I said earlier, I only ever write one book at a time, so I rarely think in terms of revisiting a theme I've visited before, or how this ties in with that from many years ago. The concentration on the single item in front of you is absolute. And so I think it would not help to read an article or a book in which this novel is related to that novel or which specifies these recurrent themes in Barnes's work and stuff like that.

I remember reading a very sympathetic review by the distinguished academic Michael Wood—it was early on, I think it was of *Flaubert's Parrot*—and he said something like, "There are strong undercurrents of marital unease running through Barnes's books," or something like that [laughs]. And it was part of a sympathetic description of my work. But thereafter I thought, "Hang on. [laughs] Am I writing another example of marital unrest?" or whatever his phrase was. And so I don't want the self-consciousness that that would bring. There's enough necessary self-consciousness about the act of writing already. I think my job is done by giving them the pleasure of my book. Or the pain of my book, whichever way it falls. And I'm not interested, except in a very, very distant way in what happens after I'm dead. I think the whole thing is chance. Not chance. Some of it is talent. But if you start second-guessing what's going to happen to your reputation or your readership after you're dead, that's another enormous distraction from concentrating on the book you're meant to be writing.

Roberts: So it's best to take up the line of "Let the books be enough."
Barnes: Well, I don't deny an interest in all the stuff that surrounds it. I read interviews with other writers. I read biographies of writers. But I think that the work should stand by itself and I can't think of any biography that I've read that has actually made me understand the work better. My friend the biographer Hermione Lee runs a course in what she calls "Life Writing." I told her that I hated the phrase "life writing." And she said, "Well I helped invent it, so you'd better like it." I've promised to go and talk to her students in a year or two. And I had said I was going to call my talk, "Some of My Best Friends Are Biographers." And that it was going to be an attack on biography. And now I'm going to call it, "Some of My Best Friends Are Life Writers."

I mean, if you ask the question the other way round . . . We don't know very much about Shakespeare. We know as much as we would know about any other successful playwright of the time. Imagine that some packet of material turned up in an attic in Stratford-upon-Avon which was either an early biography or memoir written by Shakespeare. And suppose we found that he had a very over-powering father which might have led him to have Oedipal problems, or perhaps a stepfather like Claudius. Or that he had a terrible wife like Kate in *The Taming of the Shrew*, or . . . and so on and so on and so on. If we put it that way round, while these biographical revelations may sentimentally confirm our reading of the play, none of them is going to make our understanding any better, any deeper. They're just going to be a pleasant sidebar, a pleasant parenthesis, it seems to me. This doesn't mean I don't read biographies of Flaubert, Larkin, and so on. I'm reading Claire Tomalin's Hardy biography which rightfully says that his poetry is his great work and is very much on the side of the poetry which I love. But I didn't come away with any greater understanding of any of the poems that are quoted or referred to in the book.

Guignery: Linked to that, what do you think of the interview we're doing now or other interviews you gave in the past? Do you think they can be a useful supplement to your work? In recent years writers like you have become more and more publicized: you have to go on promoting tours and go through many interviews. How do you feel in relation to that genre?

Barnes: I would warn anyone against taking an interview with a writer, however interesting and seemingly truthful, as a surer guide to the author's intentions than the book itself. There are wonderful interviews. A lot of those *Paris Review* interviews are fantastically serious, scholarly, interesting, colorful, and, at best, give you a vivid sense of the person being interviewed. It's more than just an enjoyable aside. You have another sense of the writer, I suppose. You have a sense of their own personality, their literary personality. I remember years ago very much enjoying the profile of Evelyn Waugh in the *Paris Review*, where the interviewer says: "What do you think of Edmund Wilson's view of such and such a book of yours?" And, Waugh, pretending ignorance, says: "Is he an American?" and the chap says, "Yes, Mr. Wilson is an American," and Waugh, deliberately baiting future readers of the interview, says, "Oh, I don't think they have anything interesting to say, do you?" So rude, and a fantastically good example of what Evelyn Waugh was like, though entirely—or largely—separate from the pleasure that his books give. Nowadays, given the amount writers are interviewed, they inevitably either say the same thing time and time again so they no longer know whether they believe it or not, but it will do for the occasion, or they start saying different things just out of boredom. I'm sure there are some writers like that. I try to answer the questions as accurately as possible, but it's not always the best way to pass the time to end up saying what you've said before.

Roberts: You mentioned, in relation to your papers, that you were a hoarder and a collector. You've written in the past about book collecting and the issue of "completeness."[12] We understand one of your current collecting interests involves photographs of writers. What draws you to photography? How do you find it different from more traditional forms of collecting?

Barnes: I collected stamps when I was a child. I think the only things I've collected, really, are stamps and then first editions and, nowadays, photographs of writers, composers, and painters I am interested in. I think I stopped being a fanatical collector of first editions at the point when I started to think of myself as a writer (that's to say, after publishing two or three books), and I became slightly less fetishistic about it, the mystique of it all. But to answer the main question, I think it started by seeing for sale a Nadar photograph of George Sand. It's a great photograph, which I had seen reproduced before. It's astonishing how quickly the genre of photography approached, if not perfection, certainly adulthood as an art form and as a recording form, so soon after it was invented. And how wonderful those photographs from the 1850s and 1860s, and so on, are. And I wondered if Flaubert had looked on this photograph of one of his great friends. And so I found it much more direct and touching than I would have done a painting or lithograph of George Sand.

I know about the comparison, because I, for a long time, was looking for a photograph of Sibelius and I couldn't find one. And someone offered me a large pastel drawing of him. I bought it, but there was always something unsatisfactory about it. I put it up on my wall at regular intervals, moved it around, but never felt it was quite right. Then I came across a photograph of Sibelius, an amazing image, shining bald head, in which he looks a bit like Mussolini—also frowning, tremendous frown lines—and signed by him to a Swedish woman. And the directness of the presence was a hundred times stronger than that of a perfectly decent portrait drawing. I think that if we're talking about conveying the essence of the person, photography is often more successful than painting. Even though there are still great portraits being painted—Freud, say, or early Hockney. So it's both a sort of ancestor worship, and a way of saying: these are my friends and companions. I was incredibly pissed off to miss an auction in Paris a couple of weeks ago where they sold about one hundred fifty lots of which I would have wanted to bid on forty had I known it was happening.

---

12. Julian Barnes. "Cool, Calm and Collecting." *Sunday Times* (23 June 1996): 6–7; "Introduction." *Thirty-Seventh Antiquarian Book Fair.* London: Antiquarian Booksellers Association, 1996. 5–7; "Julian Barnes on Books." *Slightly Soiled* 3/4 (December 1986): 15–16.

I have a slot immediately outside this room where there is always a photograph up, and I change it around at regular intervals, according to whom I want up there. And it's my equivalent of having family photographs, I suppose. I don't have family photographs on display, because I don't have that sort of family or that sort of piety.

Guignery: Coming back to Flaubert, I'd like to know whether your appreciation of Flaubert has evolved since *Flaubert's Parrot* and all the essays that you wrote about Flaubert over the years. As you became an established writer, did your appreciation of his views about being an artist, and about art, change?

Barnes: I can only think of one specific change. Flaubert is one of those geniuses who never wrote the same book and whose books perhaps therefore appeal differently to different people at different times; though his greatest book has always been recognized as his greatest book. Every time I read *Madame Bovary*, it doesn't really change in my mind. I'm still staggered by it and awed that it was a first novel. I also find very often that as an unworldly eighteen- or twenty-year-old, I've underlined the same lines I would underline today, which stirs a mixed feeling. On the one hand, you think: "God, you were quite perceptive then," and, on the other hand, you think: "You're no cleverer now, are you? You'd still be underlining the same piece!"

But I think my perception of the other books have changed. I think particularly *Bouvard et Pécuchet* which I reread a couple of years ago when I reviewed a new translation of it. That's a book which is very hard to understand or indeed like when you are young, and it's a strange book which resists all the seduction of traditional narrative, and it's much stranger and much weirder than one imagines, even when you've read it once or twice already. So I was extremely pleased when that novel suddenly came into focus. It may prove the case even for *The Temptation of Saint Antony*, a book which I've never read easily or with much pleasure; perhaps when I'm eighty I will see the point of it. As for *The Sentimental Education*, which I also used to love—well, I still do, but the last time I read it, I thought about it much more as a practicing novelist and wondered if it wasn't about a hundred pages too long—something which I would never have dared think when I was younger. When you are a young and innocently enthusiastic reader, you assume that anyone who is a genius automatically gets every book right, and if it feels a bit long, it's your fault, not theirs. So I really want to get back and check that and see if it stacks up as a criticism. It did seem longer than it needed to be. But maybe I was having a bad reading patch. The physiology of reading—that's something I'd like to know more about.

In terms of the personal relationship you have with the author of the letters and the travel journals and so on, I think that has remained consistent, really. That side of Flaubert first got to me when I read Steegmuller's wonderful edition of *Flaubert in Egypt* and, thereafter, the first translation of the letters I came across, also by Steegmuller; that was in 1980 or the late 1970s. From that point my feelings about Flaubert and admiration for him and amusement in his presence have remained constant, actually, and I doubt the last volume of the *Correspondence* would change any of that, though it will be a melancholy read in some ways, because you know he's going to die. Even though you know he's dead, you'll be reading his letters knowing he's going to die. When I first began to grasp his general approach to art and literature, his attitudes in such questions as desolation versus consolation, I used to think: "Yes that's right, that is essentially right." And I may occasionally now disagree with it a little more but he's still absolutely there, as a presence, icon and maestro. If only I had known about that sale, I might have succeeded in buying a photograph of him, and he would have been on the wall outside.

Guignery: What would be your favorite book by Flaubert?

Barnes: *Madame Bovary* of the novels without doubt, but if I were on a desert island, I might not want a work of literature with me, I might want a companion, in which case I'd take the five Pleiade volumes of the correspondence, because he would be endlessly companionable.

Guignery: You wrote two film scripts, *Growing up in the Gorbals* (1987), based on Ralph Grasser's autobiography, and *The Private Wound* (1989), based on the novel (1968) by Nicholas Blake (the pseudonym of C. Day-Lewis). Among your novels, *Talking It Over* and *Love, etc* are maybe the nearest approximations to a script or theatre writing. I was wondering whether you'd be interested in writing for the theatre or writing a film script again?

Barnes: If I knew I had a period of time in which I didn't have any prose to write, I might be. I enjoyed writing those two scripts, mainly because I was working with very intelligent directors: Karel Reisz who was a wonderful man and became a friend—asked me to script *Growing up in the Gorbals*—and Mike Newell with whom I worked on *The Private Wound*. It's an interesting because different technical challenge; it's not your own stuff that you're adapting, so that's an advantage. I'd never want to adapt my own stuff. Film writing seems reasonably well-paid. But then nothing happens to it; most scripts that are written, nothing happens to them. So I think the vast hazard of the industry would discourage me.

As for the theatre, I've always thought about the catalogue of novelists' disastrous attempts at writing plays. Remember the famous "Dîner des Auteurs Sifflés" in nineteenth-century Paris, which consisted of Flaubert, Goncourt, Daudet, and Turgenev. Incredible—could you get four more interesting, varied, and distinguished novelists around the table? But they were there for the "Dinner of Hissed Authors"—they'd all been hissed off the stage, some of them rightly, it has to be admitted. Turgenev certainly wrote one play, *A Month in the Country*, whose greatness is now apparent. When you see it, you can see a lot of where Tchekov comes from, but it hadn't worked when it had first been written. Also, I think, the Russian censor banned it, which didn't help. Flaubert's drama, in my view, rightly failed because at bottom he despised the theatre, or thought it a cheap way of making money.

I think that the mistake that writers make is they think they're good at writing dialogue and that that's what the theatre is: it's people coming on stage and saying things to one another, but it's not! People saying things to one another in the theatre is quite different from people saying things to one another in the novel. Ideally, conversation in the novel would have the same density and moving force that it has to have in the theatre because that's all there is. There's a bit of physical action, but not very much. I'm not sure that I have the time to learn how to be a playwright. And I'm sure it's too late now anyway in that I'm sure my creative brain is only going to produce ideas which present themselves to me as novels or short stories or whatever, rather than a play. I've never consciously had an idea in which I think: "Oh actually that's not a novel, it's a play." And if I did I would be slightly suspicious of it.

Guignery: And how do you feel when other artists appropriate your work? For example, in a few days, you'll be attending a theatre adaptation of *A History of the World in 10½ Chapters* in Antwerp.
Barnes: Yes, this will be the first time I've ever seen that. There have been various small adaptations of my work in Canada, Belgium, and Holland and other places. I don't know. I think it will be okay, because it is in Flemish, so I really shan't be able to understand it. But I don't regard the process as the work being appropriated. Borrowed for a while, maybe.

Guignery: I was thinking more specifically of the film adaptation of *Talking It Over* by Marion Vernoux, because she changed so much the end of the book—that's why I found that she, in a way, appropriated the novel.
Barnes: Right. You remember the exchange I had with her when I met her after the filming. I said, "J'espère que vous m'avez trahi," and she said, "Mais bien

sûr,"[13] and I thought: "Well, in that case it might well be a good film." In such circumstances, I don't regard myself as a betrayed novelist. The forms are so different anyway and if you had been writing *Talking It Over* as a film in the first place, it wouldn't have been like the novel, would it? The British playwright David Edgar has actually just started adapting *Arthur & George*. I had a very nice meeting with him a week or so ago. As usual I say: "I hope you'll keep the spirit of the book," but obviously it's a play and there are certain things books can do that plays can't and vice versa. You can't have a play in which the audience doesn't realize the boy's half-Indian until twenty minutes in—it won't work! And most people who come to this play will know in advance that Arthur is Arthur Conan Doyle. So there's nothing you can do about that. David Edgar says, "I have to think of some sort of theatrical equivalent or whatever," and I say, "That's your job, fine, go ahead with it."

It's hard to think of examples of bad films or bad adaptations which would actually destroy the book. Someone told me that the film of Colin MacInnes's novel *Absolute Beginners* was so bad that it destroyed the book, except that the book was slightly forgotten anyway. I don't really fear for my books; I suppose you might fear that someone would go to the film or play and think, "Christ, well I'm not going to read his stuff if that's what it's like!" But on the whole, people who go to see the theatre adaptation of *A History of the World in 10½ Chapters* in Flemish would probably have read the book anyway. They will be more likely to be on your side, I suppose.

Roberts: So, this is the last question . . . of the last interview.
Barnes: Better be good [laughs].

Roberts: The pressure's on.
Barnes: "Looking back over your sixty-one years . . . your many publications, Mr. Barnes . . ."

Roberts: Who do you feel is the more dominant athlete in their respective sport: Tiger Woods or Roger Federer?
Barnes: [laughs] That's a very good question, actually. I think probably Federer is slightly more dominant. The big question is whether he can ever master Nadal in Paris.[14] But, amazingly he's still raising his game. I don't think Tiger Woods *can*

13. "I hope you betrayed me," and she said, "Of course". See also Julian Barnes's essay, "'Merci de m'avoir trahi.'" *Nouvel Observateur* (12 December 1996): 114.

14. In 2007, Nadal won the French Open for the third straight time. Federer later won Wimbledon for the fifth straight time.

possibly raise his game. I think he's already played his perfect game many times, whereas Federer is still a work of art in the state of development. He's learned to come to the net better and he's also getting better on clay. And if he can beat Nadal on clay in Paris he will be, definitely, the greatest ever. And I adore him. His range of shots, his elegance, his utter lack of that awful strutting male bullshit, and the way both his emotions and his steely determination are hidden by a calm exterior. And I particularly love the way his village gives him a cow when he wins Wimbledon. I wish my London suburb gave me a cow when I won some prize or other.

And that is my last word on every subject . . .

Index

Absolute Beginners (MacInnes), 187
Academics, 13, 14, 21, 37, 42, 47, 50, 53, 107, 114, 180–81. *See also* Critics
Ackroyd, Peter, 72, 145
Adultera, L' (Fontane), 100
Adultery, 12, 16, 17, 172
Aging, 125, 146, 149, 150; defense against, 128; love and, 126
Agnès Varda Women's Cooperative, 177
Airplanes, as metaphor, 18
Alain-Fournier, 168
All Souls (Marías), 139
Allen, Woody, 84
America, 83, 84, 85, 87, 141, 182; compared with England, 85; exotic, 127; forgiveness and, 92; novel and, 27, 76; old age and, 150, 151; optimism and, 91; redemption and, 91; westerns, 60
Americanization, 91
Amis, Kingsley, 7, 66, 89, 109, 116, 123, 154
Amis, Martin, 66, 117, 123, 129, 165
Amsterdam (McEwan), 130
Ancestry. *See* Family
Andrieu, Lucien, 107, 113
Animals, 170; albatross, 116; cats, 6; cows, 188; crocodiles, 11, 19, 39, 40, 79; horses, 11; parrots, 18, 60, 101–4, 107–8, 113, 123, 125; pigs, 42; Ted Hughes and, 73; trials of, 41, 58; woodworms, 20, 56
Anti-Semitic Moment: A Tour of France in 1898, The (Birnbaum), 163

Architecture, 62, 166
Archives, 178–80
Arendt, Hannah, 41
Art, 60, 128, 183; Flaubert reflects about, 70, 71, 75; life vs., 16, 80; replicas and, 61; society and, 75; truth and, 88, 118
Artaud, Antonin, 17
Artists, 110, 121, 177; Roger Federer as, 188
Auden, W. H., 145
Austen, Jane, 66
Authenticity, 27, 62, 63
Authors. *See* Writers
Autobiography, 165; fiction vs., 87, 138–39, 165; in Barnes's fiction, 3, 8, 36, 56, 68, 93, 138
Awards, 7, 9, 10, 44, 115, 118, 156

Bacon, Francis (painter), 111, 115
Bacon, Sir Francis, 39
Baddiel, David, 100
Balzac, Honoré de, 69
Banality, 40, 41, 132
Banville, John, 72
Barnes, Albert Leonard (father), 8, 35, 65, 127, 163–64, 166, 168
Barnes, Jonathan (brother), 41, 67, 107
Barnes, Julian: on adapting own work, 185; adolescent rebellion, 164–65; on ageism, 151; on awareness of other writers, 23–24; becoming a writer, 23, 65, 67–68; on collecting, 178, 183–84; compared

Barnes, Julian (*continued*)
with Nabokov and Calvino,
74–75; critic of own work, 18;
and Doyle, 133; education of,
9, 67, 73, 102, 125; as essayist,
44, 87; as European writer, 29,
64; exhibitionist nature, lack
of, 165; and *Flaubert's Parrot*,
108; as frustrated historian,
121; on giving advice or trying to persuade, 48, 62, 88, 93,
121, 128, 133, 146, 167; God and,
124; grandparents of, 126–27;
growing up, 12, 66, 79; high
standards of, 116; and home
in France, 15; lexicographer,
4–5, 21, 108–9; literary theory
or scholarship, unaware of, 37,
180; means of writing, 152–53;
misinterpreted, 48; as moralist, 18; old age and, 124; past
writings, 73; as reader, 85, 184;
on reading for bar, 4, 9, 133;
on reading *Madame Bovary*,
66, 184; on reading obituaries, 152; on reading reviews, 33,
48, 94, 129, 180; on retirement,
117; and Russian language,
29, 127; search for *Temptation of St. Anthony*, 109–10; on
self-preservation, 81; as *Sunday
Times* deputy literary editor,
9; travels to Rouen in 1981, 103;
wary of biography, 53; on writing letters or notes, 152–53; on
writing one book at a time, 94,
181; youth, 7, 9, 29, 35, 119, 125,
127, 184
Characters: creation of, 78; exaggerated,
8; rein on, 78; observations of,
83, 84
Arthur & George: Maud Edalji, 138;
Woodie, 137. *See also* Doyle,
Arthur Conan; Edalji, George

Before She Met Me, Graham Hendrick,
11, 19, 40
England, England: Dr. Max, 55, 61–62;
Jez Harris, 62; Martha Coch-
rane, 27, 61–63; Sir Jack Pit-
man, 78
Flaubert's Parrot: Ed Winterton, 108–9;
Ellen Braithwaite, 16–17, 108,
112; Geoffrey Braithwaite, 13–
14, 17, 19, 21, 31, 44–45, 102,
104–5, 107–10, 112–15, 170
Metroland: Christopher Lloyd, 3–4,
7–9, 12, 15, 33–35, 69, 162;
Marion Lloyd, 176–77; Toni
Barbarowski, 7–8, 33–34
The Porcupine, Stoyo Petkanov, 46, 78
in short stories: Leonard Verity, 177;
Sylvia Winstanley, 122
Staring at the Sun: Gregory Serjeant,
164; Jean Serjeant, 12, 13, 139;
Rachel, 12–13
Talking It Over/Love, etc: Gillian Wyatt, 83, 89–90; Madame Wy-
att, 90–91; Oliver Russell, 32,
36, 83, 85–87, 89–91, 171; Stuart
Hughes, 32, 87, 89–90
Works
Arthur & George, 129–30, 132–34,
136–38, 142, 144, 146, 187; alter-
nate titles, 131, 140; cover design, 130; origins of, 131, 134,
163; religion and, 139; secondary characters, 138; themes, 132,
140; writing process, 135
Before She Met Me, 8, 11, 12, 19, 30, 39–
41, 45, 71, 79; suicide in, 16
Cross Channel, 58; "Evermore," 59; "Experiment," 43; "Interference,"
177; "Tunnel," 79
England, England, 27–29, 46, 48–50, 55,
59–62, 74, 78, 130–31, 142, 158;
farcical and political rather
than satirical, 46; inspiration
for, 27; Plato and, 49–50; re-

views of, 33, 129–30; writing process, 29, 48

Flaubert's Parrot, 13–14, 17–18, 20–21, 24, 30–31, 35, 37, 42, 44–45, 53–54, 60, 72, 84, 93, 96, 101–14, 115, 118, 123, 130, 165, 170–71, 181, 184; connections with *A History of the World in 10½ Chapters*, 21, 105; "Examination Paper," 112; as fiction, 16, 44, 54, 103; "Finders Keepers," 108; offensive chapter dropped, 14; origins of, 101–5; "Pure Story," 45, 108, 112; structure of, 17–18, 103, 105, 108, 111–12; suicide in, 16; themes, 108; three chronologies, 106–7

A History of the World in 10½ Chapters, 20, 37, 41–42, 44, 49, 54–56, 58–60, 114, 118, 176, 186–87; God and, 41; irony and, 48; origins in *Flaubert's Parrot*, 21; "Parenthesis," 54–57, 165–68; short stories vs. novel, 21; "Three Simple Stories," 56, 58; truth and, 55–56

In the Land of Pain, 96, 161

The Lemon Table, 94, 118, 125, 128, 161–62; "Knowing French," 122–24; "The Revival," 120–21, 133; "A Short History of Hairdressing," 125; "The Silence," 118, 121, 177; "The Story of Mats Israelson," 118–19, 128

Letters from London, 172–73

Love, etc. (novel), 77–79, 81, 83–88, 93, 167, 185; sequel to, 78

Love, etc. (film), 77

Metroland, 3, 5, 7–10, 12, 15, 23–24, 30, 33–35, 41, 47–48, 66–69, 71, 129, 162, 164, 169–70, 176–77; death and, 161–62; length of time to write, 3, 9, 22–23, 30, 67; wins Somerset Maugham Award, 7, 118

Nothing to Be Frightened Of, 163, 165; opening line, 41, 116, 161; origins of, 162

The Pedant in the Kitchen, 116, 146

The Porcupine, 25–26, 30, 42, 45–46, 73–74, 78, 93, 98; first published in Bulgaria, 25, 98; libel report, 49; origin of, 25, 98; reception in Bulgaria, 25

Screenplays, 51

Growing up in the Gorbals, 185

The Private Wound, 185

Something to Declare, 94, 168, 171–73

Staring at the Sun, 9, 12, 17, 30, 139, 164; death and, 16, 161–62; imagery, 17–18; structure of, 17

Talking It Over, 29, 35–37, 41, 45, 74, 77, 79, 84, 86–87, 90, 93, 167, 185, 186–87; adapted into film, 77; ending, 32; epigraph, 42; interweaving of voices/narration, 30, 37, 45, 167

Uncollected story, "The Rebuke," 171–72

Unpublished works

A Literary Guide to Oxford, 23, 66; short story as chess game, 178; travel journals or notebooks, 102, 110, 113

Unwritten works: account of Titanic disaster, 21; book on Gericault and voyage of the Medusa, 21; expanded edition of *Flaubert's Parrot*, 170; guide to houses of French writers and artists, 102–3, 110; sequel to *Talking It Over* and *Love, etc.*, 78, 89–90, 171; story of friend's father who falls in love with department store clerk, 126; translation of *Madame Bovary*, 98

Barnes, Kathleen Mabel (mother), 8, 35, 65, 66, 127, 163–64, 166, 168

Barthes, Roland, 15

Baudelaire, Charles, 66

Baudrillard, Jean, 50
Beatles, The, 11
Bedcovers, 23, 29, 68
Beesley, Lawrence, 56, 176; and Paddy Beesley, 176
Berlin Wall, 52, 143
Berryman, John, 12
Biography, 53–54, 72–73, 85, 106–9, 181–82; fiction and, 14, 31, 138; *Flaubert's Parrot* and, 53–54, 102, 107, 109; tomb metaphor, 14, 105
Birnbaum, Pierre, 163
Blair, Tony, 137
Blake, Nicholas, 185
Blue Flower, The (Fitzgerald), 72
Booker Prize. *See* Man Booker Prize
Borges, Jorge Luis, 97
Borman, Martin, 121
bourgeoisie, 34
Bouvard et Pécuchet (Flaubert), 69–70, 105, 184
Bovary, Charles, 16–17
Bovary, Emma, 16–17, 65, 137, 171–72
Bragg, Melvyn, 129
Brain, 11, 32, 39, 54, 125
Brazil, 127
Bright Lights, Big City (McInerney), 83, 85
Britain. *See* England
British, 40–41; English vs., 141; tax law, 179–80
British Council, 37, 151
British Library, 179–80
Britishness, 142
Brown, Gordon, 142
Bruegel, 109
Bruneau, Jean, 107
Bulgakov, Mikhail, 72
Bulgaria, 98; Barnes visit, 25
Burgess, Anthony, 178
Burial chambers. *See* Tombs
Bush, George W., 116, 145

Calvino, Italo, 29, 74
Camus, Albert, 77
Carey, John, 33, 129

Carpetbaggers, The (Robbins), 127
Carroll, Lewis, 28
Carter, Angela, 162
Cartoons, 78, 114
Carver, Raymond, 76
Catholics, 151, 166
Caute, David, 177
Celebrity, 84–85, 88, 156
Chandler, Raymond, 92
Characterization, 13, 17, 32–33, 69, 86, 112, 114, 121, 135–36, 140
Cheever, John, 76
Chekhov, Anton, 29, 78, 186
China, 9
Chivalry, 132, 137
Church, 131, 136, 139–40, 164, 166
Civil service, 12
Clarissa (Richardson), 32
Coetzee, J. M., 130
Cœur simple, Un (Flaubert), 60, 101, 103, 105, 113, 123
Coincidence, 16, 122–23
Cold War, 25
Colet, Louise, 70–71, 107, 171–72
Composers, 177
Computers, 81, 99, 154–55
Conferences, 43, 101–2
Connolly, Cyril, 22, 70, 100
Consolation, 128, 169, 185
Cooking, 158–59
Cosmetic surgery, 151–52
Courage: sexual, 13; social, 12, 164
Coward, Noel, 9
Creativity, 14, 119
Crepuscular, 85–86
Crime and Punishment (Dostoyevsky), 66
Criticism, 13, 115, 180; literary, and Barnes, 23, 104. *See also* Theory
Critics, 13, 14, 22, 33, 37–38, 45, 56, 73–75, 138, 162. *See also* Academics
Croisset, 102–3, 110–11
Culture, 89, 142

Dante, 97
Daudet, Alphonse, 97–98, 186

Dean, Suzanne, 130
Death, 7, 35, 101, 116, 118, 122, 128, 132, 150,
    161–63, 165–66, 181; Barnes and,
    96, 116, 161–62
Defoe, Daniel, 47
Delius, Frederick, 177
Derrida, Jacques, 37
Desolation, 169, 185
Despair, religion of, 17
Detective stories, 22, 132–33, 136, 140, 146
Dialogue, 186
Divorce, 91
Domain names, 98–99
Don Quixote, 137
Donne, John, 66
Dostoyevsky, Fyodor, 66, 68–69
Doyle, Arthur Conan, 129–32, 134–35, 137,
    140, 187
Dr. Zhivago (Pasternak), 71
Drafts of works, 3, 32, 81, 100, 178; England,
    England, 29; Love, etc., 155;
    Metroland, 169; Nothing to Be
    Frightened Of, 163; Talking It
    Over, 29; The Porcupine, 26
Drama. See Theatre
Dreyfus Affair, 131, 134, 145–46, 163
Drugs, 41, 82
Dublin, Ireland, 111, 115
Duffy, Nick, 22

Eastern Europe, 25. See also Bulgaria
Edalji, George, 130, 132, 135–36, 139–41
Edgar, David, 187
Editing, 4, 81, 163, 169–71
Education sentimentale, L' (Flaubert), 70, 184
Effi Briest (Fontane), 100
Elementary Particles, The (Houellebecq), 77
Elgin Marbles, 61
Eliot, George, 66
Eliot, T. S., 66
Ellis, Brett, 83
Ellmann, Richard, 70
Endings: ambiguity of, 4, 32, 33, 48, 62, 69,
    78, 88, 90, 113, 172
Enemies of Promise (Connolly), 22

England, 146; America vs., 85, 91; Britain,
    83, 92; condition of, 28; France
    and, 28, 40, 127–28, 131, 142, 146,
    173–74; idea of, 27, 74, 131; quin-
    tessences of, 60; state of, 27
English, 32, 40, 64, 123; British vs., 141; emo-
    tional reticence of, 132; self-
    consciousness of, 74
Englishness, 27, 28, 141–42
Epigraphs, 42, 59, 167
Essays. See Journalism
European Union, 142, 149
European writers, 29
Eurostar. See Trains
Evil, 40, 41
Existentialism, 34
Extinction, 35

Fabulation, 54–55, 63
Facts, 39, 58–59, 64, 87–88, 105–8, 118
Fame, 7, 156
Family: Barnes's, 35, 41, 65–66, 116, 138, 140,
    165–66, 184; genetic inheritance
    of, 34–35, 67
Farce, 43, 45, 74; history and, 57; semi-,
    27–28
Fathers and Sons (Turgenev), 76
Federer, Roger, 187–88
Festivals, literary, 43, 115
Fiction, 87; autobiography and, 165; biog-
    raphy and, 14, 138; history and,
    54, 59; journalism and, 23, 65,
    87; reality and, 58, 68, 104, 118,
    138; truth and, 30, 39, 64, 87,
    107, 120
Film, 38, 68; and adaptations, 77
Finnegans Wake (Joyce), 73
Fitzgerald, F. Scott, 76
Fitzgerald, Penelope, 72
Flaubert, Gustave, 13, 14, 15, 17, 20, 23, 29,
    51, 54, 60, 66, 69–70, 72, 75, 78,
    98, 101–15, 121, 165, 169, 172,
    182–86; Barnes on, 102; cor-
    respondence, 70, 75, 107, 110,
    170, 174, 185; Croisset, 102–3,

Flaubert, Gustave (*continued*)
        110–11; death of, 185; quoted
        by Barnes, 43, 80, 96, 133, 144,
        169, 178; trains and, 14, 106;
        and writing, 15; writing pro-
        cess of, 14
Flaubert in Egypt (Steegmuller), 185
Fontane, Theodor, 100
Ford, Ford Madox, 36, 75–76, 93, 128
Forster, E. M., 71
Form, 47, 49, 57, 73–74, 89–90, 165; in con-
        temporary British fiction, 57,
        77; *England, England*, 62; fic-
        tion and, 14, 21, 38, 178; in *Flau-
        bert's Parrot*, 16, 18, 54, 105; in
        A Hero of Our Time (Lermon-
        tov), 57, 58; in *A History of the
        World in 10½ Chapters*, 21, 55;
        ideas and, 20, 51, 74–75, 122,
        163; in *Nothing to Be Fright-
        ened Of*, 165; in *Staring at the
        Sun*, 18; in *Talking It Over*, 30,
        74, 86–87, 89–90; vernacular vs.
        academic, 76
Foucault, Michel, 37
Fowles, John, 170
France, 15, 24, 28, 40, 64, 127, 128, 130, 131,
        150, 173, 174
France, Anatole, 103
Frayn, Michael, 7
Free market, 74
French, 32, 64; and grammar, 124; influ-
        ence on writing, 79; invaded
        by Germans, 40; literature
        of, 24, 76, 77, 169; minds of,
        15; self-consciousness of, 74;
        Shakespeare and, 47, 169; as
        studied language, 29, 102, 127;
        views of English, 28
Fuller, John, 5

Gardening, 143–44
Genoa, Italy, 109–10
Gerhardy, William, 124

Géricault, Théodore, 20–21, 60
Germans, 40, 168
Germany, 40, 50–52, 142
God, 19, 41–42, 46, 116, 123, 124, 140, 163–64, 165
Goncharov, Ivan, 66
Goncourt, Edmond de, 98, 186
Good Life, The (McInerney), 144
Good Soldier, The (Ford), 75, 76
"Greek Street" column (*New Review*), 5
Greene, Graham, 36, 51, 66
Guardian, The, 116, 174

Hamilton, Ian, 5, 175
Handelsman, Walt, 78
Hardy, Thomas, 35, 66, 182
Harry Ransom Center, 178–80
Hawthorne, Nathaniel, 76
Hemingway, Ernest, 76, 79, 145
Henderson, Kathy, 180
Herbert, Juliet, 107–9
Hero of Our Time, A (Lermontov), 57, 58
Historians, 55, 72
Historical events, 58, 135
Historical novel, 72–73, 135
History, 27, 42, 44, 49, 55, 57, 61, 108, 120–21;
        bias and, 53, 55; evidence and,
        53, 58; fiction and, 53–54, 59;
        as literary genre, 53; narration
        and, 43, 72; rewriting, 38, 56, 60
Hogarth, Mark, 98, 99
Hollywood, 51
Holroyd, Michael, 124
Homogenization, 142–43
Hopkins, Gerard Manley, 66
Houellebecq, Michel, 77
Housman, A. E., 35
Howard, Anthony, 150
Hughes, Ted, 47, 73
Humans, 21
Humor, 4, 20, 35, 84, 109, 114, 168
Huxley, Aldous, 66

Ideas, 20, 21, 27, 42, 45, 49, 51, 59, 75, 93, 102,
        138, 174, 186

Imagination, 39, 59, 126, 137–41
Indexing, 172–73
Individuality, 34–35
Interviews, 106, 168, 181–82
Iraq, 116–17, 137
Irony, 8, 47, 48, 84, 168
Ishiguro, Kazuo, 43, 77, 130
Islam, 49

James, Clive, 5
James, Henry, 51, 76
Jealousy, 8, 19, 79
Jerrell, Randall, 21, 79
Johnson, B. S., 178
Johnson, Douglas, 131, 134
Johnson, Samuel, 36
Jonson, Ben, 36
Journalism, 4, 5, 22, 23, 25, 31, 44, 65, 67–68,
   81, 87, 88, 94–95, 171–74, 175
Joyce, James, 70, 73
Jules et Jim, 45
Julianbarnes.com, 98–99

Kavanagh, Dan, 5–6, 22, 114, 118, 133, 175–76;
   Putting the Boot In, 114
Kavanagh, Pat, 8, 117, 130
Kermode, Frank, 16
Kipling, Rudyard, 137, 174
Kissinger, Henry, 47
Koestler, Arthur, 39
Kondeva, Dimitrina, 25–26, 98
Kureishi, Hanif, 127

Lampedusa, Giuseppe Tomasi di, 71
Language, 4–5, 8, 15, 23, 29, 36, 64, 67, 85,
   102, 115–16, 124, 127, 135–36, 154,
   171; American novelists vs. English novelists, 76; influence
   on thought, 15; and reality, 16;
   syntax, 153
Larkin, Philip, 35, 182
Leopard, The (Lampedusa), 71
Lee, Hermione, 14, 54, 181
Lehrer, Tom, 47

Lemon Table (Helsinki), 116, 118
Lermontov, Mikhail, 57–58, 66
Levi, Primo, 58
Levin, Bernard, 48
Libel, 49
Literature, 64–65; British, 169; French, 24,
   169; German, 50; life vs., 79;
   Russian, 24
Love, 29, 36, 108, 119, 166–68; jealousy and,
   79; madness and, 19, 126; pas-
   sion, 11; sex vs., 121; truth
   and, 56
Lucky Jim (Amis), 116

Madame Bovary (Flaubert), 14, 16–17, 23, 43,
   45, 65–66, 69, 78, 83–84, 98, 102,
   170–72, 178, 184–85
Magus, The (Fowles), 170
Mandyn, Jan, 109
Maugham, Somerset, 13
MacInnes, Colin, 187
MacLean, Paul D., 11, 39
Magic realism, 72
Mailer, Norman, 144
Man Booker Prize, 99–100, 114, 118, 130
Manuscripts, 178–80. *See also* Drafts of
   works
Marías, Javier, 139
Marriage, 33, 92, 181
Marx, Karl, 56, 57
Maxwell, Robert, 74, 78
McCarthy, Mary, 100
McClure, James, 5
McEwan, Ian, 77, 99, 117, 130, 137, 144–45, 180
McInerney, Jay, 29, 83, 85, 144
Melancholy, 35–36, 57
Memory, 37, 39, 101, 135, 163, 167; good vs.
   bad, 38; of nations, 63; truth
   and, 38
Middle Ages, 41–42
Middlemarch (Eliot), 66, 69
Mo, Timothy, 43
Modern Painters, 177
Modernism, 165

Montaigne, Michel de, 66, 150
Montesquieu, 29
Month in the Country, A (Turgenev), 120, 186
Monty Python, 28
Moore, Lorrie, 76–77
Morality, 12, 41
Morrison, Blake, 72
Motion, Andrew, 178–79
Murdoch, Iris, 7, 12
Murdoch, Rupert, 46
Museums, 111, 115, 158
Music, 156, 158, 177–78
Myths: America as land without irony, 84;
        national, 59

Nabokov, Vladimir, 74, 78–79
Nadal, Rafael, 187–88
Napoleon Symphony (Burgess), 178
Narrative, 42–43, 45, 53–55, 57–58, 60, 64,
        69, 72–73, 78, 84, 86, 105, 109,
        111–12, 132, 177–78, 184
National Front, 11
Nations, 40, 62, 131; creation of myths, 59;
        memory of, 63; uniqueness of,
        142, 143
New Review, 5, 124, 170, 175
New Statesman, 3, 9, 21, 175–77
New York Observer, 83
New York Review of Books, 163, 173
New York Times, 33
New Yorker, 81, 94–95, 150, 161, 163, 174–75
Newell, Mike, 185
1960s, 11, 119
Nonfiction. *See* Journalism
Novels, 21, 24, 30, 69, 73, 75, 88, 102; emotion
        and, 94; essays vs., 44; and life,
        37, 80, 138; purpose of, 89; the-
        atre vs., 187

Observer, The, 21, 117
Obsession, 169; with ceasing past, 21; with
        death, 96, 116, 161–62; with
        France, 24; with obsessions,
        16; with suicide, 16
Oliver, Hermia, 109

Optimism, 91–92
Original work, 16, 20, 28, 75; replica vs.,
        48–49, 60–61
Orwell, George, 44, 145, 156
Oxford English Dictionary, 4, 9, 21, 66–67,
        108, 154
Oxford Mail, The, 176

Painters, 177, 183
Pamela (Richardson), 32
Parade's End (Ford), 128
Paris Review, 182
Parrots, 16, 18, 60, 101–4, 107–8, 113–15, 123, 125
Pasternak, Boris, 71
Perspective, 27, 37, 87, 122, 167
Phèdre (Racine), 47
Philosophy, 67, 68
Photography, 183–85
Pinter, Harold, 79
Plato, 49–50
Plot Against America, The (Roth), 144–45
Poetry, 51, 182
Point of view, 42, 68, 168; academic, 67; of
        Charles Bovary, 17; contem-
        porary, 120; German, 43; of
        Madame Wyatt, 91; racial, 141;
        of women, 9, 12; of wood-
        worm, 56
Politicians, 39, 116, 137
Politics, 11, 29, 35, 40, 74, 92, 133, 137, 143, 145,
        159–60, 164
Postmodernism, 20, 28, 37, 42, 49, 58, 73
Prayers, 148
Premier Homme, Le (Camus), 77
Proust, Marcel, 15
Pseudonyms, 5–6, 9, 175–77
Psychology, 11, 40, 67–68, 70, 77, 123, 152
Pushkin, Alexander, 66
Putting the Boot In (Kavanagh), 114
Pygge, Edward, 5–6, 175
Pym, Barbara, 71

Rabbit Tetralogy (Updike), 71, 76, 171
Race, 78, 141, 144, 163
Racine, Jean, 47

Raft of the Medusa, The (Géricault), 20–21, 60, 174
Raine, Craig, 23–24
Raphael, Frederick, 7
Rationality, 39
Readers, 4, 29, 32, 33, 43, 55, 62, 65, 73, 84, 85, 86, 90, 95, 105, 106–7, 128, 146, 147
Reading, 184
Realist tradition, 65, 73
Reality, 40, 54–55
Reid, Christopher, 24
Reisz, Karl, 185
Relationships, 19, 92
Religion, 19, 35, 41–42, 49, 61, 88, 116, 139–40, 148, 163; loss of, 165–66
Remote controls, 89, 157
Replicas, 27, 48–49, 59–60, 62–63; in art, 60–61; convenient vs. inconvenient, 61; original work vs., 48–49, 60–61
Research, 32, 54, 81, 96, 102, 113, 175
Restaurant Critic of the Year, 9
Restaurant reviews, 9, 175
Review, The, 5
Reviews, 3, 9, 22–23, 33, 48, 94, 129, 176, 180; bad, 22, 129–30; of Barnes's works, 3, 33, 48, 71, 162, 181
Richardson, Samuel, 32
Rimbaud, Arthur, 29, 66
Rite of Spring, The (Stravinsky), 34
Robbins, Harold, 127
Robinson, Jancis, 116
Rome, Italy, 110
Roth, Philip, 76, 99, 130, 144
Rouen, France, 101–3, 110, 133
Royal family, 48, 49, 132; Henry V, 59–60
Rushdie, Salman, 42, 117, 130
Russia, 24, 25, 29, 57, 87

Salammbô (Flaubert), 70, 72
Sand, George, 70, 169, 183
Satire, 29, 45–48; in *Metroland*, 9; purpose of, 46; vs. semi-farce in *England, England*, 28

Saturday (McEwan), 144
Schama, Simon, 72
Schneider, Peter, 51
Schopenhauer, Arthur, 68
Science, spiritualism and, 140
Seal, Basil, 9, 175
Sentimentalism, 96, 104, 137, 168, 182
September 11, 2001, 144–45
Sex, 12, 13, 83, 84, 93, 119, 120, 139, 146, 151; chasteness, 132; courage and, 12, 13; creativity and, 14; love vs., 121; metaphors, 14; moral decisions and, 12; 1960s and, 11, 119
Shakespeare, William, 23, 47–48, 60, 68, 169, 181–82
Shaw, Bernard, 137
Shelley, Percy Bysshe, 96
Shostakovich, Dmitri, 42
Sibelius, Jean, 116, 118, 121, 177, 183
Simenon, Georges, 153
Simpson, Helen, 77, 139
Slater, Nigel, 117
Smith, Zadie, 77, 99, 130
Somerset Maugham Award, 7, 10
Spiritualism, 132, 134–35, 140
Sports, 79, 114, 174, 187
Staël, Madame de, 28
Starkie, Enid, 13
Steegmuller, Francis, 185
Steiner, George, 100
Stoppard, Tom, 79
Stravinsky, Igor, 34
Structure. *See* Form
Suicide, 16–17, 28, 161
Sunday Times, 9, 21, 130
Swift, Jonathan, 36, 47–48

Tale of Tub (Swift), 36
Tatler, The, 9
Television, 88–90, 132, 157, 160; Barnes as critic of, 21, 117, 175; *Big Brother*, 88, 156, 157; *It's Gary Shandling's Show*, 90
Temptation of St. Anthony, The (Flaubert), 110, 184

Temptation of St. Anthony, The (Mandyn), 109–10

Terrorist (Updike), 144

That Sweet Enemy: The French and the British from the Sun King to the Present (Tombs), 173

Thatcher, Margaret, 132, 145, 151, 180

Theatre, 47, 120, 185–86; novels vs., 187

Themes in writing, 15, 46, 58–59, 68, 125, 132, 164, 167

Theory, 37, 73, 76, 180. *See also* Criticism

Times Literary Supplement, 9, 109, 174

Titanic, 56–57

Tolstoy, Leo, 23, 29, 66, 69, 128, 145

Tomalin, Claire, 182

Tombs, 14, 105, 112

Tombs, Robert and Isabelle, 173

Tone of voice, 5, 97

Tory, 11

Tour de France, 81–82, 94, 157

Tournier, Michel, 29, 76–77

Tradition, 27, 62, 74

Tragedy, 40, 57

Trains, 14, 106

Translation, 96–98, 100, 135–36

Trois Contes (Flaubert), 70

Truth, 18, 27, 30, 38–39, 43, 46, 64–65, 72, 87–88, 102, 107, 149; art and, 88, 118; fiction and, 30, 39, 64, 87, 107, 120; journalism and, 65, 87–88; love and, 56; objectivity of, 55–56; percentages of, 44, 56, 59; religion and, 88; replicas and, 60, 63

Turgenev, Ivan, 23, 29, 57, 66, 76, 78, 120–21, 133, 186

Typewriter, 22, 30, 75, 81, 99, 155

Updike, John, 71, 76, 79, 144, 169, 171

U2, 137

Values, 136–37. *See also* Morality

van Gogh, Vincent, 17

Verlaine, Paul, 66

Vernoux, Marion, 186–87

Vidal, Gore, 84

Voice, 5, 29–30, 69, 95, 97, 113–14, 171–72

Voltaire, 23, 29, 66; on Shakespeare, 47

Wain, John, 179–80

Wall Jumper, The (Schneider), 51

War and Peace (Tolstoy), 128

Waugh, Evelyn, 36, 66, 90, 175, 182

Wells, H. G., 137

Wharton, Edith, 76

Wheen, Francis, 177

White, Hayden, 42, 53

Wilson, Edmund, 182

Wine, 43–44, 83

Wodehouse, P. G., 90

Women: and cosmetic surgery, 151–52; point of view of, 9, 12, 29, 78; writing about, 78, 122, 171

Wood, Michael, 181

Woods, Tiger, 187

Woolf, Virginia, 54, 108

World Cup, 52

Writing process, 4, 9, 16, 18, 20, 28, 29, 30, 31, 45, 49, 59, 67–68, 75, 80–81, 86, 94, 100, 101, 102, 104, 117, 119, 122, 155, 162, 172–75, 178, 181; as Dan Kavanagh, 5; *England, England*, 29, 48; Flaubert and, 14; *Flaubert's Parrot* and, 14, 103–4, 111–12; *A History of the World in 10½ Chapters*, 58–59; *Staring at the Sun*, 17

Yellow Dog (Amis), 129

Zhivkov, Todor, 78, 98; trial of, 25

Zola, Émile, 98, 174